Your First Cruise

A Complete Guide to Planning and Attaining the Perfect Cruise Vacation

By T. Brian Chatfield

Your First Cruise: A Complete Guide to Planning and Attaining the Perfect Cruise Vacation

Copyright © 2008 by Atlantic Publishing Group, Inc.

1405 SW 6th Ave. • Ocala, Florida 34471 • 800-814-1132 • 352-622-1875–Fax

Web site: www.atlantic-pub.com • E-mail: sales@atlantic-pub.com

SAN Number: 268-1250

ISBN-13: 978-1-60138-151-4   ISBN-10: 1-60138-151-4

Chatfield, T. Brian, 1984-
  Your first cruise : a complete guide to planning and attaining the perfect cruise vacation / by T. Brian Chatfield.
      p. cm.
  Includes bibliographical references.
  ISBN-13: 978-1-60138-151-4 (alk. paper)
  ISBN-10: 1-60138-151-4 (alk. paper)
  1. Ocean travel. I. Title.

  G550.C53 2008
  910.4'5--dc22
                        2008019129

INTERIOR DESIGN: Vickie Taylor • vtaylor@atlantic-pub.com

Printed on Recycled Paper

Printed in the United States

We recently lost our beloved pet "Bear," who was not only our best and dearest friend but also the "Vice President of Sunshine" here at Atlantic Publishing. He did not receive a salary but worked tirelessly 24 hours a day to please his parents. Bear was a rescue dog that turned around and showered myself, my wife Sherri, his grandparents Jean, Bob and Nancy and every person and animal he met (maybe not rabbits) with friendship and love. He made a lot of people smile every day.

We wanted you to know that a portion of the profits of this book will be donated to The Humane Society of the United States.

–Douglas & Sherri Brown

THE HUMANE SOCIETY
OF THE UNITED STATES ©

The human-animal bond is as old as human history. We cherish our animal companions for their unconditional affection and acceptance. We feel a thrill when we glimpse wild creatures in their natural habitat or in our own backyard.

Unfortunately, the human-animal bond has at times been weakened. Humans have exploited some animal species to the point of extinction.

The Humane Society of the United States makes a difference in the lives of animals here at home and worldwide. The HSUS is dedicated to creating a world where our relationship with animals is guided by compassion. We seek a truly humane society in which animals are respected for their intrinsic value, and where the human-animal bond is strong.

Want to help animals? We have plenty of suggestions. Adopt a pet from a local shelter, join The Humane Society and be a part of our work to help companion animals and wildlife. You will be funding our educational, legislative, investigative and outreach projects in the U.S. and across the globe.

Or perhaps you'd like to make a memorial donation in honor of a pet, friend or relative? You can through our Kindred Spirits program. And if you'd like to contribute in a more structured way, our Planned Giving Office has suggestions about estate planning, annuities, and even gifts of stock that avoid capital gains taxes.

Maybe you have land that you would like to preserve as a lasting habitat for wildlife. Our Wildlife Land Trust can help you. Perhaps the land you want to share is a backyard—that's enough. Our Urban Wildlife Sanctuary Program will show you how to create a habitat for your wild neighbors.

So you see, it's easy to help animals. And The HSUS is here to help.

The Humane Society of the United States
2100 L Street NW
Washington, DC 20037
202-452-1100
www.hsus.org

Table of Contents

Foreword

Dear Reader,

Congratulations! By purchasing this book, you have taken the initial step in planning your first cruise vacation. And after being in the industry for 30 years and taking countless cruises, I can assure you that you're making the right decision. Cruising is by far the most convenient, cost-effective, thrilling way to see the world!

In fact, according to the Cruise Lines International Association (CLIA), the cruise industry is the fastest-growing segment of the travel industry — achieving more than 2,100 percent growth since 1970, when an estimated 500,000 people took a cruise. Industry estimates are that 12.8 million will cruise in 2008.

Choosing to cruise is a big decision, and with so many different ships and itineraries available, it's an overwhelming task to select one. Know that there is a cruise out there for everyone. Whether you prefer the activity and variety of a megaship (today's are more like "floating cities") or a more intimate experience aboard a small ship or river cruise, the possibilities are endless.

The same goes for the plethora of destinations that today's cruise ships visit. While the Caribbean remains enormously popular for first-timers and veteran cruisers alike, other popular choices include Alaska, Europe, the Mediterranean, Hawaii, South America, Asia, and beyond!

With so much to see on shore, don't forget just how much there is to do right on your cruise ship. From onboard spas and shopping to lifelong learning opportunities and workshops, your days at sea are guaranteed to be active — if you choose. That's just one of the benefits of cruising. You decide how much or how little you want to do.

It's amazing how far cruising has come in the past decade, evolving into an experience much like those at land-based resorts. When it comes to dining, for example, the possibilities are plentiful. You can choose the more traditional assigned seating in a main dining room, but there are also casual dining options, flexible dining times, healthier options, and alternative restaurants. In fact, on some ships, you can practically dine in a different venue each night!

Other onboard innovations abound. From rock-climbing walls, bowling alleys, and ice-skating rinks to surfing simulators, poolside movie screens, and state-of-the-art water parks, you will never be bored while sailing the high seas. As cruise lines continue to raise the bar in terms of onboard innovations, it's you — the passenger — who benefits by getting to truly enjoy just how amazing these ships have become.

Not only does cruising offer a wealth of entertainment and activities, it's also a matter of convenience. The fact that you can visit a handful of ports in a week — and only unpack once — is something that is only possible on a cruise. Not to mention that all the logistics are taken care of. The "driving" is done for you, as is the cooking, the cleaning, the planning, and the entertainment. It's the all-inclusive aspect that is so appealing.

So without further ado, read on to discover everything you need to know about cruising. I am confident that after you take your first cruise, you'll be planning your second.

Welcome to the wonderful world of cruising. I bid you smooth sailings!

Bill Panoff
Publisher and Editor-in-Chief, Porthole Cruise Magazine
bpanoff@ppigroup.com

Bill Panoff began his career in 1979 as a magician and entertainer aboard Carnival Cruise Lines. After nearly 10 years at sea, he jumped ship to launch a career in publishing, which catered to the cruise industry. Today, he is the publisher and editor-in-chief of Porthole Cruise Magazine, *now in its 12th year of production. The leading consumer magazine dedicated to cruising, it is jam-packed with ship reviews, destination profiles, industry news, and more. To find out more about Porthole Cruise Magazine, go to **www.porthole.com**.*

Introduction

The cruise industry is bigger than it has ever been. Since its earliest inception as a form of pleasure and relaxation for vacationers worldwide, cruise lines have cultivated and developed the cruise format to new levels of luxury and entertainment.

It may sound like a familiar sales pitch, but it is also increasingly true and, for anyone considering taking his first cruise as the next major family vacation, there are plenty of reasons to set sail. More than 11 million vacationers choose to do just that each and every year and, by joining them, vacationers are taking advantage of an industry that does quite possibly everything it can to ensure they have a good time for the seven or so days spent on-board.

With any vacation, though, there is plenty of planning that needs to be done. The first time on a cruise can seem overwhelming if it is not properly planned. There are multiple cruise lines to choose from, dozens of travel agencies, different destinations, and the ever important question — who to go with.

Luckily, because there are 11 million annual cruise participants, there is an ample group of individuals who have, in the past, experienced exactly what first-time cruise participants will be experiencing. By taking that massive accumulation of combined experience, it is possible to give a guided tour of the cruise process so that nothing is forgotten. Vacations should not be stressful experiences, which is probably why you are reading this book.

Embarking on that first cruise can be an incredibly stressful experience, but it should not be. After all, it is a vacation. No one wants to spend his time trying to figure out how a cruise ship works once he has already gotten there, nor does he want to embarrass himself in the booking process or in a port of call.

The best part of any vacation is being able to relax and unwind, and in an ideal situation, a cruise is designed to do just that. It just needs to be properly prepared. Planning is just the first step in that process. Having the perfect cruise vacation is the second. Anyone preparing for that first magical outing on the Caribbean or any number of other aquatic cruise destinations can rest assured that the contents of this book will offer exactly what you need to be fully prepared when you embark.

Start early, maybe even months before you plan on going on your vacation. By taking the right precautions months in advance, when it is finally time to start packing, calling travel agents, and organizing the family to go on that first cruise, everything will seem easier, as though it has already been done before. And with all the information gathered from years of successful cruises, you can be sure that every detail of your next big family vacation is taken care of in absolute detail.

Section 1

What You Need to Know About Taking Your First Cruise

Section 1 provides details about what to expect when you set sail on your first cruise. While selecting the type of cruise you wish to take may be a big decision, hints and tips located in this part of the book will help you have a deeper understanding of cruises. Here you will learn about how to prepare for your cruise, what to expect on-board the ship, types of cruises, types of excursions, and much more to ensure that you have an enjoyable vacation.

Chapter 1

The Cruise Industry: A Brief History

The concept of cruising as a luxury vacation option is not entirely new, although the exact method in which people currently use the vacation form to get away from their hectic every day lives is slightly different than in its earliest iterations.

Regardless, the cruise is a highly popular format that, since the 1980s, has enjoyed 900 percent industry growth. For many Americans, the first glimpse of the cruise lifestyle was made in the 1970s with shows like "The Love Boat" and early commercials that hoped to use that popularity to grow the industry.

The ploys worked and the cruise industry is now one of the largest vacation and tourism industries in the nation, with more than 11 million travelers every year visiting one of numerous worldwide destinations. With that kind of popularity and repeat business, it is no wonder so many people are interested in taking to the high seas for their summer vacations each year.

The cruise itself is a bit of a novel concept, unlike almost any other type of vacation on the planet. First, most cruises are all-inclusive. This is the most important aspect of a cruise — the one thing that sets it apart from most other vacations.

All-inclusive cruisers usually pay for the entire vacation and, when they arrive on the boat, they are treated to a suite-quality room, unlimited food, drinks, and entertainment, and dozens of other amenities that they never need to worry about the cost of. A cruise is essentially a single-time investment for an entire vacation's worth of entertainment, taking away much of the stress that comes with traditional vacations. Be sure to check with your cruise line to determine what you have paid for. While some all-inclusive cruises include extras, others do not. In these instances, you will need to budget for anything not included in the price of the cruise. Drinks on-board are commonly an additional charge. There is, however, always the option of finding an truly all-inclusive cruise package.

In contrast, a traditional vacation puts people in the position of needing to plan not only travel and lodgings, but all their meals, transportation, and activities. This can lead to much more stress than anyone could expect, especially when they are supposed to be on vacation. No one wants to spend his vacation looking for bus routes and counting meal budgets. Cruises eliminate the extra guess work, and thus have become one of the most popular ways to relax — because they are the easiest.

The First Cruises

The cruise industry first found its foothold in the 19th century when the technology behind ship building and cross-oceanic travel became more viable. As people began to grow richer due to the explosion of viable wealth in industry, they started looking for easy ways to dispose of extra income and a logical step was travel.

Another fine byproduct of industry at the time was the explosion of the shipping industry and with it the building of massive, high quality ships to carry goods across the Atlantic. The concept of the cruise was born when those ships began carrying passengers.

The early cruise ships were not anywhere near the same level of elegance someone would associate with today's small floating cities. Instead, they were primarily designed to carry goods. In 1818, the Black Ball Line became the first major shipping company to offer a passenger service between the United States and England.

The earliest voyages were one-time offerings, combining the very expensive cost of shipping goods between continents with transferring people. Immigration was ramping up at this time as well, especially as Europe bounded into the Industrial Revolution and brought along with it overcrowding and bad pay. The volume of people using shipping companies to travel rose sharply, and eventually men such as Samuel Cunard recognized this and decided to take advantage of it.

In 1839, Cunard took the concept the Black Ball Line had pioneered and expanded upon it, offering a full schedule of intercontinental voyages for anyone who had the money to buy passage. The wealthy could now book passage aboard a large ship such as the Britannia — Cunard's first vessel — and reach London or Boston in 14 days time, a trip that had taken months for early settlers to America.

Men and women at the time, such as Mark Twain, voyaged aboard the Britannia or one of Cunard's other liners for a decent price, though the accommodations were nowhere near what they are today. Twain complained in letters he wrote in 1842 that his cabin was akin to a coffin and that, during a storm, the ship was tossed around wildly. The quality of service would eventually improve, though, making it possible for one to have a luxurious time on the Atlantic.

The development of massive steam liners in the latter part of the 19th century was a major breakthrough for both the shipping and tourist industries — as the two were closely tied together at this time — and resulted in the massive cruise liners of the early 20th century, such as the ill-fated Lusitania and the Titanic.

The Evolution of the Cruise in the 20th Century

These two names capture the essence of what the cruise industry endured during the early part of the 20th century, however. The Lusitania's maiden voyage was in 1907, carrying aboard 2,000 passengers and making the trip between Liverpool and Boston in just under five days. Everything about the ship was impressive, and so it soon became a common rite of passage for the rich and famous to make the journey at least once so they could share the experience with their friends. At the time, travel for anyone below the most elite status was too expensive for a luxury liner such as the Lusitania.

There were, however, lower class accommodations that allowed those looking to emigrate from one location to the other an opportunity to take everything they owned and make a one shot trip across the Atlantic. The Lusitania met the fate of many commercial cruise ships in the early part of the 20th century, being drawn into the military conflicts that dominated at least three of those decades. However, in the case of the Lusitania, the result was much more tragic.

The Lusitania was sunk in 1914 by a German U-boat before arriving in Ireland. The incident killed more than 1,200 passengers and only incited more anger on the part of the English government, already at war with Germany in World War I.

Another company at the time, the White Star Line, wanted to compete with the Cunard Line's Lusitania and so, in 1908, unveiled its Olympic class of ocean liners, whose star was the Titanic. The Titanic was the largest ship ever built at the time and, as a result, was considered unsinkable by writers and industry men alike. As many people are well aware, though, its first and fateful journey across the Atlantic saw it run aground of an iceberg and sink on April 14, 1912.

More than 1,500 people lost their lives in the disaster, and the entire shipping industry was irrevocably changed as new regulations were introduced to ensure safety on-board, proper life-boat and life-vest allotment, and for the documentation of navigation.

Growth in luxury cruises stalled for a long time following these disasters, compounded by the outbreak of war throughout much of the world in the 1910s. Ships were commandeered for military use and, though there was a slight resurgence in the roaring '20s, the industry was not given enough time to regain its footing before the Great Depression struck in the 1930s.

In the 1930s that the two biggest names in cruise liners merged. Because of the lack of passengers in the Great Depression, the fast aging of both companies' fleets, and the extravagant cost of construction on Cunard's newest cruise liner — the Queen Mary — neither company could afford to continue operation without the help of the British government, which then required they merge. In 1933, the two companies merged their holdings and became Cunard-White Star Limited. Eventually, Cunard would acquire the remaining assets from White Star and the old Olympic class ships from the White Star company would be scrapped because of their age.

The cruise industry would not return from its tailspin, though, until the 1950s because of the Second World War, which began in Europe at the tail end of the 1930s. Many of the ships for all the major cruise lines were being used for military operations and, with no one financially or morally fit to embark on a luxury cruise during war time, the industry stalled.

Resurgence After War

Because they were so useful for transferring goods and men across the ocean, the U.S. government started subsidizing the construction of new cruise ships following World War II in the hopes that, should another major world war break out, they could once again utilize the ships for the transfer of goods. Combined with the existing fleet of ships in the Merchant Marines, the new breed of cruise ships were quickly rebuilt and in service by the 1950s.

It was in the 1960s, though, that the first noticeable growth of the commercial cruise industry was seen. While the airline industry had recently made it possible for people to travel great distances in much less time, the cruise industry started to shift its focus away from transport and more toward affordable luxury travel. Because it had worked so well in the past and because construction and navigation costs were lower than ever before, it was then possible to build much larger ships with extravagant amenities on which every day people could gather and enjoy a week or two away from their lives.

The cruise industry that we know today was born. Initially, the rise in cruise popularity was a result of nostalgia. Those who had ridden on ships during the 1920s in their youth remembered the sensation of crossing the great unknown and were intrigued by the concept of spending a week's time at sea in decadence. Similar to when any new technology arrives and expedites a common need for humanity, a certain amount of growth is seen in nostalgia — in remembering how things once were.

That is not to say that the cruise industry was not hit hard by the growth of the airline industry. The 747 airplane was something of a death knell to commercial transport and, as much of the cruise industry's money came from transport, the effects were almost immediate. It did not help, either, that the United States was in the process of creating a national and subsequently worldwide network of airports and regulatory forces in order to streamline the airline industries.

The Modern Cruise Is Born

So, it was not until the 1970s that true success was met again by the cruise industries. It was Cunard that first instigated the major changes — as early as 1974 — to the cruise industry that have made it what it is today. Business was sagging and passengers were unimpressed in the midst of an ever-more extravagant world, so Cunard started hiring celebrities to travel with the Queen Elizabeth II, their New York to London liner, and perform.

They compared the trip to that of a Las Vegas vacation, complete with numerous entertainment and amenity opportunities, and aboard the fastest ship in their fleet, the QE2, Cunard hoped they would find success and revive their failing business.

In response, cruises started to become popular for everyone, not just those interested in luxury traveling options. It also cannot go without mentioning that the debut of "The Love Boat" television show in 1977 had an effect on how individuals viewed the cruise industry. The show ran for eight seasons before being cancelled in 1986, and many consider it a driving force in the resurgent cruise line market, romanticizing the cruise as an ideal vacation option for single young men and women or couples. The show may have been a Hollywood rendition of reality, but the beautiful backdrops shown were nothing if not enticing.

In the 1980s, the new look cruise industry took off, building dozens of new ships that could each hold more than 2,000 passengers and were specifically built to carry passengers to exotic locales on vacation. They did not contain mail cargo holds or shipping containers. These new ships were solely devoted to giving vacationing passengers all the amenities they expected and desired on a multi-day vacation.

Things such as casinos, spas, and basketball courts — which had never before been built on a ship for the sole purpose of entertainment — were now common amenities and made a cruise vacation more enticing than the port of call in which it eventually landed. By advertising their amenities and their on-board entertainment options, the cruise lines were selling thousands more tickets and quickly growing into a leader in everyman vacation options. No longer is luxury only the right of the wealthy. It is a commonly available commodity for anyone who wants to take a cruise.

The Cruise Industry Today

The cruise industry today is indeed one of the largest tourism industries in the world. Having built a massive base of devoted followers and always trying to grow larger, the cruise industry has made it possible for nearly anyone on any budget to afford a cruise. However, almost 90 percent of those who can afford to take a cruise still have not done so, which has forced the cruise lines to seek continual growth and development of their marketing techniques to draw in more passengers.

The initial draw for the cruise lines that operate today was the on-board luxury offered on many boats. However, this is not enough for everyone who still has not been convinced. So, many cruise lines have started advertising the numerous options for cultural exploration and discovery that they can find in ports of call. Additionally, classes on the ship have become very popular, with some cruise lines offering classes on photography and oceanography taught by professionals from National Geographic. By offering cultural opportunities, cruises to different locations, such as Asia and Europe, are becoming more popular.

Additionally, large cruise lines have consolidated, creating even larger cruise lines that can offer different options. In the years since 2000 alone, more than 64 new ships have gone into commission, and the industry will continue to grow at a similar rate until at least 2012.

One of the more interesting developments in recent years designed to attract more passengers who have yet to enjoy a cruise experience is that of diversification. Cruise lines are starting to build smaller ships as well for those interested in more intimate experiences without the megaliner, 3,000 passenger ships that have become the face of the industry.

Many large cruise lines are starting to offer new ships that only hold as many as 200 passengers so that those interested in a vacation in which they can spend more time intimately interacting with the ocean instead of inside can do so. The goal of such expansion is to offer every possible alternative and option for those that might not be interested in one particular style or kind of cruise.

On the other side of things, the megaliners continue to evolve, offering new features designed to draw in guests — things such as shopping malls, ice rinks, and dockable catamarans within the hull of the ship for more intimate experiences on the water.

The Cruise Industry and You

The growth of the cruise industry in just the last 20 years alone shows the kind of dedication to quality and expansion the companies have. If you are just beginning the process of planning your cruise vacation, one of the first things to consider is exactly what you want to get out of your cruise. Ruminating on the history of the industry and the early necessity of boats to ship people and goods or not, there are plenty of options currently available for any of the 90 percent who have yet to take a cruise.

Chapter 2

Ten Reasons to Choose a Cruise

If you are reading this book you have likely already decided you are interested in taking a cruise. The advertisements and brochures are everywhere. A friend probably even described the wonderful experience they had last March with their husband or wife. The reasons for taking a cruise are lined up and bulleted within a Word document on the computer's desktop and serve as a daily reminder to start the planning process.

And there truly are a number of reasons to consider a cruise for that next vacation. However, if you have yet to decide that you are truly willing to pay the money necessary to take that first cruise or whether a cruise is right for you, a little persuasion never hurts.

It is vital to know exactly what is important on a vacation. When making plans and choosing between a variety of different options, having a clear picture in mind of what amenities, destinations, and activities are most important to you will serve to ensure that the correct cruise is chosen when the time comes to start making those vital selections.

The Top 10 Reasons to Choose a Cruise

For that reason, 10 of the most common reasons for selecting a cruise are listed below. Each of these offers something that can be found in a cruise package. Not everything listed below can be found in every vacation package available, though, which gives the first-time cruise planner a good idea of what they should be looking for. If someone decides that value is more important than the cuisine or the eventual destination, value packages should be considered before the specific exotic locale they have always wanted to visit.

Value Vacation

The first thing many people consider when selecting their vacation options is just how much it is going to cost them. A great deal of people cannot afford to just go wherever they like and worry about the total cost at a later date. So, it is vital to balance the amount of fun a particular destination will be against its initial cost.

Cruises have become popular in recent years because they offer such a wide variety of value vacation options depending on the guest's financial means. A five-day cruise can cost as little as $300 if the guest is willing to choose a value cruise line and a small room for the trip.

However, if you are looking to enjoy a luxury cruise at a reasonable rate, that same five-day cruise might cost around $800 — still a very reasonable amount. The eventual cost range for a cruise can be extensive, anywhere between $300 and $4,000 depending on the cruise line, the destination, and the length of the cruise. Choosing a cruise is a great vacation option because of that value.

Starting to balance the cost of a cruise against the amenities and amount of people going is a vital first step in deciding which line and destination to go with.

A Romantic Getaway

The next most popular, and often most cited, reason to go on a cruise is the classic "Love Boat" response. Many people view a cruise as an ideal option to get away from their friends and family for a few days and enjoy the company of their spouse or loved one. What better way to spend a few romantic days alone than on a boat in the middle of the Caribbean?

The cruise lines are well aware of this popular reason for selecting a cruise and have long since offered numerous amenities designed to see to the desires and wishes of couples on a romantic retreat. Secluded dining options, honeymoon suites, and intimate lounges all serve to offer couples looking to escape their lives together for a few days somewhere to enjoy that time alone.

Romance is not solely for the attached, though, as many young singles have started taking to cruises as a means by which to meet other young singles. Cruise lines have started offering theme cruises, especially in the spring and summer months, for those that are interested in going alone to find a romantic partner.

Choosing a romantic cruise can be a great boon to a marriage or a new relationship, and certain cruise lines and destinations offer amazing packages for just this reason.

World-Class Cuisine

Spending five to 10 days on a boat in the midst of a giant body of water means that passengers will be eating all their meals from the same restaurants and food services. The result is that the one thing you will most readily remember when you return from your cruise is how good the food was or was not. If the food was terrible, few people would be willing to return. The cruise lines know this, and have long since offered world-class cuisine on all their boats.

The food is almost assured to be of the highest quality for nearly anyone embarking on their first cruise. Often the food service manager on a cruise ship is required to have a college degree and years of experience in the industry before they are considered qualified for the position. Additionally, world-renowned and high caliber cooks and chefs take positions on cruise lines consistently, as they are offered good pay and a chance to see different parts of the world in exchange for their talents.

Anyone considering a cruise vacation should almost immediately expect the food to be of a high quality. If a cruise line's reviews do not speak highly, or at least neutrally about the cuisine, it is likely a bad sign for that cruise line.

Numerous Choices

At any given time, there are as many as 400 vessels departing in a given month for a given destination that a vacationer might want to visit. This means that the options for a cruise vacation are nearly endless, highlighted by the sheer number of cruise lines, boats in their fleets, and different themes for those boats.

Families interested in a group vacation can find specifically family-themed cruises from Disney, while couples and spouses can find adult-only trips. There are a large variety of different boats available, and each one is designed to ensure that those on-board are catered to directly. This means that if you have a particular reason or concept in mind for your cruise — a marriage, a reunion, or just a relaxing getaway — you can almost assuredly find a boat that will offer the services you are looking for.

Simple Vacation Options

One of the major reasons the cruise has become so popular in the last 20 years is that it does not require those embarking to do anything more than book a plane ticket to and from the boat and book the cruise itself. There are plenty of other small details that any vacation requires, but the details that tend to get forgotten or lost in the shuffle are almost immediately unimportant, as the cruise lines take care of them.

This means that, once the cruise has been booked, everything on-board is taken care of. You do not need to worry about finding food, planning activities, or paying for transportation while at your vacation destination. It makes the entire process much simpler than it ever was before, and thus a great option for those looking to relax, even in the planning process.

Destinations

There are hundreds of cruise destinations. While the inherent image of the cruise is a Caribbean destination or two, you can currently choose from numerous locales all over the world. This means if the family or spouse does not want to visit the Bahamas or Puerto Rico again, you can choose from any number of other destinations.

Alaska, Mexico, Central America, and even Asia and Europe have become much more popular in recent years, as those who do not want to go on the stereotypical cruise have made their voices and decisions heard. The cruise lines have thus expanded their options considerably and now offer destinations in dozens of different countries.

If a particular destination is more important than anything else for you, you will not need to compromise your vacation.

Satisfaction

Since solely devoting their vessels and services to ensuring the good time of their passengers in the 1970s, the cruise lines have been able to ensure the kind of satisfaction that very few vacations can, because, as a guest on a cruise ship, you are seen to almost constantly. In a far away city or foreign country, this can only be truthful within the hotel in which you are staying and only if the hotel is of the highest quality.

A cruise is different because it is specifically designed to guarantee satisfaction for the visitors. There are some instances in which a company or specific boat does not offer absolute satisfaction for its guests and, in these cases, passengers should do their best to be aware of their options and research their choices. If this kind of happiness and satisfaction with a decision is vital for a guest, it can easily be had.

Service

Going hand in hand with satisfaction, service is almost a constant on-board most cruise ships. The cruise lines go out of their way to ensure that their staff is fully trained in the most detailed of methods to make every guest feel at home on the ship. Similar to a four star hotel staff, most cruise lines offer dozens of housekeeping staff members, a world-class cook staff, and dozens of different on-board activities overseen by expert staff members.

In the 1980s, cruise lines started hiring celebrities to work on-board and improve the entertainment options. In recent years, they have taken extra steps to offer things like expert hobbyists and guides for ports of call, making trips to exotic locales much more fun and possible for those who are interested.

Family Environment

Any vacation option needs to cater to the possibility of there being a family on-board, and few vacation options are as family-friendly as the cruise industry. Cruises have long been great options for just about any combination of guests, but entire boats have been outfitted for family opportunities. These boats create a family-friendly environment that is perfect for any aged guests and has long been a very popular alternative to busy vacations with over-planning.

For any family trying to find an alternative to the typical vacation options that please everyone in the group, a cruise is often the best choice. With value pricing for families, a cruise can be the most affordable as well.

CASE STUDY: PATRICIA JACOBSON

Patricia Jacobson and her family first heard about cruising as a family vacation option through her sister's family who took a seven day cruise to Nassau in 2002. The trip was so successful and her reviews so raving that Patricia could not pass up the opportunity when husband Jason received coveted July vacation time:

"Our first cruise was something else. After seven days in the Caribbean, I did not know what I would do when we returned. The kids loved the activities available on-board — I do not think I saw them more than a half dozen times at most after breakfast and before dinner each day. Jason and I essentially had our second honeymoon and the after effect has yet to wear off.

For sure though, I wish I had spent a little more time planning the trip. I had the benefit of my sister Sara's experience. She showed me the right travel agent to talk to and gave me advice on a ship that her family had enjoyed, but I was still overwhelmed by the amount of options, the time it took to put everything together, and the budgeting. We almost did not make it at all after I realized the extra cost of flying to Miami in July.

I would definitely recommend that anyone who wants to put together a halfway decent cruise at least talks to someone who has been on a cruise and can give you their personal experience. In lieu of anything else, a good book or guide will help you through the hard parts."

Prioritizing for Your Cruise

The top 10 reasons for vacationing on a cruise ship are all compelling discussions. When combined, they offer an experience that few other vacation options can offer, and create a situation that is above and beyond many people's expectations, especially for the money being paid.

However, it is not realistic to expect everything on the list to be available on every cruise. If any vacation was that easy, no one would need the kind of extra guidance and information available in this book. You should spend extra time balancing and weighing out the viability of each thing on this list and deciding what is most important.

For instance, if the location of a vacation is more important than the price, you will likely disregard the price differential and focus more intensely on the options available for a cruise in the Bahamas or to Alaska, if those are the desired destinations.

Step one in the cruise selection process, before any paperwork, travel agencies, or cost analysis, is charting which of the above options are the most vital. For example, a romantic cruise will discount any family-oriented options from the list of potential cruise lines, making the decision more straightforward.

Chapter 3

It Is in the Details: What to Expect Before You Book

Booking a cruise vacation is a long and arduous process if it has never been done before. There is a lot of research, dozens of different cruise lines and travel agencies to choose from, and seemingly hundreds of options for nearly every aspect of the trip. It can seem at times like some of those decisions — if made wrong — will result in a stressful period of time. However, that does not necessarily have to be the case. In fact, starting early and being fully prepared for whatever might happen is almost as good as knowing which decisions to finalize.

While the list in Chapter 2 gives a detailed account of the different reasons someone might choose to go on a cruise, here is a description you can expect to find when you do book your cruise. Because the booking process is too involved and vital to the eventual success of a cruise, it is most important that you are absolutely sure you understand what you will experience during your time on-board.

Advantages of Choosing a Cruise

Besides the 10 reasons previously mentioned, there are dozens of advantages to choosing a cruise. One that can be reiterated again and again above any others is price. The cost of a cruise, when compared to other, similar vacation packages, is value packed. While it is possible to find a vacation package that will take someone to an exotic or distant locale for less than $1,000, it is very rare to find one that includes all the necessary expenses that a different style of vacation would incur.

Because a cruise is self-contained (taking place in a singular location) and pricing is done in packages wherein attendees do not need to pay anything more than their travel agent promised they would pay, it holds a higher value than most traditional vacations that incur additional expenses after arriving, before leaving, and upon returning home.

Additionally, a cruise is advantageous because of the method in which it operates. Instead of a combined vacation on which a traveler would visit three cities over the course of two weeks and need to pack and unpack in three different hotels, essentially losing entire days of their vacation, a cruise allows those same travelers to never repack and unpack again while visiting numerous ports of call.

If you are interested in the freedom of an all-inclusive environment, a cruise is that much easier as a vacation spot. It does not require extra planning or time on your part to decide what you will do when you arrive in certain cities. Instead, you can simply attend and enjoy existing activities on-board the boat.

Disadvantages of a Cruise

That is not to say that a cruise is without a few disadvantages of its own. There are those who will try to dissuade their friends and family from setting sail for any number of reasons and, in certain cases, they may be right. There are some situations in which a cruise may not be the best vacation for your family. In these cases, you should reconsider your vacation plans or the timing of your cruise. You should not let anything on this list directly dissuade you from a cruise, though. These are simply common problems that could arise on a ship that any potential traveler should be aware of. Without the proper planning and awareness before a cruise is booked, the results could be disastrous.

First of all, not everything on an all-inclusive cruise is cost free. There are certain expenses that will begin to add up, especially for those that do not expect them. The first of these is taxes. Occasionally, when calling in a port, you will be required to pay a port tax. This is sometimes covered in the ticket price, but many other times it is not. This is an important factor to discuss with a travel agent before booking.

Additionally, the cruise line might charge for excursions to land from the boat. While they might offer landside activities such as mountain biking or sightseeing, it usually has an extra cost attached. Even in the all-inclusive packages most cruise lines offer, this is not considered part of the cruise itself because it is off-board.

Expenses might include tipping the staff on-board the ship — something you should do in common courtesy and to receive decent service — buying snacks in between meals, and any gambling or souvenir expenses incurred on- or off-board the ship. One of the main disadvantages of a cruise ship can be the extra costs that are overlooked.

Additionally, not every cruise vacation is all-inclusive. A traditional cruise will often be much less expensive, but will also result in a significant increase in cost for food, entertainment, and activities on-board. Also, make sure you have a clear understanding of what is considered "all-inclusive" on your cruise. By doing so, you will not be surprised by any extra costs.

The final possible drawback of a cruise is the risk of illness on-board. This is not as large of a risk as it has been made out to be, but has plagued cruise lines in recent history because of the sheer volume of cruise ships in service. On some occasions, entire cruise ships have been stricken by illnesses such as the norovirus, a vicious stomach virus that spreads incredibly quickly. While it is technically not any rarer than a common disease that might strike while on vacation in Italy or Puerto Rico, the results can be much more devastating, as the entire ship can be stricken at once.

Weighing the Options

Many choose to overlook the slight disadvantages of a cruise right away and instead focus on the numerous advantages available to the savvy traveler. However, if you have thought that a cruise offers the easiest and least time consuming option for a vacation, you should at least think twice about the amount of work, time, and money that will go into planning and executing the ideal cruise vacation. It is much more than what it initially appears.

The Basics of On-board Life

Forget the pros and cons of the cruise industry for now, though. You have likely already decided that a cruise is the right decision for you and are more interested in how that cruise will unfold. What kind of people will you meet? What activities can you enjoy? What will cruise life be like on-board the ship? These are the vital questions that most first-time cruise participants ask themselves, and rightfully so.

Life on-board a cruise ship is much different from life on land, and it very well should be. As someone on vacation, you will not want to feel as though everything is the same as at home, and yet a certain amount can be said for that familiarity and comfort a good staff and well-accommodating furnishings can offer.

Depending on what kind of a cruise you embark on, the majority of the trip is spent in the luxury of a four star hotel. Rooms vary in size and location, but are generally well furnished and of decent quality, allowing those on-board the comfort of a familiar space no matter where they come from in life.

Additionally, especially on all-inclusive cruises, all the meals are taken care of for you. The aspect of every day life that requires people to make and prepare meals is removed, allowing more time for relaxation. Activities are planned at times, but a certain degree of freedom is given to anyone interested in exploring the ship or the ports of call on their own terms.

Life on-board a cruise ship can be one of two things. It can be extremely relaxing, spent lounging in a luxurious room, reading on the deck, and swimming. Or it can be spent engaging in dozens of planned activities, watching numerous free shows, and enjoying the sites available in each port of call. What many people enjoy about a cruise vacation is that they are given the freedom to decide between the two.

With upward of 3,000 other passengers on-board at any given time, cruise ship life is a massive social event. Unless you spend the greater portion of your time locked in their room or looking at your feet as you walk around, you will be able to enjoy the company of dozens of strangers from nearly every walk of life and location. If you enjoy meeting new people, a cruise ship is probably the best vacation opportunity available for doing so.

At first, a cruise might seem overwhelming for that very reason. Upon waking after the first day on-board, you will be surrounded by hundreds of strangers, the open sea, and dozens of staff members hoping to get you involved in on-board activities. It is definitely not like the comfort of watching television on your own sofa in your own living room. However, the brand of relaxation, though more specialized and intense at times, is equally as enjoyable.

Cell Phone and Internet Usage On-board

In years past, being on a cruise meant being cut off from the world for days at a time, waiting to make calls back home until landing in a particular port and going ashore. A lot has changed in recent years as technological dependence has made it to where people can go almost anywhere on the planet and still have cell phone and Internet access for communication. A cruise ship is not any different.

Many cruise lines feature standard Internet hot spots and connection ports in cabins, along with cell phone access in designated lounges. And usually, according to industry reports, two-thirds of passengers use the Internet access provided to them and at least half use the phone access while on-board.

There are almost no ships in any fleet that do not have some form of computer or Internet access made available to passengers these days. The exact offerings for each ship vary slightly, though, including the price of using that Internet access. So, contacting cruise lines directly before a trip to check and see what they offer is usually the best choice.

Activities on a Cruise

One of the most advertised and discussed aspects of a cruise is the number of different events and activities offered by the cruise line. Depending on the ship, there are quite possibly hundreds of different things available to enjoy on-board a cruise at any given time, making it possible to almost always be busy.

If you are embarking on a cruise for the first time, this collection of activities can seem overwhelming at first. In many cases, it very well is. However, before booking your first cruise, it is good to know exactly how expansive those opportunities are.

Most cruises offer the standard collection of top notch dining and entertainment options. This usually includes numerous restaurant choices, along with bars, nightclubs, and evening shows from first-rate performers. On an all-inclusive cruise, these are usually free and are a daily part of the schedule. On traditional cruises, the same options are likely available but probably not as overtly and may cost a bit more than desired. It is good to research the availability and selection of food and entertainment options aboard a cruise before booking.

Being at sea has its advantages, and many cruise lines take advantage of this by offering on-board Las Vegas-style casinos. While not as big or as prevalent as the Vegas strip, these casinos are often very popular, especially at night.

If you are interested in staying fit and trim aboard the boat, fitness options are almost always offered, and are usually well beyond what one would expect. Some ships sport basketball and tennis courts, while others have multiple Olympic-sized swimming pools. Additionally, spas and massages are often offered alongside the numerous fitness options, including fully equipped gyms.

Every ship has its own collection of activities, including everything from movie theaters and shopping centers to organized classes and excursions off the ship. One thing you can count on is that you will receive a detailed list of all available activities on-board almost immediately after you ask about a particular cruise.

Rain or Shine

The weather is always a major factor when preparing for a vacation. And when deciding where and when to book a cruise, it can be incredibly important to know exactly what kind of weather the ship will be sailing into. For the most part, cruise lines will not set sail in regions when the weather is unsavory. However, there are always better times of the year to travel to a particular destination, such as Alaska, Europe, or Asia.

For northern locations and cold weather cruises, you should dress and pack appropriately. Though much of the cruise might take place inside the ship, it is very likely that you will go ashore at least once or above deck. Additionally, in the case of a northern cruise, it will be necessary to organize and embark on the cruise at a good time. Winter months are not the best time in that case.

When discussing cruises to mid-latitude locations, such as France or the Mediterranean, the time frame is slightly more open, usually stretching between spring and fall. Winter months in this area still offer numerous cruise options, but the weather might make it so that they offer less activities and off-board options than a summertime cruise. Because this is considered a temperate climate, it is equally important to dress for the occasion depending on the time of year. The mid-summer months can get very warm in Europe and are often the most popular times to take a cruise. However, April and late September have also become quite popular in recent years because they are less crowded than other months at sea and because they offer moderate temperatures for those not seeking hot weather vacations.

Though not the only cruise destination by any means, the Caribbean is among the most popular available throughout the year. While it might seem the locations of Puerto Rico, the Bahamas, or Jamaica make them ideal all year cruise destinations, there is a significant time period in which cruises in this region are not considered completely safe, largely because of hurricane season.

The official hurricane season runs from June 1 to November 30 each year, though the most volatile months are August and September. Cruises run throughout the year, and cruise ships are capable of steering around projected hurricane paths, but the effects of these storms can often make it hard to visit the promised ports of call and can disrupt the overall experience.

Besides the hurricane season, weather in the Caribbean is fairly constant, remaining between 75 and 90 degrees Fahrenheit most of the year. February is considered the peak of cruise season, as it is in the midst of the calmest period of the year for storms and offers warm weather vacations for those who are still defrosting from the winter snows.

For any location, planning for a cruise should begin with the time and weather associated with the location. If vacation time arrives at a time when a particular cruise might be ruined or less enjoyable than possible because of weather, the traveler should either reconsider the destination or try to maneuver their vacation time to a better part of the year.

The Nitty Gritty

The last thing to consider before starting the booking process for a first-time cruise is the slew of minor details that can make or break a vacation. There are dozens of them, from the basic vacation materials, such as buying the right luggage and warm weather clothing to the renewal of all passports in a timely fashion.

Passports and Possible Visas

The first step in the process of preparing to book a cruise should be to renew or get that first passport. A passport may seem like the smallest and most insignificant of necessities for a vacation, but without it you cannot go anywhere. The most important thing about getting a passport cleared before a trip is planned is that it can take a long time to do so.

To start with, the basic time frame for getting a passport application cleared is two to nine weeks, as published by the State Department. However, since the beginning of 2007, the time frame for getting a new passport has ballooned up to six months because of recent law changes regarding passport usage in travel to Canada and Mexico.

With the influx of new passport requests expected to last until 2009 when the law becomes final and all border crossings will require a passport, you should start much earlier and assure that there is ample time for the State Department to process the application.

There is an expediting option that allows a passport application to be processed in as little as two to six days, which costs an additional $60 to complete. To use the fast track passport application, you must be leaving the country within a few weeks. The process cannot be used in advance for a trip that leaves in three months. It is recommended that, if there are only six weeks left before a trip is planned to commence, you should wait until you are within the one month expedited passport time frame and pay the extra $60 to ensure you get your passport in time for the trip.

How to Get a Passport

1. Gather and organize the necessary government forms and paperwork from the State Department and begin the seemingly interminable application process. These forms can be found at any local U.S. Post Office or through the U.S. State Department at **http://travel.state.gov**.

2. Pages one and two outline specific instructions that should be followed before anything else. If the forms are downloaded from

the State Department, complete and print pages three and four. The government recommends that, when printing these forms, they are printed on standard 8 ½" x 11" paper with no holes, at medium weight, and in only black and white. Any special papers or inks will be rejected.

3. You need to gather all the necessary documents requested by the State Department, including proof of U.S. citizenship. This includes:

   a. An officially certified birth certificate from the city, county, or state in which you are born (this cannot be a copy and must be officially certified by a notary of the state in which you were born)

   b. If born overseas, a record of that birth

   c. Naturalization certificate

   d. Certificate of citizenship

4. Documents to prove identity can include the following:

   a. A previous and damage-free passport that has not been altered in any way

   b. A naturalization certificate

   c. A certificate of citizenship

   d. Any current and valid:

      i. Driver's license

      ii. City, state, or federally-issued government ID

iii. Military ID issued to active or retired personnel or family members

5. Two photos need to be taken for the completion of the application. These photos should be taken in normal clothing — no work uniforms — and without anything on the head. Glasses should be worn if they are normally worn. The best place to get passport photos taken is in a post office where they already know the process and can have them ready quickly. Not all post offices offer these services, so check first before visiting one for passport photos.

6. The application will need your social security number. If it has not been memorized, it should be written down and included in the paperwork.

7. There is a standard fee for passport applications that changes on occasion. On the same Web site as the passport application, the fee schedule can be found. If you are in a hurry and will be departing on your trip in less than one month, an application can be expedited for an extra $60.

8. There are numerous passport offices around the country, so the next step is merely to find one and have the application processed. They will request the departure date and prioritize the application accordingly.

What to Remember

*   The current standard fee for a U.S. passport (October 2007) for an adult over 18 is $97. These are good for 10 years.

*   The current standard fee for a U.S. passport (October 2007) for a child under 16 is $82. These are good for five years.

❀ Contrary to past travel regulations, passports are now required for travel to Canada, Mexico, the Caribbean, and the Bahamas. This affects almost all cruise passengers.

Medical Documents and Supplies

Though more detail is given to what should be packed and remembered prior to a cruise in Chapters 7 and 8, other details should be considered well before booking even begins. Because medical issues might require additional trips to doctors and pharmacies before a trip, it is best to take care of them as far in advance as possible.

While it is impossible to know what issues might arise in the weeks eventually leading up to a cruise, it is not unforeseeable to spend time six months or so before a cruise preparing all the necessary medical equipment. For any family, it is good to have an emergency stash of medical supplies, especially if anyone in the family is diabetic or has heart problems and has daily needs. This ensures that, if for some reason unforeseeable in the future, medication is forgotten or lost, there is an extra stash always ready.

If the day of the trip arrives and that medication is nowhere to be found, it might be very hard or impossible to find replacements before the plane or ship departs. Medical supplies should thus be sufficiently backed up and always readily available.

Additionally, medical documents can be the difference between a simple visit to an on-ship doctor and a horrible vacation. Almost all cruise ships have Internet and phone access now, which makes it possible for the on-board physician to contact a family doctor or pharmacy for verification. It will be important to have this contact information. Additionally, if you get ill and have your recent medical tests and charts with you, it makes treatment much easier by the cruise physician.

Being Ready to Leave Home for Days

The prospect of leaving home for a long period of time can be both exciting and worrisome. Before you book, it is often a good idea to start thinking about some of the necessary tasks that go with a vacation. Though dealing with these problems can often wait until after the trip is booked and a concrete date is set, it is good to know early on what might arise.

By starting a list early, it is possible to add new items over the course of the coming months instead of hoping the list is comprehensive. While the large things like finding a house-sitter and taking care of the pets will probably not be forgotten, other details, such as the food in the refrigerator or having the right credit cards available, will need to be taken into consideration.

Common Cruising Myths

A common question many people ask when returning from their first cruise is, "Why don't more people know about this?" It is a good question, but it is likely the wrong one. Instead, they should ask why more people do not take advantage of cruises. The cruise industry is very well known. Advertising and travel agencies have seen to that. Unfortunately, the stereotypes and myths about cruises have persisted since the 1970s, and the childhood memories many people have of a certain television series only perpetuate them.

When you return from that first cruise, with the myths having been thoroughly broken, you will likely be unable to comprehend how others still have such odd misconceptions. Here are some of the most common of those myths and how they are misconstrued.

Myth #1: Everyone Gets Sick On-board

The Reality: Seasickness is an unfortunate reality of any trip at sea. It will happen to some people who suffer from motion sickness on occasion, but luckily the cruise lines have done a great deal of work to ensure this does not happen any more than is absolutely unavoidable.

Modern cruise ships have been reinforced with specially designed hulls that keep rolling to a minimum and have minimized up and down motion with high tech computer models and well-balanced engineering. The number of seasick individuals is very small on most cruises, as the motion is negated in all but the most powerful of storms — those being largely unavoidable.

Luckily, for those that still experience the occasional motion sickness, there are numerous means by which they can avoid excess illness. Sea Bands are popular nondrug options, while traditional seasickness medicine, like Dramamine, is available from most doctors when heading to sea. The best idea is to be prepared for the worst by visiting a doctor before embarking, but not to immediately assume sickness will occur. It is very rare.

Myth #2: Boredom Is Unavoidable

The Reality: Cruise lines have done a lot of work and spent a great deal of time ensuring that no one is ever bored when on a cruise. In fact, you would be hard pressed to find any other vacation option that throws quite as much to do at you. While each cruise ship has its own collection of activities, they are usually substantial enough to keep them entertained for the duration of their trip.

The list of possible activities is nearly endless and is covered more in depth in Chapter 11. However, if you still cling to the long-held belief that a cruise is going to involve sitting on a wet and crowded deck for five days with nothing to do, the truth is much less dull. Along with the daytime activities, nighttime lounges, entertainment and casinos, and the off-ship excursions, the likelihood is that a cruise will actually have too many things to do, making it hard to select which activities to participate in.

Myth #3: Not Fitting In

The Reality: This is just counter-intuitive. Part of the fun of being on a cruise is that everyone is slightly different and you never know who you might meet while there. With hundreds of different hometowns, cultures, and languages represented on-board, it is almost impossible not to meet someone new. Fitting in is essentially the last thing you should want to do, and being concerned about it is the same as being nervous on the first day of school or at a new job — it will pass as soon as that first friend is made.

Myth #4: Passengers Look Ridiculous without Shipboard Experience

The Reality: This is a goofy myth, but unfortunately one that many potential cruise passengers have let color their decision to attend a cruise or not. There are dozens of reasons someone might choose a different vacation, but deciding not to attend a cruise because they might look silly when they do not understand what "port side" means is unfortunate.

For the most part, everyone on a cruise ship is in the same situation. Why would they be any different? Very few people have spent all that much time aboard ships in their lives and those that have probably were not crewing them. So, it would be unrealistic to expect anyone to understand what the different terms might mean.

If you feel you must supplement your knowledge at least a little though, there are plenty of different resources to do so. Here a few of the most common terms used on-board:

Port side — left side of the ship while facing forward

Starboard side — right side of the ship while facing forward

Bow—front of the ship

Stern — back of the ship

Galley — kitchen on the ship

Bridge — where the captain and officers are usually working, navigating, and running the daily operations of the ship

You likely will not need to know most of these terms, though having them handy will serve to dispel the concern that you will make a fool of yourself while on-board.

Myth #5: Only the Elderly Take Cruises

The Reality: This is a partial truth, but not nearly as much as it once was. In the years of the traditional cruise, senior citizens took to the seas in record numbers for any number of reasons. A cruise was an easy, affordable vacation. It allowed them to escape colder climates, meet people their own age, have fun, and be active. The same is still true, but the numbers have changed significantly in recent years. While the majority of cruise passengers are between the ages of 48 and 59, there are an equal number of passengers under 40 and over 60.

Additionally, the cruise lines have grown to the point now that they can offer numerous themed cruises for individuals who are younger, older, or with families, depending on what they desire. If a 31-year-old single wants to meet other young singles on a cruise, there is sure to be a small selection of cruises scheduled that cater directly to this demographic.

Myth #6: Everything Is on a Schedule

The Reality: Similar to the myth that cruising is too boring, this has changed a lot in recent years. Cruises today offer so much variety that the regiment and scheduled activities are merely a diversion for those that want to seek them out. Think of a cruise in the same manner as a gym. In a gym, you can use any equipment you like and workout on your own schedule, or you can sign up for a class with other gym members in dance, aerobics, or yoga. You are given ample choices and a cruise is no different.

Dining options are most often wide open, allowing you to visit the restaurants when you desire, mainly because the variety of restaurants is wide enough that they are never quite overcrowded. Some cruise lines have even begun to offer freestyle cruises on which you can spend your entire vacation doing as you please, eating where and when you want.

If you enjoy the regiment and the formality of a traditional cruise, though, they are still available. The truth to this myth is that anyone can spend as much time as they like following schedules and regiments, dressing up in nice clothes for dinner, and watching scheduled shows, but for those that fear that kind of closely watched scheduling, there are other options.

Myth #7: It Is all About the Food

The Reality: This is less of a myth and more of a misconception. Cruises are laden with wonderful food, offering dozens of different options and hiring world-class chefs to operate the kitchens. However, they are not all about the food by any means.

Traditionally, cruise ships have long since offered a huge array of dining options. Beyond the three meals everyone eats on a regular basis, cruises would offer things like mid-meal snacks, late night buffets, and hors d'oeuvres at every turn, making it seemingly impossible to get away from all that extra food if a passenger wanted to.

Fortunately, if you do not want to be tempted by the overabundance of dining options every day while on-board, cruise lines have started responding with healthier alternatives. While anyone interested in having the large meals with numerous intermittent snacks can do so, there are dozens of different options available to those looking for lower calorie, light fare.

Cruises now offer numerous dietary options as well. For those on high protein, low carb, no sugar, or no gluten diets, everything is offered, making it possible to eat however they like for the entire trip without cheating on a diet or getting sick because they are on vacation. Additionally, the addition of fitness centers, pools, tennis courts, and basketball courts makes it easier than ever to burn those extra calories off while enjoying the numerous culinary options a cruise provides.

Myth #8: The Weather Can Ruin the Cruise

The Reality: This is true of any vacation taken at nearly any location in the world. No matter where someone is headed, the weather can have a profound effect on a vacation. Think of it in these terms, though. If a hurricane or large storm comes, the ship can move out of its way. If that same storm arrives while staying in a hotel in the Bahamas, you would be forced to wait it out inside the hotel. Then you are stuck with the same boring hotel food and amenities for a week while it pours rain outside. On a cruise, even if the weather gets really bad, there are so many things to do on-board, passengers will not feel as though they have wasted their vacations.

Myth #9: Cruises Are Only for Romantic Getaways; What about the Family?

The Reality: The cruise industry has strived to make cruising available to nearly anyone of any age in the hopes that they can bust the traditional image of lovers and retired couples crowding their cabins. Cruise ships, especially those designed for family vacations, are equipped with enough things to do for children that parents almost never need to be worried about there being enough to do for the entire family. Also, parents can spend the afternoon with their children and then step aside for a quiet night alone while the children are watched over in any number of different capacities by the ship's staff.

Balancing Myth Against Fact

Myths are present in almost every brand of vacation. Those hoping to set sail on their newest vacation option are often tripped up by any number of different friends and family members outlining the reasons they should scrap their plans and do something completely different. Luckily, dealing with the myths that friends and family might throw out can often uncover even more enticing reasons to set sail on a cruise. While many of the most common misconceptions about the cruise industry are slightly true, the greater majority of them have long since been remedied by the cruise industries in an attempt to make vacations on their ships much more fun for everyone involved.

Chapter 4

Choosing Your Ideal Cruise

Cruising has come a long way since its initial inception in the 19th century. The earliest cruises, designed for transport more than for luxury, were purely functional, hosting most travelers in second and third class accommodations that would be akin to the worst-looking and least appealing shacks landside.

The industry changed in the 20th century and started catering to the luxury aspect of the cruise when air travel replaced sea travel as the most effective way to get anywhere. Cruise lines saw an opportunity and exploited it, creating a new method for couples, families, and singles to get away without having to worry about the common problems associated with a vacation.

The cruise industry grew rapidly, at an almost 900 percent rate between the 1980s and today, and it now sees more than 10 million travelers a year board cruise ships worldwide. However, there are still millions of people who have yet to be convinced that a cruise is an ideal solution for their vacation needs, something the cruise lines have put all their efforts into remedying.

To do so, they have created dozens of different themed cruises on which different demographics can enjoy a specific brand of company, activities, and staff designed to make them as comfortable as possible and feel at ease while away from home. With so many options available, the next essential step before talking to a travel agent and starting the booking process is to decide which kind of cruise is most suitable.

Themed Cruises

There are numerous themed options for cruises available from the major cruise lines. Each line tries to offer its own signature themed cruises, but many of the styles of cruise are available from multiple cruise lines. If you are concerned about being able to enjoy a cruise with like-minded individuals who will not make the experience awkward or not enjoyable, there are plenty of options.

Singles Cruises

Cruise lines have long since offered the option for single individuals to seek out cruises on which only other singles are present. This style of cruise has become increasingly popular with individuals seeking love on their vacations. Most major cruise lines offer this style cruise, usually with specially designed events and activities to help bring singles together and get to know each other.

On a singles cruise, there are a variety of different options, and the cost can occasionally be higher depending on which are selected. Because the single will not be sharing a room with anyone, there is usually a higher cost per person, unless that person is willing to combine rooms with a stranger. Placing two strangers in a double room is an option on some singles cruises.

There are not specific boats created for all singles, meaning that most liners have multiple rooms with two beds. It is necessary to fill these rooms and maximize the volume of the passenger list.

A singles cruise will offer numerous special events beyond the usual amenities for its passengers, such as cocktail parties and group introduction. A singles cruise will begin with a group gathering or numerous such gatherings where those interested in introducing themselves can meet dozens of new people right away. These cruises often feature extra dances and late nightclub events that bring together singles, along with activities designed with two purposes in mind — both to break the ice and to offer ample opportunities for entertainment on-board.

There are numerous other themes that can be found within the different brands of singles cruises. Seniors, gay and lesbian, or culturally themed cruises allow singles to find specific kinds of people to connect with.

Seniors Cruises

While the majority of cruise-goers are over age 48, a standard cruise is essentially open to any age. For seniors who want to enjoy a cruise with other seniors, there are dozens of options available to do just that.

The fundamental difference lies in the freedom senior citizens have on a cruise that younger passengers do not. For example, a senior is usually willing and able to go on cruises during times and to locations that traditional passengers could not. They can travel on much longer cruises, often taking trips to multiple destinations, and are interested in visiting more exotic locales that they have not yet been to in their lives.

Additionally, senior citizens are interested in participating in any number of alternative forms of activities, with exciting new classes on computers or the arts. For that reason, senior cruises will often cater to these varying interests, offering classes and hands-on activities to take advantage of their willingness to branch out.

Fitness programs aboard a senior cruise are likely to be less intensive because of the different physical needs, resulting in offerings such as yoga or Pilates and courses on wellness. Spa and pool activities are equally positive because of their low resistance and high results for senior citizens. Additionally, dietary options are catered to the numerous different styles of diet represented by senior citizens, such as diabetic or low calorie and low salt options.

Most senior cruise options are designed with their passengers in mind, creating a comfortable environment in which they can relax and enjoy their time aboard without needing to be concerned about things such as over-excited neighbors, children, or minimal time between ports.

Romantic Cruises

For decades, the ocean has represented the ideal setting for a romantic getaway. Couples both new and old have turned to cruises for years to get away from the daily grind of their jobs, families, and neighborhoods and to enjoy a romantic getaway. The atmosphere of a cruise ship is ideally suited for a romantic getaway, catering to every need, both small and large, and allowing cruise passengers to simply enjoy each other's company.

The original and idealized image of a romantic cruise was developed in the 1970s on "The Love Boat," showing the different ways in which couples could have a romantic vacation or in which singles could hunt down and find love. That image may not be the same one represented by modern cruises, but the concept is still very much alive.

Cruise lines are very well aware that couples may look to the high seas for a romantic getaway and have developed numerous options for the couples that do. Carnival Cruise Lines has long been known as a purveyor of party style cruises, offering ideal situations for the younger crowd seeking love and for young couples looking to spend a few nights in an exotic locale.

Another popular option for romantic cruises is that of the small ship. Star Clippers Cruises is a popular alternative to oversized megaliners, allowing a much more intimate environment and a closer proximity to both the water and the nearby land. These cruises can also be purchased for shorter durations for those looking for a weekend together instead of an entire week away from home.

Luxury ships are designed to cater to romantic encounters as well. A great example is Cunard's pair of Sea Goddesses. The ships are small and only serve 116 passengers but boast 89 staff members, creating a romantic, pamper-filled experience.

For those seeking the large ship treatment, ships such as the Grand Princess are famous for their size and opulence. With room for 2,600 passengers, the Grand Princess is the most expensive cruise ship in the world to date, featuring a built-in wedding chapel for ocean weddings and more than eight restaurant options, including intimate, candle-lit seclusion. Big ships such as this and others offered by the various other cruise lines ensure that romantics are never bored.

Family Cruises

Families have long since discovered how entertaining and accommodating a cruise ship can be for just about everyone in tow. Because they offer so many different things to do, everyone in the family will surely be taken care of, leaving no bored children or over-worked parents.

Cruise lines have long since seen to making sure both parents and children enjoy their cruises with specially themed trips just for families. There are currently 60 different cruise lines that offer family themed cruises, with a total of 300 different ships and thousands of annual trips to choose from. It is merely a matter of deciding which one will work best.

Carnival Cruise Lines was one of the first cruise lines to market itself as a family-oriented option, playing up the fun factor with which they operate and ensuring the entire family has something to do. Babysitting options, as well as special programs and classes for everyone ages two and up, ensure that parents are not overwhelmed with their children the entire vacation.

Celebrity Cruises is a relatively new cruise line that has recently added numerous ships to its fleet, along with dozens of different options for families. Activities are designed for children ages three to 17, and themed nights, such as talent shows, keep children busy so parents can relax.

Crystal Cruises is a luxury cruise option that has become popular for their ability to offer cruise passengers children's programming when there are enough children aboard. Anyone who wants to go with an upscale solution for their cruise instead of the more common megaliners can work with Crystal Cruises and still find the family-friendly environments they need.

The Cunard Cruise Line features two of the largest cruise ships in the world — the Queen Elizabeth 2 and the Queen Mary 2. Both ships offer children's services, such as British nannies and nurses, along with more developed children's programs for older children.

Disney Cruise Lines has done the most substantial work in outlining the exact reasons why children would have fun aboard. Taking the style and flair of Disneyland and putting it on-board a cruise ship, they bring Disney characters, events, and a theme park atmosphere to the ship that provides children and parents alike plenty to do for the duration of the cruise.

There are numerous other cruise lines that offer specific programs for children and families. Holland America Line, Norwegian Cruise Line,

Princess Cruises, and many more offer programs for children as young as two-years-old, all to ensure that no one in the family goes home having had a bad time while on the cruise.

Disability Cruises

Cruises do not discriminate against those with disabilities. However, the majority of activities and events on-board a cruise ship are designed for those who are not and, therefore, cruise options have developed for those individuals who need more attention because of a disability.

These disability cruises are often on smaller ships and offer the same world traveling and culture exploring opportunities of a traditional cruise, but with a slightly different approach to ensure a better experience for the passengers. Most of all, these cruises are often customizable for each passenger, allowing them to work with travel agents to decide how they will travel, where they will go, and what activities will be available.

Also available are third party services, such as Accessible Journeys, that will contact and work with the cruise line to ensure the same features are available for disabled travelers. They can even be hired or worked with to provide support while on-board.

Gay and Lesbian Cruises

Gay and lesbian cruise-goers looking to attend an all-gay cruise have many options. There are both pros and cons of taking a gay themed cruise, but many gay cruisers find it to be more relaxing as it affords them a much greater level of comfort. A non-themed cruise may force a gay individual to feel much less comfortable aboard the ship because they do not feel they can act like themselves. An all-gay cruise frees them to act like themselves and be willing to talk to nearly anyone they meet.

For a gay cruiser looking to find romance or new friends, an all-gay cruise is a popular choice. It ensures a higher degree of comfort than a traditional cruise and more options for meeting new acquaintances. This also results in a younger collection of fellow passengers. For those gay and lesbian cruisers looking to avoid middle-aged married couples, a gay-only cruise is a good choice.

Major cruise lines do not offer gay-only cruises on their lines in particular. However, through a gay tour company, cruisers can find tour takeovers in which enough gay passengers book passage that the cruise becomes gay-only. For those looking to find a cruise with all the amenities of a megaliner, though, these same gay tour companies often put together tour groups that will stay together aboard the cruise line and schedule multiple parties and activities.

Popular options for those looking to find gay and lesbian cruises through travel agencies can contact companies such as the following:

RSVP Vacations — specializes in cruises for gay and lesbian cruisers; singles and couples

Atlantis — offers gay cruise and resort options; mostly for males, though

Olivia Tours — lesbian-only tour company; offers special options

David Tours — luxury tours for both gay and lesbian cruisers

Freighter Cruises

One of the most interesting new forms of cruising that has developed in recent years is that of the freighter cruise. Harkening back to the early days of cruises in the 19th and early 20th century, a freighter cruise allows passengers to take passage on-board a commercial vessel that is delivering cargo, visiting numerous ports in the process.

For the most part, organized freighter cruises offer the kind of luxury accommodations the captain and crew of the ship enjoy during their overseas journeys. In some cases, the rooms might even be bigger than on a traditional cruise liner. Additionally, meals can be had with the captain and the other officers, and the view is usually much better.

There are usually less people on-board a freighter cruise, in comparison to a megaliner cruise, at any given time. Additionally, most freighter cruises do not offer much to do for those on-board. For those solely seeking seclusion and relaxation, a freighter cruise is ideal. For anyone seeking the kind of unlimited entertainment options available on a luxury liner, a freighter cruise is a bad idea.

With only 12 passengers on-board and limited options for staying busy, a freighter cruise is an ideal option for anyone looking to get away from it all. They generally cost $100 to $150 a day, though tramp cruises with lower quality accommodations will cost a bit less. For those looking to travel the world on a budget and not be distracted by the energy of a megaliner, this might be exactly the right decision.

Special Event Cruises

Beyond the traditionally themed cruises, there are dozens of different options available for people looking to enjoy particular events. Smaller cruises cater to golf excursions that take golf fans to dozens of different golf courses over a given time period. Cruises are available for specific event styles, such as ballroom dancing or a work-related retreat. The possibilities are nearly endless. The best way to know exactly how many different cruise options there are from any given cruise line is to contact them directly or talk to a travel agent and ask for a cruise schedule. Travel agents will have additional information available about themed cruises from smaller lines as well.

Reunions and Family Cruises

Family reunions are major events, often costing large sums of money to organize and get underway. For that reason, cruises have become increasingly popular in recent years as a place in which family reunions can take place without worrying about details, such as feeding everyone, finding things to do, and organizing space to gather and visit.

Because a cruise line will often accommodate any such large group and has the space in which to do it, planning can be a tandem process in which the person in charge of the family reunion is given ample assistance from the cruise line or the travel agent.

Affordability

The most important thing to do when organizing a family reunion on-board a cruise ship is to ensure that everyone will be able to afford the trip. Cruises range greatly in price, and a short, inexpensive cruise may be better than a multi-week $3,000 cruise, depending on the family. Planning time is another major factor. Some individuals are unable to take time off without substantial notice. Planning early gives family members plenty of time to plan and set aside the money necessary to attend the cruise.

Family-Friendly

The list above is a great place to start when planning a family reunion. Without a family-friendly cruise line, the children will be incredibly bored. Unless it is an adult-only excursion or a very short trip, a cruise ship that has plenty to do for participants of all ages is an ideal selection.

When to Go

Christmas and summer are the two best times of year to organize a family reunion. Most people will be immediately available and children will not need to miss school to attend. If the cruise is planned for summer, though, remember the weather's effect on the excursion in certain instances. Hurricane season begins on June 1st, so that is something to keep in mind when planning your cruise.

Destinations

Simply choosing where one person wants to go on a cruise is not going to be a successful means by which to plan a reunion. Dozens of people will probably be attending, so having at least a consensus on the destination is a good idea when starting the planning process. Contact each family that will be attending and ask them where they would be most interested in visiting. By going with the plan of least resistance, the planner will be less likely to hear "I told you so" on the trip from the dozens of family members who wanted to go elsewhere.

Start Early and Keep Everyone Informed

The planning process begins very early and should include everyone the entire way through. Consider creating a blog or a bulletin board on the Internet and having everyone post their thoughts to it. This also allows the planner to post any updates as they come along and ensure everyone has the time line and schedule at hand.

Finding the Right Cruise Package

There are plenty of cruise lines that cater to group events. However, some in particular will actually cater to a family reunion. One of the most popular such cruise lines is Royal Caribbean Cruises. Royal Caribbean Cruises specializes in family reunion packages in which passengers can receive discounted tickets and enjoy carefully designed activities, such as scavenger hunts, VIP amenities, and reserved meeting space for family events. Disney Cruise Line also offers a good family reunion package with plenty of great options, such as custom t-shirts and event organization.

The Schedule

One thing many people try to do with family reunions aboard a cruise ship is over-plan. It is too easy to immediately assume that the extra planning is necessary. Instead, planners should stick to organizing the very basics, such as booking the cruise, informing family members of when and where it will be held, and telling the cruise line that the cruise is a family reunion so they can plan accordingly. Consider planning only a couple of simple events, such as an opening night dinner and a day four excursion. This ensures the family spends some time together, but also that they receive the freedom to enjoy the cruise as they see fit.

Family Reunion as a Special Event

A family reunion can occur for any number of reasons, whether it is the 60th wedding anniversary for the patriarch and matriarch of the family or an event held every five years. Regardless of the reason for the family reunion, cruise lines will often provide special consideration for specific events. If a family reunion takes place during Christmas vacation, the cruise line can often ensure a special Christmas Day event with the right preparation time.

Other cruise liners have chapels aboard and offer chances for wedding vow renewals or religious ceremonies if they coincide with the time and purpose of the reunion. If planning begins early enough, most events of this type can be accommodated.

Getting Married on a Cruise

Like a family reunion, a wedding can be held on a cruise ship with the assistance of the cruise line and be a wonderful event. Because of the vast resources and built-in locale, the ship is a great opportunity to make the most of that special day. However, there are numerous factors that come into play for such an event, including cost, location, date, and the amount of planning desired by the bride and groom.

The Basics

Most cruise ship weddings actually take place on-board the ship while in port. Because of the legal implications of the wedding and the paperwork required for marriage certificates, this is much easier and often required.

The marriage license will need to be obtained from the location in which the marriage takes place. If the marriage will take place in Miami before the ship sets sail, the marriage license needs to be obtained from the state of Florida through Miami. Different locations have different rules regarding how this works, though, so prospective brides and grooms should contact the cruise line prior to planning their cruise for more information on how to do this for the location they have chosen.

Marriage at sea is not impossible. There is one ship in the Princess Cruises fleet that has a chapel aboard — the Grand Princess. In the instance of the Grand Princess, wedding licenses must be issued from the country of Liberia, as that is the home port of registry for the ship.

The Cost

Weddings are expensive. It is an unfortunate side effect of having that one perfect day finally arrive. Current estimates according to *Bride Magazine* range between $15,000 and $20,000 for an average wedding. The alternative to this outrageous cost is eloping somewhere like Las Vegas or Atlantic City. In this case, however, the amount of money saved is offset almost immediately by the anger it might breed in friends and family.

A happy medium between eloping and an expensive, traditional wedding is to get married on a cruise that offers a gathering place for as many friends and family members as wish to come in an exotic location for less money than a traditional wedding would likely cost — thousands less in some instances. It also allows couples to combine their wedding with a luxury honeymoon.

Of course, the process is not nearly as personal and magical as some couples might desire, especially for those getting married for the first time. If a couple desires hundreds of guests, the cost of a cruise ship wedding can actually become substantially more when purchasing so many tickets.

There are some ships that will allow couples to hold their wedding in port and invite a much larger selection of guests before the ship sets sail. These guests will then leave before the ship sets sail and the newlyweds set sail on their honeymoon. The cost for such a ceremony varies depending on how elaborate the wedding is designed to be.

CASE STUDY: SHEENA DELLING

Sheena Delling and her husband Darron were married in July of 2007 on a major market cruise line ship. They were able to invite all of their friends to a ceremony that took place before the ship set sail and afford to take two of their closest friends along with them without paying an excessive amount of money.

"My first marriage was a big event. I hired caterers, had a $3,000 cake made, and am still paying off my dress. It would still be the most memorable day of my life if I had not gotten divorced three years later. So, when I finally met Darron, we both decided to skip the expensive, unnecessarily large proceedings and put together a simple, easy to organize ceremony.

I saw a special on the Travel Channel about being married on a cruise ship and was immediately intrigued, so I contacted the agent who had handled my most recent trip to Europe and asked him what I would need to do to get married on a cruise

CASE STUDY: SHEENA DELLING

ship. He laid the options out for me along with the ships and lines that offered the service and how much it would cost.

In the end, I paid less than $1,000 for the wedding, another $3,400 for tickets for me, Darron, and our best man and maid of honor. It took less than three weeks to put together, with the cruise line taking care of almost all of the preparations and I paid the bill off before we set sail. The cruise was everything we had hoped for and we spent two separate meals at the captain's table, something I'm told does not happen unless you do something very special — like get married on-board! It was an unforgettable experience and much easier than I could have expected."

The Options

There are dozens of different cruise lines, and many of them offer some form of wedding option. Each package is slightly different, though. The following cruise lines offer packages that will allow couples to get married in any number of different methods at varying costs.

Carnival Cruise Lines — As the traditional fun ship, Carnival Cruise voyages are generally for smaller ceremonies and Vegas-style eloping. A wedding ceremony generally costs about $2,200 and covers both the bride and groom for the full trip. There is plenty of room for a full reception, but because of the nature of the ships, this is usually not an option selected for this cruise line. The basic ceremony itself comes with an official civil ceremony, champagne, flowers, wedding cake, and photographs. Larger ceremonies with private receptions cost about twice as much. Guests are not included in the package price and will need to be paid for separately.

Norwegian Cruise Lines — Norwegian has a slightly different take on the cruise ship wedding, offering the bride and groom an opportunity to bring aboard dozens of guests with minimal additional cost. The basic wedding package costs $799 and includes a small ceremony with a cake, champagne, and photographs. On-board weddings cost about $1,100 and run as high as $2,000, depending on what is requested to go along with the ceremony. The cost per person for a cruise ranges between $500 and $1,000 depending on what time of year it is.

Princess Cruises — Princess Cruises is able to claim what no other cruise line can — an on-board wedding chapel. No other cruise line can actually marry individuals while on international waters, forcing other couples to marry while docked at an island port. The reason for this is slightly convoluted, but essentially has to do with the legal status of Liberian wedding certificates. Liberia gives legal right to the captain to perform weddings and, as a result, the United States recognizes those weddings. The cost is significantly higher, though, and is thus better suited for a couple interested in getting married alone. A standard price for a wedding/honeymoon cruise on a Princess ship is about $3,000.

Holland America Line — The rates for this upscale line of cruise ships are a bit higher than any of the others. They offer varying wedding packages for different on-land destinations. Each destination varies in cost. For example, Jamaica costs between $1,700 and $2,000, while Alaska costs between $1,400 and $2,500 depending on the exact location of the marriage.

Royal Caribbean Cruises International — Royal Caribbean's wedding ceremonies on land are among the most expensive available but offer high quality services. The cheapest package available is $1,395 for a landside wedding in most of its ports of call. Add the cost of the cruise fare and a standard wedding without any extras will cost about $2,500 total. The cost rises a bit for each additional amenity added — including things such as extra photographs, guests, and champagne.

Cruise Ship Wedding Tips

Getting married on a cruise ship is among the easiest and least expensive wedding options. However, do not forget these common factors when planning a cruise wedding:

❋ Start the planning and booking process very early. Cruise ship weddings may be booked up to 18 months in advance.

❋ The only ship's captain that is able to perform a wedding ceremony is aboard the Princess Cruises Line. Other captains do not have the license to do so because of the laws associated with the countries in which they are based.

❋ Balance cost against needs for a particular cruise. First-time weddings may be better suited aboard the ship before leaving port so more guests can attend. Vow renewals and second or third marriages are great opportunities to take a small romantic cruise/wedding/honeymoon, though, with fewer guests.

Different Styles of Cruises

There are innumerable different styles of cruises, depending on the desires of those attending. The best part about the variety of cruise options is that each option allows you to diversify your cruise plan with as many destinations, options, and styles of cruising as possible. Often, the difference between cruise styles lies in the destination. Some depend on the build and style of the boat used in the cruise and others depend on the time of year in which the cruise is taken.

Destination Cruises

While many of these cruises may be taken on traditional cruise ships, the entire experience is altered by the variation of the ship and the location to which the ship is destined. For example, those cruises that end in Alaska are much different than those bearing into the Caribbean. Often, the ships are slightly smaller and the itineraries are a little shorter. While on-board activities might be similar, the common result is often very different, resulting in an exceptionally unique cruise experience.

For those embarking on their first cruise, a common desire is to visit the tropical locales that have been made so famous by cruise commercials and entertainment depictions. However, anyone looking to diversify can stretch into any number of exotic locales, including the colder northern destinations, the temperate European locales, or the Far Eastern locales that vary substantially in both weather and cultural differences.

Ship Styles

There are numerous styles of ships as well. The traditional image of a cruise is that of a megaliner, those massive cruise ships that act as small towns, home to 3,000 passengers and dozens of crew members. These ships boast numerous restaurants, facilities, and activities. However, there are several other cruise ship offerings, ranging in both size and style.

Catamarans and other small ships cruises are also available from the major cruise lines. These ships, often allowing as few as 12 passengers, are much cozier and allow passengers to get to know their neighbors intimately. They often feature much shorter cruise options, though, shoring back their excursions by days because of the nature of the ships themselves.

River Cruises

This commonly overlooked cruising option was made popular in the 19th century along the largest rivers in the world in numerous countries. Ships would casually work their way up massive rivers and drop off passengers along the way. Today, river cruises are popular in various locations, including Europe, China, and the United States. In Europe alone, Uniworld operates more than a dozen different ships along the major rivers of the continent, allowing visitors to easily view all their favorite locales.

In China, the Yangtze has become a very popular river cruise destination because of its size and length, allowing for two week cruises between Shanghai and Chongqing, among other locales. The cruises allow visitors to enjoy the various cultural offerings of China alongside the hundreds of different climates, geographical locales, and villages passed along the way.

River cruises are often much smaller but can be just as long as an at-sea cruise and nearly as luxurious if booked with the right company. They allow for more secluded vacation experiences, less crowding, and more culturally specific encounters along the way. Depending on the river as well, the cruise ships used might vary in sizes. Smaller touring cruises along European rivers are often streamlined and slick. In contrast, a river cruise along the Yangtze might be a bit larger than other rivers because of the berth of the river.

River cruises are ideal opportunities to take a slightly different look at a country while on the water than anyone could get from landside.

The Holidays

The fall and winter holiday season is a very popular time for cruises, as it offers a variety of different opportunities if you are looking to take some time away from the usually busy fall and winter holidays and have an easy, relaxing vacation. Most cruise lines offer more than a dozen different cruises between November and January. This variety makes a cruise a great option for a family vacation for Thanksgiving, Christmas, or New Year's.

While special discounts or packages are not quite as common as one would expect for the holiday time of year, cruise packages that carry on over a holiday are often unique in that they offer a specific experience for anyone looking to get away from home for that time period. A cruise over Christmas often features specific events particular to that holiday, while a New Year's cruise will feature fireworks and special cocktail celebrations. To research and learn more about the specific options available from each cruise line for the holidays, contact them directly and inquire about what they offer.

For many destinations, especially the warm weather arenas of the Caribbean and Mexican Riviera, holiday cruises are considered a short peak in the middle of low seasons. These cruises often fill up early on, as much as a full year or more in advance. If you are considering a holiday cruise for the big holidays in December and January, planning needs to start early. Also expect to have heavy crowds and children on-board the ship.

Choosing Your Destination

The final piece to the puzzle after deciding what kind and style of cruise you want is to plan out the exact location of the cruise. Fortunately, there are dozens of possible locations for your first cruise, so no matter which one sounds most interesting, there is a viable solution. For the first-time cruiser who does not know for sure what they want to experience beyond their first elusive cruise vacation, the decision might seem oddly hard for the first time. For those few, it is necessary to decide what kind of experience is most important.

With the more than 60 different cruise lines currently in operation, cruises currently travel almost anywhere in the world, from the Caribbean to Europe to Alaska to Asia. No matter where someone is interested in traveling, there are plenty of opportunities to reach those far-off locales via a cruise.

The most popular destinations are those in the tropical climates of the Caribbean. Key West, Jamaica, Grand Cayman, Aruba, and Curacao are very popular destinations for anyone traveling west and interested in the year-round warmth of the Caribbean Sea.

There are other routes in the same vicinity that are slightly less popular but equally as enjoyable, including the Eastern routes of Puerto Rico and the Virgin Islands along with the Bahamas. Nassau, in particular, is one of the most frequented ports for the cruise industry, featuring numerous world-renowned resorts and hotels. Occasionally, luxury cruise lines feature private island destinations in the Bahamas or Caribbean for those with the money to afford such a trip.

From the Western side of the United States, cruises depart from California and visit Puerto Vallarta, Acapulco, and Catalina along Baja and the Mexican Riviera. These cruises are no different than the Caribbean style cruises except for the flavor of the ports of call and duration spent at sea (often slightly shorter).

There are other locations that allow cruisers to focus solely on destinations instead of the cruise itself. Alaskan cruises often feature numerous different ports of call, as do Bermuda cruises. Additionally, Canadian coast cruises are designed for anyone seeking an excursion during the spring or fall seasons to see the beautiful foliage of the Northern half of the continent.

There are numerous other destinations available on much longer cruises. These cruises include locales as far-off and diverse as Panama and even Antarctica. These cruises are much more expensive and can take weeks or months to complete, but offer once-in-a-lifetime experiences. By far the most extensive and expensive cruises, though, are those that travel around the globe. They can take as long as three months from beginning to end.

Regardless of the concerns you might have about the repetitive nature of certain locales, there are plenty of things to do no matter where a cruise is destined. If a cruise is set to land in four different Caribbean island ports of call, there will still be numerous options for activities and entertainment on each island, regardless of the preconceptions you carry that the situation might be repetitive.

Ultimately, the best thing you can do is decide early on what you would like to do and subsequently what you would like to visit. If you are interested in a tropical, warm weather experience, you will want to look at Caribbean or Mexican cruises. If you are looking for culturally rich, architectural cruises, you should consider Europe or Southeast Asia. If you are looking to enjoy the raw power and majesty of nature untouched regardless of the weather, you should seek out the northern territories of Alaska or Canada.

The options are nearly endless, and with exception of the Arctic, every region on Earth is reachable via a cruise ship. It is only a matter of deciding which trip is most suited for you and your family's personality. After that, it is time to start booking and enjoying your first cruise.

Chapter 5

Big Decisions: Selecting Your Cruise

By this point, the final decision as to which cruise line, what style cruise, and how far you want to travel should be within grasp. Now it is time to start looking at the important details, such as the options made available when you enter a travel agency and ask for more information about a particular destination. You will need to gather everyone involved in making the decision together and ask them exactly what they are interested in doing when they embark.

It is time to start researching each of the major cruise lines, comparing their services, your desires, and the cost of the cruise you are looking to take. The cruise industry is a massive one with more than 60 different lines and 300 different ships on the water at any given time, making your decision both easy and hard at the same time. It is easy because there are so many choices. No matter what you are looking for (in terms of a cruise) you will likely find it. However, it is also hard because there are so many choices. It is a bit of a catch-22 in that regard.

On top of everything else, this is the time when actual planning and a time line start to come into play. Because of the cost of booking a cruise, the best method of cruising is to book as early as possible, meaning anywhere between six months and one year before you depart. This is a lot of time, but you need that time to do the proper amount of research, prepare your home and your family, and ensure you know exactly which cruise line, package, and excursions you want to book.

The Best Time to Take a Cruise

In Chapter 3, the weather was briefly discussed as a factor in deciding when and where a cruise is taken. There are plenty of additional factors having to do with the time at which a cruise is taken, though, and each of them is related directly or indirectly to how much fun your family will have in that time frame. No one wants to miss large chunks of school for a vacation only to make it all up in a rush two weeks later. Additionally, no one wants to be stuck inside, missing all the pre-booked excursions that were planned because of a tropical storm or hurricane.

So when is the best time to take a cruise? It depends on a number of variables. First, what kind of locale and what kind of backdrop do you enjoy? A midsummer cruise to Canada is not nearly as enjoyable as one in October when the fall foliage is in full color. However, if you want a warm weather vacation for the whole family, you want to head south during the summer months.

Also, the people going on a cruise directly affect where and when it should be taken. If children will be going, the vacation should be taken during a break, either in the winter, mid-spring, or summer. If it is a reunion cruise, a holiday is almost essential to assure everyone has time off. If none of these are a factor, off season might be a good time because money can be saved more readily.

Hawaii

- **High Season:** March, April, and June to August, and Holidays

- **Low Season:** End of August, End of November, February, May

Benefits of High Season: The same is true for Hawaii as is true for the Caribbean. When children are out of school, high season starts. The weather is comparable year round, save the rainy seasons, so the benefits of high season are generally best felt for those families with children.

Benefits of Low Season: Ships are much less crowded and the weather is equally wonderful in the low season, meaning that these are great options for couples without children or even families that are able to get their children out of school for a few days. The prices are much nicer in the low season as well. Because the off season months tend to be the wettest and coolest months of the year throughout the islands, they are less popular. However, they are also prime times for whale watching and water sports, as water temperatures are still quite warm. The only months in which severe weather is a possibility are August and September when hurricanes come closest to the islands.

Mexican Riviera

- **High Season:** Holidays, January to April, June to August

- **Low Season:** Early January, May, October to November

Benefits of High Season: The usual applies for the western side of Mexico, as much warmer temperatures are prevalent. Families and vacationers often choose to visit in the summer months when the weather is consistently in the 70s and 80s. It becomes increasingly popular throughout the winter months for those in the north because of those year-round highs. The summer has slightly less options, though, as many ships are moved north to Alaskan cruises, which are slightly more popular that time of the year.

Every region has a peak and a low period for cruises. The summer is generally a peak period in most locations, though some areas tend to have peak travel in odd months. This is important, though, because if a family wants to go on a cruise during a peak month, they need to book as early as possible to assure space on the boat.

There are very few low seasons left anymore, as the cruise industry has continued to grow and year-round travel has become more possible. Cruise lines have the added bonus of being able to move their ships to a different location if the weather is bad for a few months, allowing them to offer year-round cruises in the top locations. However, there are a few low season cruises that can save money for potential cruisers. The following list outlines the various high and low seasons of each major destination.

Alaska

- **High Season:** June to August

- **Low Season:** May and September

Benefits of High Season: For Alaska, the weather is fairly warm this time of year, upward of 70 degrees at times. Wildlife is at its peak during this time period as well, ensuring that travelers who go on numerous excursions will likely see a good deal of creatures. However, this time of year is extremely popular for Alaskan cruises and sees very high demand. Those considering a summer trip to Alaska must book far in advance to ensure seating is available. Also, most cruises depart and arrive on the same days, so to avoid the crowds in port towns, choose an off schedule cruise line.

Benefits of Low Season: The obvious benefit of any low season cruise is that there are fewer people, small crowds, and slightly lower prices than high season. The weather is questionable though, usually in the 50s and 60s during the day, and snow is a possibility at night, especially further north. Additionally, excursions are riskier this time of year because of the weather. Cancellation is a possibility.

Bermuda

* **High Season:** June to August

* **Low Season:** April, May, September, and October

Benefits of High Season: Traveling in high season always means a greater selection of ships, especially to popular destinations like Bermuda. The water is warm and perfect for anyone interested in water sports, and numerous families are usually on-board, making it easier for children to blend in and make new friends. The ships are more crowded, however, and the humidity can be unpleasantly high during the hottest parts of the summer.

Benefits of Low Season: There are numerous benefits to traveling in the low season in Bermuda. The humidity is much lower than in the high season, something many people almost require for their vacations. However, the rain in October is slightly oppressive, lasting much of the month and, at least once every year, a hurricane will affect the island in some manner. For the best low season month, May is a good choice.

Canada/New England

* **High Season:** September and October

* **Low Season:** July and August

Benefits of High Season: The biggest draw of these northern cruises is the fall foliage, so the high season is brimming with beautiful scenery along the New England and Canadian coastline. Children are often back in school by this time, so the cruises are less hectic while the temperatures are still moderate enough for comfortable walks and excursions.

Benefits of Low Season: Because of the summer weather, temperatures are much nicer, making the excursions off the ship much more pleasant. Usually hovering in the low 70s, the small Canadian towns in which the ship docks are great places to spend a quiet afternoon in the summer weather. Additionally, water sports are possible in the warmer weeks of these months as well. Because there are no real negatives of taking a summer cruise in New England or Canada, the price difference is almost non-existent.

The Caribbean

* **High Season:** June to August, Holiday Weeks, February to April

* **Low Season:** April, May, and September to January (except holidays)

Benefits of High Season: There are two different brands of travelers in peak season. There are those on vacation with their whole family during school breaks and those trying to get away from the cold weather of the north. Summer months on-board are great for children because children's program are extensive. Also, plenty of other children will be on-board for them t make friends with. The price in the high season, though, is much highe along with the cost of flights and possible delays in winter months. Eve without the cost of flights, high season is more expensive than low season.

Benefits of Low Season: The weather in the low season is wonderful a the crowds are limited. Plus, the price is much lower this time of the ye than any other period and makes the trip much more enjoyable. Hurrica season is a big concern for many travelers, as it carries on from June November; however, because the ships are given ample time to maneuv it usually just means changing ports of call to avoid the storm. Howeve embarkation is in a city being affected by a hurricane, it can be very h to get home. Also, for those with odd school calendars, such as early rele in summer or late start in fall, the low season can represent a chance to s a lot of money on a family vacation.

Benefits of Low Season: Without as many children, the low season is more relaxed and offers the kind of adult atmosphere some cruisers might prefer. Most cruise lines still offer a good selection in the fall months, while the cost in early January and late April is much lower than in high season.

Eastern and Western Mediterranean

❀ **High Season:** May to August, some fall and spring dates from those lines that offer them

❀ **Low Season:** March, April, and September to November

Benefits of High Season: Summer dates are extremely popular for both American and European citizens. The weather is much more volatile in Europe than in the Caribbean during the low season, with rainy seasons occurring more than once each year. This makes summer months much more popular. You should expect high humidity, higher prices, and big crowds during the high season, though.

Benefits of Low Season: As with many destinations, low season is the best time of year to travel without children. Weather in the early fall and late spring months is ideal as well, though by November the rains start in earnest, making cruises unpleasant. Airfare specials this time of year are often run at special rates, making it possible to travel two-for-one. There are some cruise lines that only run cruises during high season in Europe, though, so the right cruise line must be checked to find such special discounted rates.

So Many Ships, So Little Time

The worldwide fleet of cruise ships is substantial. Combining the ships of all the different cruise lines, there are slightly more than 300 ships available to choose from throughout the world. In some instances, it might not be possible to make a selection between these ships. However, in some other situations, the sheer volume of lines and cruises makes it possible to go with nearly any size and style of ship.

The megaliners are all similar in appearance but are very different in what they offer inside. Sure, they all offer the same basic amenities — the fitness centers, the dining options, and the casinos — but they also offer certain other extras that go above and beyond that of other lines. Only one ship has an on-board wedding chapel, for example.

Additionally, the size difference and style of construction varies between the different cruise ships. There are numerous styles of ships available, such as wooden mast sail ships, smaller tour-sized ships, and dozens of different middle-sized ships for shorter cruises in more diverse locations.

The Large Ships

Starting at about 70,000 tons and holding 1,500 to 2,000 passengers and up, the mega cruise liners are the largest and most amenity-packed options on the sea. Everything you can imagine in a cruise ship can usually be found on the super large ships — from 24-hour activity schedules to lounges, children's programs, and Vegas-style shows. Ships continue to get even larger as well, hoping to pack more passengers and even more elaborate options into each sailing. Here are some highlights of the largest cruise ships in the world.

Royal Caribbean Cruises Fleet — The largest of Royal Caribbean's ships weigh in at 160,000 tons and hold over 3,600 passengers. In fact, eight of the 10 largest cruise ships available are in the Royal Caribbean fleet. In 2009, they plan to unveil a much larger and infinitely more elaborate ship, the Genesis of the Seas, a 220,000 ton megaliner which will hold more than 5,400 passengers.

The Queen Mary 2 — Considered one of the most elaborate cruise ships on the water, Cunard's 150,000 ton megaliner can hold 2,600 passengers and is considered a premiere destination for luxuriant features and amenities. Launched in 2004, the ship is one of the largest in the world and features spacious staterooms and plenty of on-board activities.

Princess Cruises — The largest ships in the Princess fleet weigh in at 116,000 tons and hold more than 3,000 passengers. Their Grand Princess ship is among the most well-known cruise ships for its on-board wedding chapel, while newer ships, such as the Emerald Princess, feature a wide array of casual cruise options.

Carnival Cruise Lines — The Carnival megaliners include ships such as Carnival Conquest and Freedom, each weighing in at 110,000 tons and carrying just under 3,000 passengers. They are known for their collection of some of the best exercise and spa facilities at sea.

Mid-Sized Ships

The next grade of cruise ships is a little harder to quantify, as it contains any ship between 25,000 and 70,000 tons. These smaller, yet still lavish cruise options can hold anywhere between 380 and 1,800 passengers, depending on the style and line of the cruise. Many of the same features, such as night shows, casinos, and spas are still available but much smaller in scale than the traditionally huge megaliners. While ship features may be scaled down, there is usually more space per passenger on-board the ship, allowing passengers more freedom to move about without feeling crowded.

The Queen Elizabeth 2 — After 40 years, the QE2 is a staple of cruising history. Nostalgic yet luxuriant, the one-time megaliner is now in the upper tier of mid-size ships and offers cruises throughout the world.

1990s Fleets—Many of the major cruise lines' fleet additions in the late 1980s and 1990s fall into the mid-size fleet category. These older ships often offer more space on the ship for passengers than larger ships that are booking more and more passengers.

Small Ships

The smallest cruise ships fall into any number of categories depending on the cruise line. There are ships as small as 95 tons ranging upward of 25,000 tons that cater to different locales, passengers, and activities. Usually these ships are designed for relaxation and self-entertainment rather than the whirlwind tour of activities a megaliner might offer. They usually offer more intimate settings and can carry passengers to ports of call that are harder to reach with a big ship. Service and dining are usually the most important aspects of these smaller cruises, making them a great chance to relax and sit back.

Windstar Cruises — This small cruise line features a selection of sail ships ranging from just under 10,000 tons to 15,000 tons. They generally hold fewer passengers but feature some of the nicest spas at sea.

Cruise West — This classic cruise line features a fleet of much smaller ships, made from the 1970s through the 1990s, that hold as few as 85 passengers on cruises to Alaska or down the California coastline.

Other Options — The Yachts of Seabourn, Silversea Cruise, and Regent Seven Seas Cruises are other cruise lines that offer smaller ships for more intimate cruising experiences. These ships are often available for much smaller parties and hidden away destinations on islands you might not otherwise see on a larger cruise ship.

Size Matters as Much as Circumstance

When selecting which cruise and what size ship you want to embark on, there are a number of factors to consider. One important factor to keep in mind is what size ship will be appropriate for your vacation.

If you are going on a short anniversary expedition with your spouse, a smaller cruise ship might be the best fit as it offers more space for you to be alone, a more intimate setting, and more romantic, secluded destinations and ports of call.

However, if you are planning your next family reunion or vacation, a larger cruise ship is almost required. They are generally less expensive for groups and offer enough amenities and features that anyone in your party will be able to remain entertained for the duration of the trip. You should always look at all the options as well as the factors that may affect those options before making a final decision on which ship and what size it needs to be for your next cruise.

The Cruise Lines

There are many cruise lines from which to choose. For a megaliner cruise alone, there are more than a dozen different options available. For that reason, it is important to have all the necessary information available when you make your cruise decision. There are a number of factors that might affect which cruise line you select, so it is important to know what they offer, where they visit, and how much you can expect to spend.

Provided below is a listing of each of the major cruise lines and their pros and cons. Each cruise line has a different theme and target audience. However, many of the larger cruise lines offer similar features in an attempt to appeal to wider audiences of vacationers.

Carnival Cruise Lines

Generally considered a good choice for first-time cruisers, Carnival Cruise Lines markets itself as the "fun" cruise line, striving for fun-filled outings to multiple locations in the Caribbean, South America, and Alaska. Each ship in the line's fleet strives for a different theme of some sort, featuring a wide variety of family-friendly offerings. Groups and families are most welcome on the line, as activities are marketed to nearly anyone who might go on-board. Dinner times and activities are usually freeform.

Celebrity Cruises

Striving for a unique, luxurious experience, Celebrity Cruises offers five-star options in an affordable, convenient package. The Celebrity Cruise Line ships cater more toward individuals and couples seeking an elaborate vacation. However, they also offer options for family cruising, albeit not as extensively as some of the more family-oriented ships. Along with fine cuisine, high quality art shows, and a collection of events designed to cater to those looking for a more relaxing, elegant experience, Celebrity is a unique option among the major cruise lines.

Costa Cruises

Originally based out of the Mediterranean, Costa Cruises is a budget cruise line that offers a unique, Italian flavor to its cruises. There are plenty of destinations available, ranging from the Mediterranean, Middle East, and Africa to the Caribbean. Featuring a slightly different selection of events and offerings on-board, Costa adds a special flavor to the traditional, low cost, seven-day cruise that many other lines offer.

Cruise West

With its fleet of small ships built as long ago as the 1970s, Cruise West runs and operates a variety of cruise options throughout North America. Primarily known for its Alaskan cruises, Cruise West features small ships that hold as few as 85 people for short three- and five-day excursions to the northern states. Cruise West also offers cruises to Mexico, the Caribbean, and to places as far away as Japan in the other months of the year. Generally, Cruise West is ideal for couples or singles hoping for a short getaway, as rooms and activities are sparse for families.

Cunard Cruises

As the oldest and at one time (many decades ago) largest passenger shipping company in the world, Cunard Cruises still stands as one of the most decadent. Although Cunard only features three ships in their fleet, they are among the nicest at sea, hoping to hark back to the days of cruising being synonymous with wealth and elegance. The Queen Mary 2 is among the largest cruise ships on the ocean and most of its amenities cater toward a more luxurious vacation, offering less for children and families and more for couples. Cruise options feature Mediterranean, Caribbean, Transatlantic, and worldwide trips.

Disney Cruise Lines

The Disney Cruise Line caters to families and children, in particular. The ships in the line do not have casinos or too many nightclub options, instead choosing to host as many family-oriented activities as possible. There are a wide range of opportunities for children, including shows and Disney characters walking the decks.

Holland America Line

The size and options of the Holland America Line fleet are often aimed toward the older generation. There is a slightly smaller selection of activities for families, but the ships are usually more spacious. With a dozen ships and 280 ports of call, Holland America has one of the largest selections of cruise destinations in the world, going as far as Antarctica.

Majestic America

Offering a slightly different opportunity for cruisers, the Majestic America cruise ships visit various river destinations throughout the United States, including the Mississippi, Columbia, Snake, and Alaskan Rivers. Using smaller, elegant river cruise ships, Majestic America is a unique and entertaining chance to take a floating vacation without the cost or time commitment of an ocean cruise.

Norwegian Cruise Line

The Norwegian Cruise Line features freestyle cruising and a worldwide selection of destinations. Each ship offers a slightly different set of options regarding the degree of casual dress or entertainment involved. Norwegian offers classes and programs for passengers to learn more and enjoy their cruises in a slightly more unique fashion.

Princess Cruises

Made famous by its original partnership with the television program "The Love Boat," Princess Cruises is known for its wide selection of on-board activities, romantic getaways, and West Coast cruising options. They also feature the only at-sea wedding chapel aboard the Grand Princess. Based out of Libya, this classic cruise line has a lot of features to offer.

Regent Seven Seas Cruises

Regent Seven Seas launched a new look in 1994 along with four ships designed to offer luxuriant, smaller ship cruises to exotic locations for couples and the wealthy. The ships hold only as many as 700 passengers and visit locations that the larger ships often cannot. Private suites and balconies make the Regent fleet unique in the amount of space allotted for each room.

Royal Caribbean Cruises

Featuring a wide array of destinations in more than 160 ports of call and some of the largest ships on the sea with its newest additions to the fleet, Royal Caribbean is a fast-rising and very popular cruise line with a great deal of options. Activities and on-board entertainment are consistently top notch, while more ships are added to the fleet every year, offering more unique and timely vacation options for nearly anyone who is interested in taking a cruise.

The Yachts of Seabourn

Among the highest regarded cruise lines in the world, Seabourn features a luxury-oriented fleet of ships that visits numerous destinations across the globe. New ships have been added annually in recent years as the Seabourn cruise line continues to grow.

Windstar Cruises

With a unique, smaller-style cruise experience, in comparison with its major competition, Windstar allows cruisers to enjoy more space, more seclusion, and unique destinations that other ships cannot reach. These sail ships hold as few as 300 people and contain some of the most interesting and immense at-sea spas available.

Quick Comparison

For a quick and easy comparison of the major cruise lines, refer to the following chart of specific offerings. Each cruise line usually offers a decent variety of options and each varies in cost. The options on the following chart outline general recommendations for passengers and their families based on specific criteria.

CRUISE COMPANY COMPARISON				
Cruise Line	Family	Cost	Destinations	Standard - Luxury
Carnival	Yes	Low-mid	Worldwide	Standard
Celebrity	No	Mid	Worldwide	Affordable luxury
Costa	Yes	Low-mid	Five Continents	Standard

CRUISE COMPANY COMPARISON				
Cruise West	Yes	Low-mid	Alaska, South Pacific, Mexico	Standard
Disney	Yes	Low-mid	Worldwide	Standard
Holland America	Yes	Mid	Worldwide	Standard
Majestic America	Yes	Low-mid	US River Cruises	Standard
Norwegian	Yes	Low-mid	Worldwide	Standard
Princess	Yes	Low-mid	Worldwide	Standard
Regent Seven Seas	No	Mid-high	Worldwide	Luxury
Renaissance	No	Mid-high	Europe, Caribbean	Luxury
Royal Caribbean	Yes	Low-mid	Worldwide	Standard
Seabourn	No	Mid-high	Worldwide	Luxury
Windstar	No	Mid-high	Worldwide	Luxury

Cruise Packages

Once you have decided which cruise line and style of ship will best suit your family's cruising needs, it is time to start searching for the best options for getting them there. Luckily, in the digital age, there are thousands of possibilities to help seek out and find the cheapest or most efficient means of taking a cruise. Once the candied fruit of travel agents everywhere, now anyone can find and book a cruise package on a variety of travel Web sites such as Expedia, Travelocity, Priceline, or Hotwire. These travel Web sites allow anyone to purchase airline tickets, rental cars, cruise tickets, and any other necessary vacation tickets all at once. This saves both time and money.

What Kind of Package to Get

Cruises are usually purchased in conjunction with a number of other options, so there is an equally endless selection of cruise packages to choose from. Many times, you can select and create your own custom package through a travel Web site by telling them exactly how long a cruise you want, what your budget is, and the distance you have to travel from your home to the departure port.

If you are working with a traditional travel agent, you can equally customize your options, and you have the added advantage of an agent who can help make the right decisions for transportation, departures, and final booking. Possible options you will need to consider when booking a cruise package include:

- Airfare to the departure port

- Rental car or transportation from the airport

- Additional cruise passengers

- Additional on-board amenities

- Port excursions while on a cruise

Any of these can usually be purchased directly through whatever resource you use to purchase cruise tickets, as most travel agents and Web sites try to offer extended services to make booking as easy as possible.

What to Remember When Choosing a Package

As the percentage of people using Web sites to book their vacations rises every year, there are a few important tips to ensure the cruiser gets exactly what they want. While they may offer substantial discounts on travel, online booking Web sites can become confusing and often feature a variety of hidden terms and fees that a user may not notice. Be wary of any travel booked online and make sure to read all the terms before sending credit card information.

You will want to double check all dates and ensure that everything coincides with the cruise itinerary. Especially if you selected your cruise line and destination before you started booking, you need to make sure the flights and the excursions they book in addition match up with the itinerary. Most booking Web sites will automatically match up itineraries. However, there are times when arrival times and dates overlap. Travelers should watch for these and give themselves enough time to travel.

If a traveler decides to use a travel agent, they should have all the information they will need prepared before speaking to the agent. This means they should be ready and willing to discuss the length of the cruise they want to take, the destination, the preferred cruise line, the number of people in the traveler's party, the ports they want to see, the excursions they want to embark on, and the flight times that are best for them. If the cruiser is not prepared to commit to a flight or a set of excursions when they book their cruise, they may end up paying more than necessary by splitting it up.

Excursions

A cruise, when booked on the ship you know will be most enjoyable for your family, is a great chance to take advantage of a nearly endless number of activities. But what fun is it to travel 4,000 miles across the country and into the midst of the Caribbean if you do not get the chance to see and experience the islands and native culture of your destinations? Doing so often involves a completely separate booking process that requires contacting of third party companies and payment for additional activities.

Many travel agencies and online travel companies offer options that allow passengers to book these excursions through them, using their services to contact third party companies and set up such outings as an island-side bike ride or sightseeing of a coral reef. Using a travel agent or online travel company allows travelers to create a more complete vacation package and generally makes the agents or companies more money. By researching the different excursion options available, you can be ready to choose a vacation package when the time arises.

Kinds of Excursions

There is a nearly endless variety of excursions available to you, largely depending on the cruise line, the port of call, and the time of year. The best way to research and choose an excursion is to contact the cruise line or a travel agent directly and ask a few questions. Here are some of the most popular and common types available.

Catamaran and Yacht Tours

Many destinations offer opportunities for you to go aboard a smaller, more intimate ship in order to explore the various nooks and crannies of an island's shores. These short, two- or three-hour trips allow a better chance to see and experience wildlife and sea life in a specific region.

Shopping Tours

Cities across the world feature unique and entertaining shopping experiences. A shopping tour can guide you through crowded city streets to find souvenirs, particularly in countries in which you do not speak the native language.

Nature Hikes

Why visit a Caribbean island and not view the waterfalls, forests, or paths that dot the countryside? These excursions take on many different variations, from simple hikes to Jeep expeditions.

Cycling

Rent a bicycle and take a guided tour of your destination while getting a breath of fresh air. Cycling tours are great for almost any destination.

Swimming or Rafting

In certain destinations, rivers and lakes are particularly interesting locales to visit. Rafting or swimming expeditions may involve exciting whitewaters or simple, relaxing coral reef snorkeling.

Historical and Cultural Sites

Exploring and becoming familiar with a different culture is a fun addition to any vacation. Cruise excursions can take you to historical sites in a foreign country and show you various current and past cultural differences.

Wildlife Tours

The wildlife of a different country is sure to be different and exotic compared to your home. Wildlife tours range from simple nature hikes in the Caribbean to carefully guided tours in Alaska to look for bears.

Factors that Affect Excursion Booking

Excursions from cruise chips are a great way to enjoy a new angle and aspect of a different culture and country. However, you should remember a few key points. Excursions usually book months in advance. A single cycling excursion may have space for 20 individuals and, with 3,000 passengers on a cruise ship, it will fill up quickly. If you have specific excursion needs, you should book as early as possible.

Additionally, the time of year and weather may indirectly affect the availability of a particular excursion. The water temperature in some destinations, such as New England, may drop too low for water sports, while Alaska's winter months are usually not suited for wildlife tours because of the snow. Research when the best time for a particular excursion is before booking a cruise.

Avoiding Cruise Scams

Finally, before booking and making any travel decisions final, you need to be aware of the possibility of being scammed. Legitimate travel agencies are highly regulated for this very reason, ensuring that the vacationers using their services feel safe and secure handing over their money for a trip that will not occur for another six to 12 months.

Travel scams are among the most common and pricey of scamming methods used by those who seek to defraud unwitting customers. Because of the hectic and confusing nature of booking a vacation, these scams often result because a traveler is unable to keep track of everything around them and wants to save a little money. Unfortunately, that can often lead to them losing more money than they ever would have saved.

According to the National Fraud Information Center, $803 per scam incident was lost in 2004 as a result of travel-related scams. The previous high had been $468 in 2002. Today, travel fraud is ranked number two on the NFIC list of fraud complaints, just below online auctions. There are plenty of people trying to take a traveler's money. If wary of a possible scam, cruisers can ensure a safe, scam-free booking process.

Travel Company Scams

One of the biggest advantages of using an online booking company is that travelers know they are trustworthy (if they have used one of the well-known booking Web sites). Travel agencies, on the other hand, can all look the same, and the only real way to be sure of their legitimacy is to research and check their credentials before working with them.

Discount Travel Clubs

Many times, a perfectly good deal that seems too good to be true really is. Discount travel clubs have popped up in ever-increasing numbers as scammers seek to trick travelers into thinking they are getting a great deal on a top notch travel opportunity. Membership is usually a bit higher than they would expect, followed by what appear to be discounted trips. In truth, these are usually discounts a traveler could find anywhere and, in the end, the scammer takes away both membership fees and the commission from the supplier for selling the trip. A legitimate travel club is one that features realistic dues and caters toward specific gatherings rather than "discount" travel.

Pricing Scams

A passenger might expect to be taken for a fool by a guy in a back alley trying to sell a discount trip to a far-off destination. Passengers should be wary of anyone selling discount travel. Airlines and cruise industries use deceptive pricing techniques consistently to trick travelers into thinking they are getting a better deal than they actually are. Whenever an airline prints that a ticket is only $79, it usually is based on a one-way flight taken from a roundtrip fare, meaning the actual cost is twice as much. Plenty of industries use the same techniques, putting the truth in the fine print. Unfortunately, scam artists can get even more creative and defraud travelers of much larger sums of cash, while maneuvering around the squiggly line of the law by using small print. Triple check what a trip should cost, read the fine print repeatedly, and cross check your projected fares before signing or paying for anything.

A Failing Business

Because of the nature of travel, passengers may pay for a trip more than 12 months before they actually intend on taking it. In this case, it is vital to ensure the company the passenger has purchased their tickets from is a financially secure company. If a cruiser buys tickets from a failing travel agency and then, 10 months later, they start preparing to leave for their trip, only to find out that the travel agency went bankrupt and the tickets were never valid, they probably will not be very happy. Research is vital to ensuring they do not get taken for a fool by enterprising thieves or failing businesses.

The Free Cruise Scam

One of the most common and, unfortunately, most enticing scams around is the free cruise. It consists of a pushy salesman or woman calling and informing someone that they have won a free cruise. The lucky winner may have put a card into a box at a fair or in the mall because they were promised a legitimate drawing. By whatever means the scammer got the individual's phone number, the free cruise is only a ruse to get information and, subsequently, money from a victim. Usually, before the phone call is over, the scammer will convince the potential victim that they need a credit card number to cover any deposits, fees, or future taxes. They do not guarantee a room, any dates, any destinations, and usually the victim is left paying for airfare and travel. This is only if the cruise actually exists. If the cruise is a fake, they will merely charge the credit card, disappear, and never be heard from again.

The easiest way to deal with this form of scam is simply to hang up the phone on the scammer. Never listen to anyone on the phone who wants credit card information, anyway. It is almost always a scam and, when it is not a scam, it is a horrible deal that will cost more money in the end than it will save.

CASE STUDY: THOMAS BELTON

Thomas Belton is a freelance writer who has worked for Cruise Mates, Cruise Touring, and various other travel publications. He most recently studied and wrote extensively on the effects fraud and scams can have on the travel industry if they remain as prevalent as they are today. He offers his thoughts on how the industry might change or adapt to the growing effect that the Internet and untrustworthy salesmen have on first-time buyers.

CLASSIFIED CASE STUDIES

directly from the experts

CASE STUDY: THOMAS BELTON

"Like any industry, cruising has its fair share of ill-mannered individuals — those men and women who simply want to take your money and run. It is a shame really because the cruise industry has enjoyed such extraordinary growth recently and along with it, the quality of cruises has skyrocketed. I recently interviewed a couple who returned from Bermuda after a 12 day cruise that only cost them $750 a person. They sailed on a brand new ship and had the time of their lives.

But for every dozen success stories, there is one more story of deceit and, unfortunately, scamming. The results vary from case to case, but when a family or individual is scammed out of their vacation, they are usually crestfallen. I have interviewed dozens of these cases and the most common thing in any one of them is that they had no idea they could be targeted so easily. They did not realize that the travel agent or the Web site they were dealing with did not have its licensing or that their money could be stolen with no guarantees. They thought they were paying the cruise lines directly.

All of these common mistakes can be avoided by doing a little research. Anyone preparing to book a cruise with a travel agent or booking Web site should make sure they are legitimate first. This means they need to ask for licensing from a travel agency or check for comments on a particular Web site. If the prices look too good to be true or the method of interaction appears to be disorganized or lacking in formality, they should do some double checking, just to be sure. I warn first-time cruisers whenever I talk to them — do your research, only then should you trust your travel agent, and enjoy your trip."

Steps to Take in Protecting a Travel Investment

There are specific steps you can take to protect your future investment in travel. Each of these steps involves working with existing, well-known organizations to keep scam artists from winning.

Research the Companies You Deal With

You never want to deal with a company that might be intent on scamming you. However, you cannot merely rely on instinct to tell you when that is about to happen. You need to do a little research beforehand to be sure that the individual you are dealing with is legitimate. Travel agents should be members of the American Society of Travel Agents or the Association of Retail Travel Agents. For booking a cruise, you need to look for members of the Cruise Lines International Association. Trustworthy businesses are often members of the local chamber of commerce. You can ask for any of this certification and a legitimate business will gladly and proudly provide it.

Tenure of the Business

Even well-meaning businesses may have poor practices or bad finances. Check on the amount of time the employees have worked for the company and if they have received any complaints through the Better Business Bureau. Ask them the questions that matter and be sure to follow up with research of your own. In today's digital economy, a company can be started and look professional in less than day. A scam artist can then take the money of dozens of unsuspecting people before disappearing a week later without a trace. Just because they look legitimate does not mean they are. Do the research and always remember not to pay with cash or a check.

In Case of Fraud

If you are defrauded somehow, there are a variety of tasks you can perform to ensure no one else falls victim to the same scam. If you do fall victim to fraud, you should call the NFIC or ASTA immediately at (800) 876-7060 and report the situation. Additionally, you should contact law enforcement and the local Better Business Bureau to see if you can be of any assistance in combating the scam artist. Do not just let it go. Help stop the scammer from striking again in the future.

The Stress of Booking Is Worth the Pay-Off

The booking process for a first cruise will seem like an ordeal. It might take days or even weeks to finally get all the information you have been seeking prepared for the actual process of walking into a travel agency and paying for tickets. However, by doing the necessary research described in this chapter, much of the stress and worry that accompanies vacation planning can be alleviated.

By ensuring that you and your family have chosen the cruise line and ship that best suits your needs and that the associated excursions, activities, and accommodations are the best available, you will not have to put up with pushy sales pitches, unsure decisions, or months of uneasiness wondering if you chose the right package.

Chapter 6

Booking a Cruise

After going through every option available and ensuring that no stone has been left unturned, it is finally time to book your first cruise. There are a lot of details, mostly having to do with your budget, that will now need to be dealt with.

The Cost of a Cruise

Cruises vary greatly in initial cost. However, a great deal of the cost will come after payment for tickets. This is where many cruisers get confused and make mistakes with their budgets. Beyond knowing just what affects the cost of a cruise, you should be prepared for the extra charges and costs that will begin to accrue.

What Affects the Cost

There are a lot of factors that affect the cost of a cruise. Here is a list of the most common, each of them likely to have been affected by the decisions made earlier in this book:

- Time of the year

- Length of the cruise

- Destination

- Type and style of cruise

- Cruise line selected

- Ship selected

- Room and accommodations

- Extra additions to the package

- When the trip is booked

- How far you must travel to the port of departure

The list of possible differences in the price any cruiser pays for their trip is almost endless. However, many of these factors are going to be set by now, according to how pre-booking was completed.

Generally, the cruise itself will cost anywhere between $300 and $5,000, depending on a number of the factors above. During peak travel periods, costs tend to be a bit higher, but traditionally, a megaliner cruise ticket is relatively inexpensive. Luxury cruises, such as the Queen Mary 2 or any of the other higher quality ships on the sea, will cost a bit more but usually offer a more inclusive package. Additionally, there are some cruises that cost much less but are not all-inclusive, forcing passengers to pay a little extra for food and other features on-board.

Travel will vary greatly depending on where the traveler lives and how far they are willing to go from the airport to the port. Travel agents can often package air and cruise tickets together, but ultimately the cost of the plane tickets will vary depending on the time of the year and the port from which the cruise departs.

Secondary Costs of a Cruise

There are a great deal of smaller factors that will begin to add up and affect the cost of a cruise as well. Tipping is a major factor to include in the incidental costs you may incur. Also, while meals are free, snacks and drinks can often cost extra and may add up to as much as $20 per day, per person — more for those who plan on late nights.

Casinos are present on almost all large cruise ships, and the cost of visiting one can be substantial, even for those who do not gamble much. You should budget a set amount of money for activities and casinos alone while on a cruise (assuming the ship you choose has a casino) to best ensure you do not go over budget.

Souvenirs and other items that might be bought while in port can be another unexpected expense. You should have an extra bit of cash on you during the cruise to cover these extra expenses.

While knowing exactly how much a cruise will cost is hard, it is possible to have a general idea of how much money should be set aside. The cost of the cruise itself is often only one-third of the total cost that should be set aside when booking. Take into account total airfare, cost of packing, travel, tipping, food, and excursion costs.

The Cruise Budget

You do not have to simply spend the money a travel agent suggests you do. There are many ways to go about cruising on a budget, from finding discounts for the cruise itself to flying halfway or just driving to the port of departure. There are multiple discounts available if a cruiser knows where to look and what to request.

Below is a chart that shows how much a traditional cruise budget is. As it gets higher, the number of choices and possibilities increase accordingly. It is not impossible to have an entertaining cruise for less than $500.

CRUISE BUDGET	
$500 and Less	A cruising budget of less than $500 might seem a tad small to start, but as you begin researching you will find that it is not impossible to find short or low period cruises for $300 and up. These cruises often do not include the cost of food or excursions and may require you take a room without a view.
$500 to $750	Slightly nicer, yet still in the affordable range, a cruise between $500 and $750 will often be on a larger ship during an acceptable time of year and with minimal features beyond the standard amenities.
$750 to $1,000	When you start getting upward of $1,000, your cruise will be much nicer. You can often afford a larger room, even one with a view, and usually a ship with all-inclusive meal plans and activities, resulting in extra payment for travel and excursions only.
$1,000 to $2,000	The nicer ships on the sea will cost between $1,000 and $2,000 but are well worth the extra cost for anyone wanting a luxury cruise. These cruises might last longer and offer larger rooms, a more direct staff, and a greater selection of options to keep your family occupied.
More than $2,000	Anything more than $2,000 can range greatly in terms of what you receive. There are some seven-day cruises that can cost as much $6,000 or more. You can often choose to sail on a smaller ship with the same amenities and much more room than a megaliner, while making specific decisions regarding your meals and what you will do while on the ship.

The Budget Cruise —
How to Pay Less for a Cruise Booking

Before the end of the last decade there were plenty of options for people looking to book passage on an older ship for a lower rate. Numerous ships from the 70s and 80s, run by smaller cruise lines, still operated on a regular basis at rates sometimes as much as 75 percent lower than their larger, more modern competition.

Eventually, those cruise lines went out of business, though, driven by the massive growth and popularity of cruises that the larger lines offered. As cruise lines such as Carnival and Princess began building massive ships capable of carrying close to 3,500 passengers, smaller ships lost their share of the market.

This does not mean it is impossible to find a discounted rate for a cruise anymore, though. Because they have grown so large, have so many ships in their fleet, and spend the whole year at sea, megaliners can afford to offer massively reduced fares to almost any destination, if a traveler knows where and when to look.

Large Budget Cruises Available

Usually a budget cruise will be a much shorter, three- or five-day trip offered by a major cruise line on their smaller, older ships. Smaller does not refer to a significant drop off in size, though, but rather an older ship that may be 60 percent of the size of today's newest, most impressive cruise ships. There are cruises available for as little as $189 from companies like Carnival and Royal Caribbean whose fleets are growing by as much as one ship every year, allowing them to offer reduced rates on soon to be retired ships.

Another great way to find an inexpensive cruise is to look for repositioning cruises in the transitional months of September or April. When the ships from Alaska or New England move south toward California and the Caribbean, fares can usually be had for as little as $149 to $199. These are only offered sporadically throughout the year and usually only once per cruise line or cruise ship, but for a cheap vacation away from home, they are good options.

Small Budget Cruises Available

While the larger cruise lines have taken a great deal of the market up, there are still a few smaller cruise lines that offer one or two day outings for very low prices. It is possible to find day cruises to the Bahamas from Florida for as little as $129, allowing passengers to spend approximately 14 hours at sea before returning. Lines such as Discovery Island and Imperial Majesty Cruise Lines offer these shorter, single and two-day cruises for a short, weekend getaway.

Interesting Options — and Changing Perspectives

A recent startup company in Europe has started a budget cruising program that allows passengers to essentially set their own prices based on their budget and the length of vacation they want to take.

The cruise line, EasyCruise, allows passengers to book passage on any of a growing number of 100 passenger ships for as long as one week. They can choose how many days they want to be on-board, though, and pay accordingly. The prices start as low as $24 a night and go up according based on the demand for each day. If there are only three rooms left for the sixth day of the trip, the cost of those rooms would rise accordingly, to as much as $149 for that night.

The cost is based on passengers receiving absolutely no extras on the cruise. The ships are plainly painted and decorated with no activities or amenities, and food costs extra. House cleaning is extra and passengers are expected to entertain themselves. The approach offers those with small budgets a chance to get away and relax without worrying about endless vacation plans.

What to Look For to Keep a Budget Down

When looking to keep a budget down for a first cruise, the cost of the cruise itself is going to be only a fraction of what you eventually pay. You will want to not only seek out budgetary shortcuts for cruise tickets but for airline tickets and excursions as well. Follow these seven easy steps to keep costs down as much as possible:

#1 — Compare Prices

Always look around for the best prices. While the cost of a cruise itself might be set for any given time of the year, each cruise line will offer different discounts, as will travel agents and travel Web sites. Ideally, you should contact a combination of travel agents, Web sites, and cruise lines to find the best prices available. This also applies to airfare. Do not accept the package a travel agent offers right away. Research if it will be at all cheaper to pay for airfare through a separate party for bigger discounts.

#2 — Travel in the Off-Season

The off-season varies for every destination and is increasingly shrinking as more and more people go on cruises every year and ships become more accommodating. However, there are still certain times of year in which you can find significant discounts on tickets for a cruise, as well as air travel, if you know where to look.

#3 — Drive to the Port if Possible

As many as 40 percent of Americans live within driving range of a departure port. If it is possible to get to the port of departure without paying for transportation, do it. Have a friend or family member drive you to and from the port and pay only for gas. Additionally, busses, trains, and other forms of transportation can save you a large chunk of money when traveling before and after a cruise.

#4 — Get a Smaller Room

The cost of rooms on-board a cruise ship make up a significant portion of the cost. By seeking out a smaller or less ideal room on-board a cruise, you can save large sums of money. Travel agents will often have room charts and price comparisons available for your trip. If you plan on spending very little time in your room, it might be best to cut out the cost of a large room with a view altogether and save a couple hundred dollars.

#5 — Bring Snacks and Drinks

Most cruises offer meals as part of the cost. However, they usually only cover the three central meals of the day and usually only during certain times. If you are interested in opening up their dining options or snacking during in-between hours, the cost of food can begin to add up very quickly. By bringing extra snacks and drinks, you can save as much as $20 per person, per day on-board. For a family of four on a seven-day cruise, that can mean saving $560 just in food costs.

#6 — Book Your Excursions as Early as Possible

The additional cost of excursions often does not factor into early budgeting. By booking them as soon as the cruise and time is established, you can be sure you have enough money set aside and that the excursions you are interested in do not fill up. Also, the closer you get to the date of an excursion, the more likely the price is to increase, directly affecting the budget.

#7 — Set a Specific Budget for On-board Expenses

While it is all well and good for you to say you will not spend any additional money on-board, it will happen. There are simply too many things to do on-board and too many opportunities to spend money. Food may look too enticing and casinos are a nice vacation-only opportunity. Set aside a decided amount of money for on-board expenses and tips before even booking the cruise. By having that money prepared, you can ensure the budget remains set and that upon returning home, there is not a four-figure bill waiting for you.

Be Realistic

Ultimately, a cruise is a rare occasion in which you and your family can get away from your lives and spend a few days at sea enjoying the luxury and accommodations that only a select few are able to enjoy on a regular basis. Setting a budget for a cruise should be a realistic process. You should decide early on what you can afford. You should similarly not try to underestimate your budget. You should seek out a cruise schedule that best fits your family, your lives, and your budget, and work from there. If a budget is too high, you might consider pushing the cruise back a couple of months and working within the confines of a new budget.

Above all, you should remember that there are a seemingly endless number of options available, allowing you to be incredibly flexible depending largely on what you decide you want to do.

How to Book

It is now time to start the booking process by contacting a travel agent or travel Web site and ordering the cruise. The first step in this process is gathering all the information that has been discussed, perused, and finalized. All research materials, Web sites, and travel documents that have already been figured out should be on hand for the booking process.

Next, a list should be created which answers the following questions:

- ❀ What dates are you willing to go?

- ❀ Where do you want to go?

- ❀ What cruise lines do you prefer?

- ❀ What amenities are most important?

- ❀ What is your maximum budget?

- How far are you willing to travel to a port city?

- How many people and of what ages are traveling?

- What excursions do you want to go on?

With this information, any good travel agent should be able to assist you in creating a package that covers all the necessary aspects of your first cruise vacation, and customize it exactly for your needs.

Travel Agents Versus Travel Web Sites

In today's digital economy, you have more than a handful of static choices for your booking needs. You can select to either deal with a traditional travel agent in person, or you can opt to do what an increasing number of people are doing and use a travel Web site with automatic booking (and usually bigger discounts).

The answer is not as clear cut as it might sound. The major travel Web sites include:

- Expedia

- Travelocity

- Priceline

- Hotwire

- Orbitz

These Web sites all offer a series of extensive discounts, usually found by ordering last-minute packages and trips that would normally have extensive markups for travel agents. Without the need of a human agent selling every ticket, the Web sites can reduce costs significantly and save travelers a great deal of money.

Additionally, packages can be booked together with airfare, rental cars, and excursion packages for an easy itinerary creation.

The main drawback of travel Web sites, though, is the limitations present in trying to navigate complex travel regulations and purchasing options alone. While discounts can be had at will, you might not be getting the best selection of choices because you do not know where to look.

A travel agent is trained to not only know where to look, but to package things in a manner that saves you the most possible money, sets up the most efficient package, and meets all the needs outlined by the questions above. While a travel agent might be a little more expensive to work with, travelers can all but guarantee that, by doing so, they are able to get all the most up-to-date and relevant options delivered to them — after all, travel agents want to sell vacations.

Ultimately, the decision between a travel agent and a Web site should boil down to a few select factors:

1.   How important is cost to you?

2.   How important is meeting all the criteria outlined above?

3.   Is personal interaction important to you?

With these factors in mind, the decision between an agent or a site should be made to reflect the specific needs of you and your party, optimizing choices at the time of booking.

Rules and Regulations

When booking a cruise, it is a good idea to request all the pertinent information regarding updated travel regulations. At any given time, there are a number of different regulations that may have changed, either in the country from which a traveler is departing or any one of the countries you may be visiting. By staying up-to-date on all those changes, you can remain prepared as you get ready to leave on your trip.

The main thing that has affected cruises in the last two years is the change in passport requirements. For a long time it was permissible to use a photo ID and a birth certificate in lieu of a passport for travel to many North American countries. However, after January 23, 2007, those rules changed and now any international trip requires a passport. Because of State Department backlog, the rules have been delayed and revised multiple times so it is best to check with the State Department and a travel agent before setting sail. Travelers should assume they will need their passport for any trip out of the country.

Most cruise destinations do not require visas because of the nature of the travel. There are certain instances in which this rule varies, such as in Brazil and Turkey. You should check with a travel agent before assuming you do not need a visa. To receive a necessary visa, contact the State Department or embassy of the country to which you are traveling.

Air Travel

Generally, you are now recommended to give yourself 90 minutes for domestic flights and two hours for international flights when arriving at an airport. In addition, you should give yourself 45 minutes for check-in and security, and be at the gate at least 15 minutes prior to departure.

Carry-ons have been restricted recently to disallow any gels or liquids in containers larger than three ounces. You must also place those small liquids into a plastic bag and keep it sealed. The usual restrictions on sharp objects and other questionable carry-on items are still in effect.

Checked luggage has been limited to less than 50 pounds by most airlines recently and no more than two bags. International flights often allow as much as 70 pounds. Anything above these limits is subject to a surcharge.

To best prepare for the packing limitations now in place for air travel, check with the Department of Homeland Security and the Transportation Security Administration. Both agencies keep lists and pertinent information on their Web sites.

Cruise-Specific Rules

Rules for travel aboard a cruise ship are subject to change at any time. The most common rules limit women from traveling in the third trimester of pregnancy, and a single parent traveling with a child without a permission slip from the second parent.

The Department of Homeland Security also requires cruise lines to provide a list of all passengers 96 hours before entering any U.S. port. For this reason, cruise lines request that all passengers provide the necessary information as early as possible, often offering incentives for the pre-registration process. It also helps to ensure embarkation takes much less time.

Because all countries have different regulations and requirements for international travelers, it is best to contact the State Department or embassy of whichever country you will be entering on your cruise. Cruise lines and travel agents will generally provide this information, but in a constantly shifting political environment, the extra surety provided by doing research directly into matters will be well worthwhile.

Deciphering the Options

When booking a cruise, there is a seemingly endless supply of options that the travel agent or Web site will ask before a cruise is finalized. Some of the most common options and how the decisions you make in the booking process might affect your cruise experience follow.

Dining Times

Traditionally, many cruise lines would require that dining times were selected during the booking process. This will affect which restaurants and what time of the day you are allowed to dine. In recent years, many cruise lines, as they build bigger and more feature-rich ships, have made it so passengers can eat whenever and wherever they want.

When booking, it is important to check how meal times are handled for the particular cruise being selected. While it is growing more common to have open meal times, there are still smaller cruises and budget lines that will require you to choose your times early.

Room Position

Where your room is located will usually directly affect the cost of the cruise. With so many rooms on such a massive ship, the options are nearly endless. Rooms with views are generally more expensive. The larger, more luxurious rooms will usually have a better view. Smaller rooms located within the ship, without a view, are usually less expensive. If you do not expect to spend more than a few hours a day in your room, a smaller, more secluded room for less money might be a good option.

Guaranteed Cabins

This particular method of selecting a cabin on a cruise ship allows a bit of flexibility on the part of the cruise line and may even result in an unexpected upgrade. There are two main types of cabin guarantees.

ROS (Run of Ship)

This type of cabin guarantee is often misunderstood and results in a situation in which someone thinks they are paying for one type of cabin and ends up getting something completely different. Usually a travel agent will describe an ROS cabin as being a minimum requirement for a cabin purchased by the traveler. They usually mention the possibility of receiving an upgrade to a better cabin, as the cruise line will put the traveler in the best possible cabin still available. This is not always the case, though. Rather, the cruise line usually places the traveler in the first available cabin, which could end up being an undesirable, small one.

Minimum Category Guarantee

This style of guaranteed cabin is much different than an ROS. It allows passengers to select the minimal quality cabin they are willing to stay in on their cruise. The cruise line can then place them in any cabin, from that minimal choice up to the best cabins on the ship. There is less of a gamble, and this always provides the chance of getting a last minute upgrade to fill a nicer cabin.

Private Receptions

In the case of a wedding or a family reunion, a private reception in one of the cruise ship's reception halls or restaurants needs to be booked well in advance when paying for the cruise. All the information related to the reception should be made available immediately so the travel agent or Web site can inform the cruise line of how the reception room will be used.

Who Needs Insurance?

Consumers are told they need insurance for just about everything. Their homes, their cars, their televisions, and even their cellular phones are all insurable and, in fact, are often insured because it is the smart thing to do. It makes sense, then, that travel is another aspect of a consumer's life that should be insured.

Too many people feel as though there are reasons not to get insurance. It is yet another expense tacked onto an increasingly expensive vacation that is only useful in the worst case scenario. Who wants to think about everything that can go wrong before they even set sail? However, regardless of the situation, there are dozens of different reasons why a cruiser needs to have insurance. If anything were to go wrong, the amount of money invested in a cruise vacation that would be lost is huge.

What Does Insurance Do?

The problem many people have, and do not immediately consider when booking their first cruise, is that their existing insurance does not cover what it might normally cover while in the United States. Medicare and many private insurance companies will not necessarily cover medical expenses incurred at sea, because cruise ships are often registered in another country, such as Panama or Libya.

Additionally, the cost of the cruise does not cover any medical care provided by the on-board nurse or doctor in the medical facilities. After returning home and receiving the final bill for the cruise, you will find additional charges for such services to include thousands of dollars in extra medical charges. Usually, the standard doctor visit on-board will cost about $40, but if anything else is required, such as medicine, equipment, or procedures, the cost can rise quickly.

The only exceptions to the amount an on-board doctor's visit might cost is when the cruise line takes responsibility in the case of an on-board incident or a breakout of the norovirus, both of which cruise lines usually cover the cost of.

For these reasons, travel insurance can be a very important addition to a trip, saving thousands of dollars if something were to go wrong. Beyond health problems, travel insurance covers a list as diverse as weather problems, missed flights, missing passports and luggage, or anything else that might go wrong before, during, or after a cruise. Any of these problems can put a massive financial drain on a traveler and force them to cancel a trip completely in some instances. If a traveler thinks of it in this manner, they cannot only keep from losing money on their trip, but they also keep from losing the money they spent on their trip altogether.

Special Exceptions

Travel insurance is a vital addition to any trip, but it does not cover every possible contingency in the event of something going wrong. It would not be fair to expect it to. This means that, if luggage is lost or a flight is delayed, there is nothing the insurance company can do to fix the problem or cover the cost of replacing lost clothing right away.

The luggage is insured, but because there is a six-hour time frame before it is considered officially missing, the claim might not be filled for a while. This is yet another reason to always have extra cash and a credit card on hand. If luggage is lost and clothing needs to be purchased, the insurance company will fill the claim eventually, recuperating the cost of needing to replace that luggage.

Missing the Boat

A good addition to any insurance coverage for a trip is "catch-up" insurance. This is a very helpful addition, as it will take care of anyone who has missed their boat because of a late flight or travel delay. The insurance company will then pay for a flight to the next port of call for the ship where they can catch the boat. The cruise line is not responsible for ensuring anyone gets on the ship, even if air travel was purchased in a package. However, with the additional insurance coverage offered, you can make sure nothing keeps you from catching the cruise.

Medical Emergencies

The cost of a medical emergency at sea can skyrocket quickly. Consider this: If someone becomes ill or injured while on-board, they not only have to visit the on-board doctor, but may need evacuation to the nearest hospital, hospital care, and a possible flight back to the United States for further care. The cost of doctors, air travel, and additional medical expenses can lead to a backbreaking pile of medical bills if they are not properly covered.

The actual cost of such an incident is much higher when at sea and should be insured accordingly. While an illness at home might cost thousands, the same illness at sea with medical evacuation involved might cost as much as $100,000. Insurance should be purchased to cover at least this much and even more if the cruise is in a more remote destination, such as in the Eastern Hemisphere.

Where to Get Cruise Insurance

There are plenty of options available for cruise insurance, but the most immediately available and easiest to get is the policy offered by the cruise line itself. On occasion though, it may not be the best option available. In these instances, there are plenty of third party insurance providers that work directly through travel agents to offer coverage. Companies such as Travel Guard and CSA are good choices — they offer comprehensive coverage for almost any contingency.

Reimbursement Policies

Many times, travelers might assume that, if they cancel their cruise reservations, they will receive their insurance premiums back. However, especially through the cruise lines themselves, the money is only refunded in special cases such as medical emergency. If a cruise is cancelled, the traveler will need to make a claim, and the insurance company will investigate before refunding the payments. If the cruise line itself goes bankrupt, they will not guarantee reimbursement. These are both good reasons to consider a third party insurer, as they will offer better reimbursement terms.

The Cost of Insurance

There are plenty of different insurance providers, each of them offering different rates for travelers. CSA is a good example of one of the largest and most widely used travel insurance companies.

The following coverage is for two individuals aged 52, traveling for one week in the Caribbean. The cost of insurance for both individuals was $159.19 and includes the following coverage:

* Trip Cancellation — 100 percent of trip, up to $2,000

* Trip Delay — $150 per day, up to $2,000

* Baggage Delay — up to $400

* Trip Interruption — 150 percent, up to $3,000

* Baggage and Personal Effects — up to $2,000

* Accident and Sickness Medical Expenses — up to $50,000

* Emergency Evacuation — up to $250,000

* Collision Damage — up to $25,000

* Air Flight Accident — up to $200,000

For an additional $81, both passengers can receive enhanced protection for the following areas of their trip:

* Baggage Delay — up to $1,000

* Accident and Sickness Medical Expenses — up to $250,000

* Post Event Accidental Death and Dismemberment (up to 180 days after accident) — up to $100,000

A good option for researching and finding out how much insurance will cost for specific trips is to go to **http://www.InsureMyTrip.com**. You can enter your information directly into the Web site and receive quotes from different companies based on the criteria of the trip. There can be as much as a $75 per person difference in some rate plans, depending on age, destination, and coverage of the individuals. Pre-existing conditions are another major deciding factor in the process.

Not Covered by Insurance

Almost all contingencies are covered by your insurance policy. However, there are some instances which are not. As unlikely as it may seem, the break out of war is not included in the list of things covered by your insurance, while a terrorist attack is covered. Additionally, the negligent actions of a travel agent are generally not covered. This means that, if the travel agency with which you work goes bankrupt, there is no coverage for the missed cruise. Also, flights purchased with rewards programs or frequent flier miles are not covered by insurance. The insurance company sees them as being free and, thus, there is no monetary value to cover.

Cancelling a Trip

Most travel insurance packages will not cover a trip if there is not a good reason for cancelling. There are some companies that will offer the option to cancel a trip for any reason and refund a portion or of the entire cost of that trip. Two companies that offer such coverage are TravelSafe and M.H. Ross. For these companies, the rules are as follows:

* Coverage must be purchased within 15 days of making the trip deposit.

* Trip must be cancelled two or more days before a trip begins.

* 75 percent of the non-refundable trip cost will be reimbursed.

Additionally, some cruise lines will offer "Cancel for any Reason" policies that allow you to have a smaller portion of your money returned to you. Some of these companies will keep a flat fee of $100 per person, cancelling more than 30 days out, while others will charge as much as a 50 percent penalty. Without insurance, the non-refundable deposits remain non-refundable regardless of the reason for cancellation.

Important Facts About Insurance

If the question being asked is, "Do I need insurance?" the answer is a resounding yes. For any other questions, here are some common things to remember when getting that insurance established:

- ❈ Insurance policies become active at 12:01 the day after purchase.

- ❈ Most insurance policies require purchase within 14 days of the first deposit on a trip to receive the absolute fullest benefits.

- ❈ Insurance providers offer 24-hour phone help if anything goes wrong on a trip. They cannot always offer help right away, but they will be there to answer questions.

- ❈ Always have extra money on hand and be ready to pay for any expenses right away. The insurance company will often be able to reimburse the costs, but only if receipts are retained.

- ❈ Claims can take days to process and usually at least 14 days to review.

- ❈ Be willing and prepared to prove the reason for trip cancellation, including medical documents, possible death, or other unavoidable causes.

How to Book — A Cruise Booking Outline

Thus far, all the necessary information needed to book a cruise has been uncovered and discussed at length. It can still be a confusing process to try and balance all that information. Compiled into 10 easy steps is everything needed and expected for the booking cruise to make sure that no one forgets anything important.

Step 1

Gather all the necessary information regarding cruises that might be of interest. Research different cruise lines through brochures and Web sites, as well as the ships, deck plans, and available amenities for each line. Research possible destinations, as well as ways to get to them.

Step 2

Decide on a final location. Talk to a travel agent or cruising expert who has specific knowledge about the various destinations and who might be able to recommend somewhere that suits everyone going on the trip.

Step 3

Select the duration for the cruise. Most cruises are between three and 14 days. Choose based on budget and destinations.

Step 4

Choose a final budget for the trip. This will determine which kind of cruise is selected, how luxurious accommodations might be, and how long the cruise will last. Consider all necessary factors, such as air travel, excursions, tipping, and on-board expenses.

Step 5

Research and find a travel agent with solid references and a lot of experience. Contact them directly and discuss your budget and the type of cruise that has been chosen. Make specific references to ships, destinations, and brochures to get the best advice and package for a cruise.

Step 6

Choose a point of departure with the assistance of the travel agent. This will affect the cost of travel and where the ship might eventually visit.

Step 7

Select how many port calls are desirable for the duration of the cruise. Select at this time which destinations are most important and what activities are desirable for those destinations. The travel agent will help book these extra excursions, though they will cost more.

Step 8

Choose a room. Rooms on-board vary in size and services, and should be selected based on both budget and desired features. Brochures and information from the travel agent should help make the decision easier.

Step 9

Learn about cancellation fees, restrictions, and assorted rules and regulations for the specific cruise line and ship you selected.

Step 10

Book the cruise through a travel agent or a Web site if a travel agent was not used to gather the information listed above. Record all the booking information and set it aside in a separate file, including bills, insurance information, and itineraries.

Congratulations! Your first cruise is booked, and you are ready to prepare for and embark on your ocean vacation. It is still early in the process. Keep your documents safe and check on bills and other necessary information to make sure nothing has changed. For more detailed preparation instructions, see the time line provided in the section after this chapter.

Making a Time Line

With a budget in hand and a clear understanding of what choices are available, it is time to set a solid time line that allows the first-time cruiser to ensure all the bases are covered as the embarkation date draws nearer. By starting as much as six months in advance, it is possible to outline and be ready for any and all future situations that might arise.

Here you will find a detailed checklist and time line that allows you to follow the standard cruise booking process from inception to embarkation. Some of the details involved in this list will be discussed later in the book. Keep these pages handy — they will serve as good reference points for the preparation process.

THREE TO SIX MONTHS OUT	
Start the process of getting or renewing a passport. Passports, especially after January 2007, have a significant backlog with the State Department and should be acquired early to ensure cruise passengers are ready to depart.	
Check with a travel agent or cruise line to find out if any other identification is needed, including visas or further proof of citizenship.	
Apply for any visas or additional documentation required to enter a foreign country.	
Start gathering necessary paperwork or information for a marriage or family reunion. Contact the cruise line and request additional paperwork or requirements they might have.	

ONE TO THREE MONTHS OUT	
Make final payments on your cruise fare. The actual due dates will vary depending on your cruise line, but this should be taken care of as early and quickly as possible to make sure it is out of the way. If you fail to pay off the balance before the due date, your reservations may be cancelled.	

ONE TO THREE MONTHS OUT	
Review and create a detailed packing list for every member of your party. Using Chapter 7 as an outline, be sure no one forgets anything.	
Check all your packing materials early. Set aside formal clothing and anything you plan on taking with you, making sure it is clean and ready to pack.	
Start shopping for necessary items early. This allows you time to afford the necessary items and to remember anything you may forget when you first go shopping.	
Make reservations and arrangements for your pets and your home. Contact kennels and line someone up to house sit for you while you are gone early.	
If children are staying at home, arrange a reliable babysitter (and a backup) for the duration of your trip.	
Outline and prepare everything the children will need while gone. This includes school supplies, sleepover materials, birthday gifts, and special meals.	
Make all reservations for shore excursions and possible spa and fitness programs on-board the ship. These fill up fast and need to be dealt with early in order to ensure space.	
Have a credit card set aside with a substantial line of credit for your room deposit and on-board charges. You may have paid off your tickets already, but it would do no good to get on-board and be unable to visit the casino or buy drinks one night because your card is full. Most ships charge such extra expenses to your card, but only after the deposit is charged. If you cannot cover both, you will be without any money.	

30 DAYS OUT	
Call and get the details for your airline schedule at least one month before departure. Check and make seating and meal arrangements now.	
Check clothing and packing lists for your children if they are going with you. Do not do this too early or clothes set aside for a cruise may not fit when it comes time to leave.	

30 DAYS OUT	
Make personal appointments for your family and pets now. Any doctor's visits, haircuts, manicures, or assorted other appointments should be handled now.	
Check and review your luggage. Pull everything from the closets, make sure locks and zippers work, and empty any previous leftover traveling gear.	
Purchase any additional luggage, clothing, or other materials you may have forgotten or just now realized you need.	

TWO TO FOUR WEEKS OUT	
Contact your travel agent and receive any necessary cruise documents. Review them for accuracy and record your final itinerary.	
Check the names on your reservations, the cabin numbers, the date of departure, and make sure to ask any and all questions you have now of your travel agent.	
Read the cruise specific information provided to you by your travel agent. Included should be information about your specific cruise, the activities on-board, and the ports of call.	
Complete your packing and shopping now if possible. Minimize the chance of last minute runs to the store.	
Place all your packing materials in one place and finalize your packing organization. Communicate to your family their packing needs as well. Double check that your children have completed their packing lists as well.	
Buy film for and check the batteries in your camera. For digital cameras, make sure you have enough batteries and memory space available.	
Fill any prescriptions and ensure you have enough with you for the duration of the trip (as well as an emergency stash).	
Bring copies of all medical documents, including prescriptions, recent health problems, and tests in case of a medical problem on-board.	
Make copies of your passport, photo ID, and credit cards and keep them in a separate, secure location.	
Acquire cash for tipping and on-board purchases. Make sure you have enough one dollar bills on hand at all times.	

TWO TO FOUR WEEKS OUT

Exchange any money you may need to make purchases in ports of call. Check which currency is used and exchange accordingly.	
Consider placing items in a safe deposit box at the bank to keep them safe while you are gone.	
Make arrangements for your mail — either to be held at the post office or picked up by a neighbor.	
Have newspaper delivery stopped or held.	
If it is appropriate, make arrangements for snow removal or lawn care in your absence.	
Leave all your ship's itinerary information, phone numbers, and an extra key with a close friend or family member in case something happens.	
Purchase entertainment to keep your children occupied on the trip to the port of embarkation.	

THREE DAYS OUT

Confirm all your flights, tickets, and departure times for the entire trip.	
Tag each of your suitcases with your name and address, along with instructions for reaching you.	
Complete and have ready all the necessary documentation your cruise line has requested. This may include customs forms, immigrations forms, and other documentation needed to enter into another country. You will regret not doing this now if you wait until the day of departure.	
Complete any last minute laundry, housework, or shopping that needs done.	

ONE DAY OUT

Take your pets to the kennel or talk to the house sitter about necessary care. Have all documents ready.	
Water plants and the lawn as needed.	
Throw away any food that will go bad before you return from your trip. No one wants to come home and find spoiled milk or rotting leftovers.	

ONE DAY OUT	
Send off any bills that might be due while you are gone.	
Remove any information or cards you will not need from your wallet or purse and store them safely where they will not be lost while you are gone.	
Finish packing and lock your suitcases, double checking all lists and necessities.	

THE DAY OF DEPARTURE	
Set the thermostat and test all your door locks and windows.	
Turn off the water in the winter time and check all gas pipes and lines before leaving. Ideally, if you are gone for more than five days, turn these all off (unless a house sitter is staying there to watch them).	
Ensure you arrive at the airport at least two hours early for security check in. Be prepared to follow all airport instructions and security precautions.	
Ensure you have all tickets, keys, and necessary documents in your carry-on luggage. These should never be checked. They are the most important thing you have.	

The goal when you set sail is to be so fully prepared for any possible thing to happen that you do not need to spend more than a few minutes getting things in order when you get aboard the ship. You want to be able to sit back, relax, and enjoy every moment of your cruise without worrying about what your children may have forgotten or whether you forgot to turn the gas off before locking up the house. With the right time line and itinerary in place, your vacation can actually be a vacation.

Chapter 7

What to Bring: Packing for a Cruise

With the seemingly arduous process of selecting and booking a cruise out of the way, it is now time to start the packing process. Packing actually begins many months before the cruise embarks. No one wants to forget those important formal clothes or the paperwork required to get on the ship or off the ship in a port of call.

Therefore, you should start the packing process as many as three months in advance, starting with the creation of packing lists and inventories of necessary goods. This gives you time to not only start shopping for necessary additions to those suitcases but to make sure everything needed can be set aside and triple checked in the time before the vacation starts.

What You Need for Your Trip

What better way to be prepared for a vacation than to have a detailed, checklist of everything that will be needed when it comes time to embark.

Using the lists provided below, create specific lists for each of the members of your family now, print them out, and distribute them. This allows everyone to start packing or setting aside items now so they are ready to pack when the time comes.

Additionally, it allows you to create a second set of lists containing everything that will need to be purchased for the trip. There are a lot of small, easily forgotten items that can sneak up on you at the last second. By having these lists checked off early enough and the shopping list prepared, everything can be purchased, set aside, and be ready for packing when the week of the trip arrives.

Reading Material and Necessities

* Glasses, contacts, contact solution, contact case

* Reading glasses

* Sunglasses

* Sunglasses for reading

* Books and information for each port of call

* Language phrase books or dictionaries

* Maps

* Reading materials for the plane, pool, or trip down time

* Notebook to take notes and share with friends back home; plenty of pencils or pens for writing in the notebook

* Business cards or information cards to share with any new friends met while on the cruise; include phone number and e-mail address

❋ Addresses and e-mail addresses of anyone back home who might be sent a postcard, letter, or souvenir from a port of call

❋ Photo album

Electronics and Camera Equipment

❋ All adaptors, converters, or chargers for equipment

❋ Cellular phone with charger

❋ Personal digital assistant with charger

❋ Film camera and manual

❋ Extra film; always place undeveloped film in carry-ons

❋ Disposable camera; for beach days, port-side trips, and the like

❋ Digital camera

❋ Digital camera memory cards

❋ Digital camera batteries

❋ Laptop computer

❋ Binoculars

❋ Battery chargers

❋ Extension cord/power strip

❋ mp3 player for exercise or fitness classes

❋ Battery operated alarm clock

❋ Small lighted clock for cabin

❀ Flashlight

❀ Nightlight

Other "Necessities"

❀ Duct tape or strapping tape

❀ Plastic cable lock ties to secure baggage on return trip

❀ Extra luggage name tags

❀ Multiple different sizes of Ziploc® and garbage bags

❀ Corkscrew (place in checked bags)

❀ Umbrella

❀ Travel pillow and blankets for long flights

❀ Glue for broken items

❀ Playing cards

❀ Sports gear (rackets, scuba gear, basketball, etc.)

❀ Shoe horn

❀ Sewing kit and scissors (place in checked bags)

❀ Woolite®

❀ Clothespins

❀ Empty tote bag for easy souvenir storage while on land

❀ Coffee mugs or tumblers

Women's Cruise Clothing

❀ Undergarments

❀ Nighttime clothing

❀ Compression stockings for long flights

❀ Exercise socks

❀ Pantyhose

❀ Camisole or slip

❀ Purses for day and night

❀ Gloves and stocking cap (if expecting cold weather)

❀ Walking shoes

❀ Walking sandals

❀ Rubber sandals

❀ Evening shoes

❀ Swimsuit

❀ Evening sweater

❀ Raincoat with hood

❀ Thongs or flip flops

❀ Workout clothes and sports bra

❀ Belts

❋ Scarves

❋ Dress or outfit for informal nights

❋ Dress or outfit for formal nights

❋ Dress or outfit for casual nights

❋ Shorts

❋ Multiple kinds of tops

❋ Slacks

❋ Windbreaker

❋ Sweatshirt

Women's Hygiene Items

❋ Blow dryer

❋ Hairspray

❋ Shampoo

❋ Curling iron or curlers

❋ Moisturizer and freshener

❋ Nail polish and remover

❋ Nail clippers and file (in checked bags)

❋ Razor and shaving cream

❋ Comb or brush

❀ Hair gel

❀ Toothbrush

❀ Toothpaste

❀ Dental floss

❀ Mouthwash

❀ Conditioner

❀ Shower cap

❀ Bar soap

❀ Deodorant

❀ Tweezers

❀ Makeup mirror

❀ Makeup and makeup bag

❀ Makeup remover

❀ Cleanser

Men's Cruise Clothing

❀ Undergarments

❀ Belts

❀ Gloves and stocking cap for cold weather cruises

❀ Walking shoes

❋ Walking sandals

❋ Evening or dress shoes

❋ Tuxedo jacket and pants (or dark suit)

❋ Tuxedo tie, suspenders, and cummerbund

❋ Tuxedo cufflinks/studs

❋ Pajamas and robe

❋ Compression socks for airplane flights

❋ Exercise socks

❋ Black dress socks

❋ Sports jacket

❋ Regular ties

❋ Shorts

❋ Casual shirts

❋ Slacks

❋ Jacket

❋ Sweatshirt

❋ Raincoat with hood

❋ Tuxedo shirt

❋ Dress shirts

✿ Swimsuit

✿ Workout clothes

Men's Hygiene Items

✿ Comb or brush

✿ Shampoo and hair products

✿ Mouthwash

✿ Tweezers

✿ Nail clippers (in checked bags)

✿ Shaving materials

✿ Toothbrush

✿ Toothpaste

✿ Bar soap

✿ Deodorant

✿ Dental floss

Paperwork, Travel Documents, and Financial Information

Besides the cruise ship essentials, you will need to have all the necessary travel documents for their trip. While it might seem as though passports, visas, and tickets would never be forgotten, it is important to have a list of the necessary documents set aside, along with copies of everything on it.

Additionally, wallet contents and financial materials should be kept in a separate location where they cannot be lost. Information such as this should never be placed in checked luggage and, if possible, all original wallet and purse contents not needed for a trip should be left at home or in a safety deposit box in a bank. Items to keep in a separate location include:

❈ Airline tickets or confirmation numbers

❈ Cruise documents

❈ Passports and visas (when necessary) or proof of citizenship

❈ Vaccination certificate (when required)

❈ Driver's license and auto insurance card — for shore-side care rentals, and a second picture ID

❈ Medical insurance cards and medical history

❈ Copy of prescriptions and current medications

❈ Credit cards; call companies to inform of overseas travel

❈ ATM card

❈ Phone cards

❈ Traveler's checks (and some cash)

❈ Contact numbers for lost or stolen travelers checks or credit cards

❈ Home emergency numbers

❈ Currency conversion chart

❈ Wallet, money clip, money belt, or fanny pack

What to Expect. Be Prepared For

Earlier in this book, the importance of travel insurance was discussed. Additionally, you should consider the importance of every day items that might be needed while on the ship. Beyond the basic entertainment, clothing, and travel materials that any trip requires, a cruise has a long list of necessary secondary items, such as medical equipment or medicines, lotions, and sunblock.

While it might not seem like any of the items on this list will be used while on the ship, they should still be brought along, in a special emergency-style kit, so that if anything goes wrong, extra money does not need to be spent visiting the on-ship doctor or nurse.

* Hand lotion and foot lotion

* Rubbing alcohol

* Bug spray

* Prescription drugs and any other essential medications

* Ear plugs

* Sunscreen and sunblock

* Hand cleaner

* Hand wipes and cleaner

Choosing Luggage

Many people already have a decent selection of luggage on hand for the annual trips they take — visiting parents for Christmas, spending

Thanksgiving with a spouse's family, weddings, or anniversaries. However, many people, especially when preparing for their first cruise, might not be fully prepared with the right quality and range of luggage necessary for a 14 day trip at sea.

Luggage That Will Not Disappear

Consider how many bags at baggage claim tend to look identical. It will astound you to see the dozens of black and tan bags from the same companies filing around the carousel in succession as people check the name and address tags. While most people may assume there is no problem because of those tiny address tags, it would not be difficult for someone to grab the wrong bag without checking the tag and then taking it home with them?

The biggest problem here is if someone else takes a bag that does not belong to them, it is no longer the responsibility of the airline to return it to the person who lost the luggage. It then becomes the responsibility of those who lost the bags — a cruel twist of fate, merely because someone else did not look at the tag.

So, one of the most important aspects of buying luggage for a cruise trip, or any long trip where bags will be checked, is to ensure they are easily identifiable. One of the easiest things that can be done here is to choose luggage with a distinctive pattern and colors or to mark that luggage with tape or pen so that it stands out. It may be ugly, but it will never be lost or stolen on accident.

Luggage Types

There are a number of different kinds of luggage available for those embarking on long trips. For long trips and air flights especially, something durable is always best. Soft-side luggage may be a better looking, generally more appealing choice, but it is also often an easily destroyed, easily mistreated choice. For those checking multiple bags, the contents of the bags should be considered along with the aesthetics. Clothing may be important, but as long as it is not lost, it can be refolded and placed in a new bag.

Medical equipment, electronics, or other fragile, packed goods can be destroyed if a bag is mistreated, and soft-side luggage can result in both. For long-term travel and fragile luggage, hard-case and reinforced luggage is always a good idea. The airline will usually replace or pay for destroyed or mistreated luggage, but if something important was in the luggage, they will not necessarily cover the cost of that.

The ideal luggage combines a variety of different styles. For anything important, especially non-clothing items, small, hard-side luggage is the best choice. It adds additional protection without the extra weight that some luggage can tack on.

Medium-size, soft-side luggage is good for clothing and other mutable goods that will not be easily destroyed if the baggage handlers are unkind. For longer cruises, though, it might be necessary to have multiple bags, and then a large soft-side bag is a good idea as well, as long as it does not contain anything that is easily destroyed and can be replaced.

Ultimately, the best addition to any luggage is a good travel insurance policy to cover the cost of any damage incurred to the luggage or bags that might be lost. If the airline is unwilling to replace what they have ruined, this is a good fail-safe way to cover the cost of any clothing or goods that must be paid for while on the trip.

How to Pack

New rules are set in place at any given time by Homeland Security and Transportation Security Administration (TSA), and cruise lines also have requirements about how luggage is packed and how many bags can be brought. Generally, though, the strictest are set in place for air travel.

Packing for Security

In today's security environment, new rules and regulations dominate how you pack your bags. Because of the nature of the Department of Homeland Security and the TSA, bags are checked more thoroughly than ever before, and a mispacked bag can lead to extra time being spent in a security checkpoint or with bags being opened and handled before boarding.

To best prepare for a trip, the first thing you should do is visit the TSA Web site and read all the current travel requirements. Currently, travelers are not allowed to bring any liquids with them in their carry-on luggage unless they are less than three ounces and in a sealed plastic bag. Additionally, the same rules regarding dangerous objects, sharp grooming tools, and other possibly security risks are still in place.

When packing bags, always remember to keep items that could set off security checks in checked luggage. Many of the items not allowed in carry-ons can be carried in checked luggage. Another thing to remember for anyone traveling overseas on their cruise and stopping in a foreign port of call is the various customs laws that may be in effect upon returning to the United States. Certain items, when packed in luggage, can result in being stopped at customs or security.

Careful Packing

To be sure that nothing is lost when traveling, packing should be done with the utmost attention to the items being packed, how long the trip will be, and how important certain items are. Paperwork, tickets, and essential or expensive items should always be kept in carry-on luggage.

It is also a good idea to keep duplicates of all important documents. If two people are traveling, keep the travel documents in one carry-on and duplicates of those documents in a second carry-on to ensure that, if something happens to one bag, the information is still available.

Items should be dispersed throughout luggage so that, if one bag is lost, a collection of items or clothing for one person is not completely lost. Split up medicine and medical equipment into multiple bags to make sure everyone has the items they need. It may result in a slightly harder time packing and organizing items into bags, but it will ensure that no one person will suffer because of lost medicine or medical equipment if a bag is lost.

Frugal Packing

Many airlines have rules for the weight and the number of bags allowed on a flight. For a 14-day cruise, though, a lot of items will likely be needed, so it is important to make sure everything needed for the trip is packed without needing to pay too much extra for luggage space on the plane. There is a system in order to accomplish this.

Pack essentials first, adding any entertainment or additional items only after initial packing is complete. Additionally, you should communicate with fellow travelers about the importance of the weight of their luggage. A bag cannot weigh more than 50 pounds if it is being checked. If it does, the airline will request that the bags be repacked to meet their guidelines. This can lead to a series of delays and unwanted additional changes being made at the airport.

Be Prepared for Everything

The lists above may seem like a complete outline of everything that could possibly be needed for a 14-day cruise. However, there are a number of contingencies that may apply to specific individuals or families. When packing, you should do more than just follow the lists provided. You should outline specific needs that you and your family have. If a specific medical condition requires extra equipment or medication, you should have more than one on hand.

Medical equipment, especially, should be stored in multiple bags. If, for some reason, luggage is lost, there should be no reason to cancel an entire vacation because medical equipment and prescriptions were not packed in different bags (carry-ons should include all necessary medical equipment). If a prescription supply is put into both a carry-on and a checked piece of luggage, it is unlikely that both will be lost and the person needing the medication will be able to continue on with their cruise.

As little fun as it may be, sit down and outline any possible thing that may go wrong for a trip or that has gone wrong in the past and pack accordingly for it. Bring the right materials, be ready for anything (including situations in any port of call), and have extras of everything on hand (including copies of all documents).

Special Passenger Needs

For passengers with special needs, each cruise line has a different set of accommodations, usually consisting of specially-sized rooms, extra bathrooms, and any other needs someone might have while on the cruise. However, it is important for anyone with special needs or the family of someone with special needs to be appropriately prepared for whatever might happen while on-board. The cruise lines cannot be solely relied on to provide necessities.

For those that need to bring special equipment that might be volatile, such as insulin for a diabetic, the ships accommodate by providing storage facilities and extra equipment. Refrigerators are placed in every room for such a purpose.

While on-board doctors can make medical supplies available, it is important that anyone traveling with special needs brings their own equipment. Things like oxygen, wheelchairs, and medicine are not provided by the cruise line and should be brought in ample supply.

The best way to ensure someone is fully taken care of for the duration of a cruise is to bring more than the necessary allotment of medical equipment. Store an emergency kit in separate luggage that will tide them over if luggage is lost or something happens while on-board.

Chapter 8

Setting Sail

With the trip booked, the months passed, and the bags packed, it is finally time to set sail on your first cruise. With the sail date approaching quickly, it is important to check and double check all the necessary actions that must be taken before a vacation is undertaken. Being absolutely prepared to leave will allow everyone to finally relax and enjoy the cruise rather than having to spend the next two weeks stressing about whether the gas was turned off in the house.

The Vacation Checklist

Referring once more to the list located before Chapter 7, it is time to make sure every detail has been handled appropriately before setting sail.

Confirming Flights and Departures

As with any trip, it is important to confirm all flights and tickets at least three days prior to departure. This should not be done too much earlier than three days, as anything can change in the final days before a trip.

Additionally, while contacting the airports and airlines for final flight information, double check any hotel reservations that may have been made in the port city, and check the luggage to make sure it has been tagged and properly identified for the trip.

The Last of the Chores

It may be the last thing anyone preparing for vacation wants to do, but within the final week, all the necessary household chores should be accomplished. If they are done early enough, the last day or two before departure can be spent making sure the bags have been packed properly and other important errands are covered.

Taking Care of Children and/or Pets

Before leaving, final arrangements should be made for children (if they are being left behind) and pets. Parents should contact and discuss final child care arrangements with the babysitter or housesitter and take their pets to the kennel. Ideally, a backup should always be in place for child care in case something happens in the final days before departure. A relative or close family friend is often a good choice, as they are most reliable.

Last Minute Errands

This includes anything that might need to be done while on the trip that could result in problems upon return. Pay any bills that are due in the next three weeks, water the lawn, and clean out any perishable foods from the refrigerator. No one wants to return home from a relaxing vacation to find spoiled food, a dead lawn, and past due bills.

Finish Packing

All packing should be completed a full day before departure. Any items that were not included from the lists compiled earlier should be found or purchased now. Locks and zippers should all be tested and checked, and preparations should all be finalized for transportation to and from airports and to the port of embarkation.

General Travel Safety Tips

Before setting sail, it is a good idea to familiarize yourself with common safety tips while in a foreign country or on-board the ship. Hopefully, no one ever needs to use this information, but it can bring increased peace of mind to passengers who do not want to worry about some small detail or concern while on vacation. Many of these tips are directly related to spending time in a foreign country while on your cruise. Many of these tips can also be equally applied to anything that happens while actually on-board a ship.

* Carrying lots of cash is a risk in almost any situation. Acquiring traveler's checks is a good security precaution because they can be replaced if stolen or misused.

* Keep jewelry, wallets, and purses carefully stashed away — either at home before leaving or in a locked drawer in the cabin. Money should be hidden on the body, in a money belt, or a jacket pocket if possible.

* Try not to stand out as a tourist when visiting ports-of-all in other countries. Wear casual clothing and blend in as best as possible to avoid being victimized.

* Store tickets and important information in a secure location, away from your passport. Do not let anyone have access to those tickets, as they often contain credit card information.

* Always have travel documents, passports, visas, and tourism cards on hand when visiting a foreign country.

❋ Be wary of unwarranted attention in another country — scam artists are rampant.

❋ Always tell a family member of your plans when in another country. This ensures someone knows where you are.

❋ Always comply with a mugger if attacked while in another country. It can keep you safe from physical harm. Money and items can always be replaced.

❋ Hide any cameras away until they are ready to be used. This keeps from drawing extra attention to yourself.

❋ Copy and leave duplicates of all credit card, travel, and passport information with friends and family back home in case something happens while on a cruise.

Cruise and Cabin Safety Tips

❋ Always carry room keys when leaving the cabin, no matter where you are going.

❋ Read up on and familiarize yourself with the security options and services made available on-board the ship. Contact the cruise line directly if need be.

❋ Check and lock all doors before leaving a room or going to sleep.

❋ Ask or request use of a safe for valuables. Some rooms will have one already in place (you should know beforehand if this is the case).

❋ Even on a cruise ship, always be wary of dark corridors or late nights by yourself. Ask a friend or family member to walk with you if possible.

* Wedge the bathroom door shut while showering for added security and safety.

* Be ready for a fire, as rare as it may seem.

  • Be aware of all fire exits and emergency access routes.

  • Pull the fire alarm if necessary.

  • Call the emergency number provided by the cruise ship for fires.

  • Stay as low as possible, retreat with a room key, and open the door only after checking for heat.

  • Block vents with a wet towel or clothes to keep smoke out.

  • Fill tub and sink with water for re-wetting any towels and keeping smoke out.

  • Cover face with wet cloth.

It may not seem likely that anything on this list would happen, but by being prepared and ready for the worst — either from fellow passengers or from time spent onshore — passengers can better relax and enjoy their time on-board.

Getting to the Cruise Terminal

While most travel agents and cruise packages will attempt to sell upgrades in airline flights in order to reach the cruise terminal, there are a variety of different ways to reach the terminal that may save travelers money on their way to their cruise port of embarkment.

Living Close By

For anyone that lives nearby a cruise terminal, the options are plentiful. Almost 40 percent of the U.S. population lives within driving distance of a port city, making it much easier to get there without spending any additional time or money on air transport. Driving to the terminal is a viable option, but may cost more because of the cost of storing a vehicle.

Good secondary options are to get a ride from someone who can drive to the terminal or to use a shuttle that many cruise lines provide. Public transportation, for those in or near large cities, is always a good option.

Living Far Away

Unfortunately, the majority of the populace does not live near a cruise port. Additionally, many cruise lines or ships do not call in more than one or two ports in the United States, meaning that any cruise taken on that ship must start from a specific location, which most often needs to be traveled to. In these cases, options are slightly more expensive, usually starting with air travel.

Cruise lines will often provide information and packages for reaching the terminal of departure. Air travel varies greatly depending on the airline, the destination, and the duration of the flight. Luckily, travel agents can be very useful in acquiring this extra information and describing the necessary steps needed for air travel.

Contacting the Cruise Terminal

Most cruise terminals have a Web site or information hotline that can be visited or contacted to receive more information about directions, travel, and ultimately the cost of doing so. A trip to a Web site will often reveal driving directions from all major directions, as well as the cost of parking long- and short-term and the shuttle options made available by the terminal.

Also, you can contact the cruise line directly and request additional information only they may have available pertaining to the cost of a shuttle or related transportation methods for reaching the terminal.

There are always a variety of ways to do so, but the best way to get a good deal on travel to and from the cruise terminal is to do research beforehand.

The Right Time Line

Another important aspect of traveling before a cruise is the amount of time it may take to do that traveling. If you do not give yourself ample time to reach a cruise terminal before embarkation, you may stand a chance of missing the boat altogether. Unless specific kinds of insurance were purchased, the cruise line will not reimburse the cost of a trip if you miss the boat.

Even if the air travel attached to a trip is thrown in as part of a package, if it does not appear to give you enough time to reach the terminal, you may want to repackage your trip with an additional travel day.

For example, someone living in Oregon and traveling to Florida where their cruise terminal is located may not want to catch a morning flight for an evening departure in Florida. It may cost a small amount extra, but a good idea is to book a hotel room for one night and fly in early rather than risk possible delays.

Weather becomes another major factor in these instances. If the weather is poor in the winter months leading up to a cruise, air travel may be much more risky. Plan accordingly and add enough extra time between a flight and a cruise departure to make sure nothing goes wrong.

The same applies for driving or public transportation. Cruises are rarely directly affected by bad weather, unless it is severe. However, the roads or the bus systems may be affected if a snow storm or particularly poor weather blocks roads. To get around these problems, plan early and be ready for the worst. The small extra cost that may be involved is well worth not wasting the entire investment of a cruise vacation.

The Cruise Staff

On-board a cruise ship, there are hundreds of staff members whose daily job is to make passengers feel at home and comfortable. The amount of contact had with any given staff member varies greatly, depending on the amount of activities undertaken and the degree of social interaction performed on the ship.

Ship Crew and Hotel Staff

While it may seem as though a constant interaction between passengers and the captains, ensigns, house cleaning staff, and cooks may occur, this is rarely the case. More often than not, the ship's crew is only seen at night, when they may take in a show or visit a lounge or bar for socializing. The rest of the day they are hard at work, maintaining the ship and remain out of view of the passengers.

The same can be said of hotel staff. These individuals clean rooms and carry bags — performing whatever tasks are required of them on a daily basis. However, they rarely, if ever, spend their free time among the passengers. When they do interact with passengers, it is good to be courteous and polite to anyone who offers assistance, tipping the hotel staff for cleaning services, bag check, and for any meals aboard. These may not be individuals who are visible throughout the trip, but they will be consistently cleaning, fixing up after, and helping out passengers.

Cruise Staff

The cruise staff is a different matter altogether. These individuals, led by the cruise director, are responsible for ensuring everyone on-board has a good time. They are excellent communicators, working every day with people. The cruise staff is the passengers' first and often only link to the ship and its operations. For that reason, you should be as courteous and kind to them as possible. Their assistance will be needed time and time again.

The Cruise Director

Alongside the ship's captain, the cruise director is essentially the most important person aboard. This individual will organize and carry out all on-board activities and entertainment and is generally in charge of the social events and ceremonies performed on-board. Because of the nature of a cruise ship — holding more than 3,000 passengers at times — they are often surrounded by assistants who can more immediately see to the needs of passengers.

Assistant Cruise Director

The next in line for the duties of keeping the cruise ship operational is the assistant cruise director. This individual will often be in charge of the coordination of the rest of the individuals on the ship, making sure all cruise staff members are on task and that events and activities are consistently running smoothly. When the cruise director is not available, the assistant cruise director will often fill in to oversee ceremonies and special events.

Social Host or Hostess

This individual acts as a liaison between the ship's passengers and its crew, introducing people to the captain as time and circumstances allow. Additionally, the host or hostess performs duties in lieu of the cruise director or assistant cruise director, introducing events and activities. The social host or hostess is also responsible for helping to maintain ship morale for the passengers.

Assorted Cruise Staff

These individuals are in charge of running and maintaining ship board activities, such as golf or basketball games, and are always available to answer questions from passengers regarding the activities available or the times and locations of certain events. They answer directly to the assistant cruise director and can usually be found throughout the ship, ready and willing to answer any question you may have.

Fitness Instructors

On-board most cruise ships there are a variety of different fitness options. These can range from gyms to sports equipment and pools or organized classes. Fitness instructors are often certified in various forms of sports training and will hold several different types of classes during a cruise. For passengers seeking to remain fit and active on-board, they contact one of the multiple fitness instructors on-board as soon as you embark on a cruise.

Disc Jockey

Throughout the ship there might be nightclubs, lounges, or deck parties in which a disc jockey is responsible for not only the music but the ambience of the event. These individuals may not have direct contact with those on-board, but they can often be good acquaintances when looking for a perfect song to dance to.

Youth Activities Coordinator

For families with young children, the youth activities coordinator will be the most important person on-board. This individual acts as a cruise director for children, ensuring parents and children alike remain happy for the whole trip. They will oversee child care, child entertainment, and the various classes and activities designed to keep children active.

Golf Instructor

For many cruises, especially those stopping on islands with numerous golf courses, a golf instructor is an important individual on the cruise staff. They will play golf with passengers, offer classes, and, in some cases, may operate the golf simulator on-board for individuals looking to practice while they are at sea. Any passengers hoping to play golf at a port of call can talk to the golf instructor to learn more about what golfing options are available throughout the cruise.

Other Assorted Staff Members

Aboard every ship there are a variety of different activities that may be directly related to the specific cruise line or ship. Usually, for every general activity offered on-board, there will be at least one individual who is both familiar with the activity and willing to offer advice or guidance. While the cruise literature provided by the cruise line and the travel agent will be helpful in knowing what will be available on-board, the first thing a new cruiser should do is contact the cruise staff and inquire about activities on-board.

Interaction with the Cruise Staff

The cruise staff is on-board to help you. Customer service and interaction is the essence of their jobs, and they are more than happy to assist you with any of the available on-board activities. However, you should remember that they are people still and have other passengers and duties to attend to. Much like anyone in a service position that you might deal with in real life, a cruise staff member should be treated with the proper respect. Tip individuals who offer extra assistance or help and always be polite to cruise staff. They will be around the you and the other passengers for the rest of the cruise and can be very helpful.

Cruise Communication and Etiquette

For many years, families worried about how they would communicate while on-board a cruise ship. Because of the nature of a cruise — thousands of people in a single space — and the wide variety of activities always available, it was often the case that establishing meeting points and buddies for perusing the ship were necessary to keep anyone from getting lost, especially children.

However, as technology has developed, so too have the options for communication while on-board a cruise ship. Even as cellular phone technology grew in the 1990s, it was still not as developed as it needed to be for use on-board a ship hundreds of miles away from land.

That has changed with today's technology. Today, with the strength of smaller cellular towers and satellites, most cruise ships offer cellular phone access, either through enhanced signals or by hookups on-board the ship. These can, on occasion, cost a little bit of extra money, but they work well and allow families to keep in touch while on-board and to call back home in between port cities.

Additionally, most ships offer Internet access now, often from within the room. This access can cost extra, but it is usually high speed and reliable, allowing passengers to stay in touch with their lives while at sea.

Alternate On-board Communication

There are still more options for staying in touch while on-board that do not cost extra money. Using walkie talkies or text messaging are both good options that allow people to stay in touch without the high cost of cellular phone use on-board. Walkie talkies can be cheap and even fun for children to carry around, but can also lead to problems if they get lost, are misused, or become annoying to other passengers.

Etiquette On-board

While the different options made available for communication are numerous, they need to be used carefully when on-board. It is one thing to make an occasional cellular phone call on-board, but the overuse of phones, or walkie talkies especially, can be considered rude by fellow passengers and ship staff. The best way to ensure the proper use of communication devices is to use them sparingly.

Do not allow children to run around playing games with communication devices unless they are in designated children's play areas and try not to carry on full conversations on them when it would be just as easy to walk and talk to someone in person. Keep in mind that nighttime, restaurants, and shows are not always the best places to use these electronic devices. It can be considered rude to the other passengers.

The Purser's Desk

Usually located in a central location on the ship, the purser's desk is essentially the information hub of the cruise ship. It is here that you will find any information that you have not gathered before setting sail.

On each ship, the hours and services offered by the purser's desk vary, though most larger cruise ships offer a 24-hour service desk for their passengers. To find the hours for the purser's desk, you can either consult the Daily Bulletin of activities and events on-board (it is usually printed there somewhere) or you can find it posted on or around the actual reception area.

Usually, if you have any questions related to the events on-board, meal times, upcoming ports of call, or child care, you can find information with the purser's desk. Additionally, if you have any money issues you need handled, the purser's desk can usually assist you. Updating credit card information for on-board expenses, getting cash from an account for tipping or off board excursions, or discussing a bill can also usually be accomplished here.

A good general rule is if you have any questions with answers you cannot find, visit the purser's desk and they will either have the answer for you or point you in the right direction to find out what the answer is.

Chapter 9

Safety First on Your Cruise

A cruise environment is unlike any other on the planet. You are in the midst of a floating city, with 2,000 to 3,000 fellow passengers, all of you having the time of your lives, away from your homes and the confines of dry land. The brochures, sales pitches, and travel agents trumpet the benefits of a cruise vacation repeatedly, trying to remind you just how different and fun a cruise can be.

No matter how much fun a cruise is or how much you enjoy the prospect of hitting the high seas and spending a week away from your job, bills, and ordinary life, you must still consider a few details that can become easily lost in the shuffle of a busy vacation. Never forget that when you set foot on any boat, or outside of your home for that reason, you should be prepared for anything to happen.

Luckily, since cruise lines are well aware of the possible issues that may arise from setting sail and having something go wrong, they are among the best prepared vacation settings to assist in taking care of or assisting with any number of issues that may arise.

When you set foot on a cruise ship, you can expect that a full staff of security personnel, a medical staff prepared for most situations, and departments for filing any complaints or worries you may have are in place. If someone becomes violently ill or hurts themselves beyond the capabilities of the on-ship medical staff, you can rely on a number of air evacuation units that are on call for the various fleets of cruise ships at sea at any given time.

With hundreds of sailings each year and millions of passengers, the cruise lines have dealt with almost every possible situation you can imagine and are prepared for what may occur. However, you should still be ready for these situations by knowing what resources are at your disposal, how you can access them, and what you should do in a specific instance.

Whether it is a problem with your luggage, a suspicious encounter with a stranger or empty bag, or a massive outbreak of illness, you should be well aware of the possible outcomes of any situation on-board.

Security On-board

Cruise ship security has long been a major concern of the cruise lines. Well before the current awareness in travel security arose after September 11, 2001, cruise lines were running well groomed, tightly designed security operations in almost every case. That does not mean there have not been changes in the years since the airlines, trains, and bus systems overhauled their security protocols.

Many of the security measures implemented by the cruise lines are taken from the U.S. Coast Guard's "Security for Passenger Vessels and Passenger Terminals" guidelines. Since 2001, they have been operating under what are known as Level 3 security measures.

Standard Security Measures

The measures implemented by the cruise lines under the Coast Guard's guidelines include the following:

- ❇ Access to the bridge, engine room, and other sensitive areas of the ship are limited to security cleared personnel only. Passengers can no longer visit the bridge on a tour.

- ❇ Extra screening of all baggage, carry-ons, ship cargo, and stores is conducted.

- ❇ Extra screening of the passenger list and identification. Passenger information is needed at least 24 hours before setting sail.

- ❇ Coordination with the Immigration and Naturalization Service in the United States to ensure that any individuals who should not be on-board are removed immediately.

- ❇ Additional on-board security to ensure that no illegal activities or unauthorized entry occurs.

- ❇ Commercial vessels are now required to give 96 hours notice before entering a U.S. port, whereas previously it was only 24 hours. A full passenger list must be provided at this time for security purposes.

- ❇ The maintenance of a 100-yard security perimeter around all cruise ships.

These are the most basic rules set in place by the Coast Guard and the cruise lines. There are also additional measures that cruise lines have been following for some time now.

Controlled Access

A cruise ship is a unique security environment because it is so much easier to control access. While in port, there are only two viable exit and entry points on the ship and there are security personnel in both locations checking IDs and manifests, and making sure everyone is who they say they are. Terminal and docking areas are also secured. Together, the extra levels of security make entry by someone who does not belong on the boat very hard.

Anti-Terrorism

In the security climate that hangs over traveling today, terrorism is one of the greatest threats. The cruise lines, like other travel industries, have taken the extra steps to make sure that passengers remain safe. Security checks are now performed on all passengers and on all baggage. While airlines do not necessarily have the time to x-ray every piece of luggage that enters a plane, the cruise lines have plenty of time before embarking and will x-ray everything that passes through their hands. Metal detectors are placed in all cruise terminals now as well; passing through one is a requirement for anyone about to enter a ship. Shipments of supplies are measured and checked by the ship's crew as well as the port officials to make sure they are safe. While a ship is docked in port, there are crew members on watch at all times on deck. At night, the ropes are let in and access is cut off to the ship completely.

In addition to increased operating security, ships are also keeping very close track of passengers in their logs. Electronic monitoring systems allow security personnel to keep close track of who is on the ship at any given time. If passengers disembark unexpectedly or if someone is missing, the security on-board can find out with the press of a button, and follow by taking the appropriate measures.

The Security Staff

The actual security staff for any given cruise ship will vary depending on the cruise line and the ship. There are some cruise lines that hire ex-army and naval personnel to watch over their security. Others will hire private security forces or former police officers to oversee their security needs.

At one point, the sole purpose of security was to handle any disturbances that might arise between passengers. Today, however, they are present to add peace of mind to the ship and its passengers, making sure they remain safe throughout the cruise. Some ships have now hired additional security personnel just to assess risks and communicate with the shipboard crew to keep things safe.

The ports of call are measured and researched for their potential history of security problems and are handled with an according amount of care. The ship's staff and crew are also given additional training to make sure they handle any possible problems that might arise — whether it is an unfamiliar face, unsecured cargo, or an unclaimed bag.

Security Cameras

The security cameras on-board a cruise ship are everywhere. In every public space on-board the ship, there are cameras making sure the boat runs smoothly and nothing goes wrong. They are generally placed in embarkation areas, public rooms, out-of-bounds areas, crew spaces, machinery spaces, corridors, and the common deck areas around the pool.

Port Security

When you disembark in another country's port, you can be sure that there will be just as much security as in a port in the United States. European ports, for example, are much more security conscious than most other ports, requiring many more actions from ships and cruise lines when pulling into port. Additionally, there are certain expectations laid down for any port to which a major cruise line frequently visits. If St. Marten and Nassau want the tourism dollars that the cruise industry brings them, they need to provide the high levels of security that the U.S. government and the major cruise lines expect.

Additional Post-September 11 Security Measures

Beyond the heightened security that cruise lines now follow in the Coast Guard manual, there are additional security measures in place for U.S. ports as defined by Homeland Security.

Cruise ships now have a 300-foot, no-float zone around them. This zone ensures that a space in which no private vessel is allowed to enter around the cruise ship exists. Cruise ships are also given an armed escort in and out of port now by the U.S. Coast Guard.

Passengers must show their tickets to enter or access any part of the port area or terminal now, similar to the rules set in place in airport terminals. This means that embarkation parties, like those on scenes from "The Love Boat" are a thing of the past. Visitors will have to wish you goodbye from the parking lot outside the terminal. Many terminals now have as many as four separate security check points to pass through before actually getting on-board a cruise ship.

Be Ready for Drills

When you set foot aboard a cruise ship, you are not stepping onto a purely privately run enterprise in which safety is a concern of the cruise line only. Since the early part of the 20th century, safety regulations set by the U.S. government have had a major effect on how safe ocean passage is. There are many rules in place designed to maintain the safety of a ship's passengers, crew, and staff.

Cruise Ship Safety Compliance

Every U.S. registered cruise ship must undergo a careful series of Coast Guard regulation checks every year to ensure they comply with the general safety guidelines set down. These guidelines include things like hull structure, watertight integrity, lifeboats and other lifesaving equipment, vessel control, firefighting, and navigation. After passing the annual inspection, a ship is given the Coast Guard Certificate of Inspection, which will last for the following year. The certificate is usually posted at or around the purser's desk where passengers can see it.

Most major cruise lines register their ships in other countries, though, and are thus subject to different inspection laws, according to their country of origin. While these countries can set their own safety guidelines, the United States still requires that all foreign ships taking on U.S. passengers at U.S. ports follow the International Convention for the Safety of Life at Sea or SOLAS. SOLAS requirements are usually in line with the same Coast Guard requirements listed above regarding fire prevention, lifesaving equipment, and ship integrity.

The Coast Guard will inspect all ships as they go into service at a U.S. port, repeating these checks every three months. They will run various drills and require the ship's crew to take on a variety of different tasks in the case of various kinds of emergencies, including fire, flooding, or evacuation. If the Coast Guard feels the ship does not meet SOLAS requirements, it can require that the ship repair any problems before taking on passengers at a U.S. port. You can view the records of these inspections at the Coast Guard Marine Safety Office or at the Port State Information Exchange Web site at **http://www.psix.uscg.mil**.

Crew Member Licensing

All crew members employed by a U.S. passenger ship must meet specific guidelines laid down by the U.S. Coast Guard. After a crew member has been licensed, the Coast Guard can revoke these licenses and remove someone from a cruise ship for any acts of misconduct or inappropriate behavior. SOLAS requirements permit that only qualified, competent individuals man a ship and any foreign awarded credentials are checked by the Coast Guard for ships that dock in any U.S. port.

Drills

Both the U.S. Coast Guard and International SOLAS requirements state that fire and lifeboat drills must be held regularly. While the crew is generally well practiced in these routines, they are designed to show the passengers what they should do in the event of an emergency. As such, you will likely perform a series of safety drills when you set foot on the ship to start your experience.

Depending on the length of the trip, there may be multiple fire and lifeboat drills on-board. Usually, there is one drill for every week of a voyage. If you are traveling for less than one week, you may only need to perform the first drill that occurs within 24 hours of embarkation.

In addition to these regular drills, the Coast Guard requires the posting of a notice in each cabin and stateroom that describes what to do in the case of an emergency. It will describe the various emergency signals on-board, such as a whistle or alarm for different types of emergencies. It will detail the locations of various safety equipment, such as life preservers, and the proper way in which to put them on for both adults and children. The lifeboat to which each stateroom is assigned will also be posted.

The actual lifeboat and fire drills are usually carried out with crew members guiding you in performing the necessary tasks. There are signs in all of the corridors and passage ways to show you to where the lifeboats are located. Each lifeboat has a crew member assigned to it whose responsibility it is to make sure everyone is aboard and understands the situation. They will also go over additional instructions for donning and preparing your life preserver. At this time, ask any questions you may have about the drill.

Sanitation Oversight

For U.S. registered ships, the U.S. Public Health Service takes responsibility for making sure cruise ships follow the necessary sanitation guidelines. This includes surprise inspections and regular checkups for food preparation and handling, use of drinking water, and general sanitation in public spaces. With so many people in one confined space at sea, there are many health risks that could arise if the ship is not kept sanitary.

Medical Staff

There are no federal regulations that require a cruise ship to carry medical personnel on-board. However, essentially all cruise ships have a shipboard doctor and medical staff for minor to intermediate problems. If a substantial injury or illness occurs, though, the most common route of action is to have the passenger airlifted off the ship and to the nearest port city where a major hospital is located. You should contact your cruise line specifically to learn more about their medical facilities.

Making Complaints

Whenever you notice something out of the ordinary or unsafe, you will want to make a complaint to the ship. If the situation is severe enough, you should contact an authority that can investigate the problem and make sure the ship is secured and safe in future voyages. While at sea, no one wants to feel as though their vacation is in any way unsafe. Do your part and report the violations you witness.

Ship Safety Complaints

For most shipboard safety issues, you can make your complaints to the

Coast Guard Marine Safety Office. Use the following phone numbers to contact and file these complaints:

Coast Guard Toll-Free Hotline: 1-800-368-5647

Coast Guard MSO Miami Office: (305) 535-8705

Coast Guard MSO Juneau Office: (907) 463-2450

Coast Guard MSO San Juan Office: (787) 729-6800

Sanitation Issues

If you notice or experience unsanitary conditions aboard a cruise ship, you should contact the following office to report your experience:

U.S. Public Health Service
Chief, Vessel Sanitation Program
National Center for Environmental Health
1850 Eller Dr. Suite 101
Ft. Lauderdale, FL 33316
954-356-6650

Safety Equipment On-board

When you set foot on-board, be well aware that there is a substantial supply of safety equipment located throughout the ship. This equipment will ensure your well-being and safety throughout the cruise. The crew of the ship will direct you to the location of any of these items, as will the posted safety documentation in your cabin or stateroom.

The following safety equipment list is an average of equipment as supplied on an ICCL Cruise Ship with an average weight of 86,000 tons. For reference, the larger ships in most current fleets are around 110,000 tons. These numbers will adjust accordingly for size and passenger load of a ship.

- ❀ Five separate firefighting teams

- ❀ 170 personnel trained to assist the firefighting teams

- ❀ At least 20 crew members with advanced firefighting training

- ❀ 5,000 sprinkler heads

- ❀ Over 450 fire extinguishers

- ❀ More than 4,000 smoke detectors

- ❀ More than 400 fire stations/hydrants

- ❀ Lifeboats and preservers for more than the maximum capacity on-board

The Dreaded Norovirus

For your first-ever cruise you may be worried about the possibility of illness. You may have heard horror stories about a ship full of 3,000 passengers becoming violently ill and returning home early, and the truth is that the norovirus does occur. However, with thousands of annual sailings and only a small handful of such outbreaks, the actual risk of illness is not significant enough for you to worry about.

History of the Norovirus

The norovirus was named after an outbreak that occurred in Norwalk, Ohio, in November of 1968. The outbreak caused gastroenteritis in dozens of elementary school children and was studied for some time until it was finally identified as a new strain of virus in 1972. There have been numerous reports of outbreaks since that first reported case, and the one thing that usually remains the same is that the virus spreads very rapidly and hits a high percentage of those it comes in contact with.

The disease itself can be called any number of things, because it carries the same symptoms as a number of other viruses. It may be referred to as gastroenteritis, food poisoning, or the stomach flu, depending on the situation and circumstances of the outbreak.

Symptoms

The symptoms of the norovirus are usually very similar, if not identical, to the flu virus. They usually occur with nausea, vomiting, diarrhea, and stomach pain. Additionally, weakness, muscles aches, headache, and a slight fever may accompany these symptoms, which may last for a few days before getting better. Symptoms can become life-threatening in children, the elderly, and those with immune deficiencies. The biggest risk associated with the norovirus is dehydration.

Stopping the Norovirus

Because the norovirus is most often spread through food and skin-to-skin contact, one of the most effective methods of preventing it is simple handwashing, both for food handlers and regular individuals. When someone is diagnosed with the disease, the areas they have been in contact with should be sanitized to reduce the risk of it spreading.

Common Food Carriers

There are often specific foods that can carry the norovirus, resulting in what many refer to as food poisoning. These foods are not naturally prone to carrying the disease, but carry a higher risk if proper preparation methods and sanitization guidelines are not followed. For example, when the CDC studied 11 different outbreaks that occurred in New York, they found that seven of them were because of person-to-person contact, three were due to food and water borne infection, and the final outbreak cause was unknown. Usually, when transferred through food or water, it is because of fecal contamination — as a result of water that was not properly purified or food that was contaminated at some point.

For this reason, shellfish and salad are most commonly associated with norovirus outbreaks. Raw seafood, especially, can be a major source of the disease because of the various pathogens that clams or oysters may come in contact with before being eaten. If you become ill from any food other than shellfish, it is most often because the food handlers were ill themselves.

How Often Do People Get the Norovirus?

In terms of general frequency, stomach related illnesses are the second most common in the United States, behind only the common cold. Of those stomach illnesses, one-third can be attributed to the norovirus, making it a common illness. In most cases, however, it is diagnosed as a stomach flu or food poisoning and treated as such. It is only in the rare case when a mass infection occurs, such as on a cruise ship, that it becomes a more substantial, worrisome issue.

How Long Does It Last?

After being infected with the norovirus, the actual duration of symptoms can vary greatly. Generally, the symptoms of the disease do not appear until up to 48 hours after infection. They will then last as little as 24 and as long as 60 hours as your body fights the virus. The mortality rate due to the norovirus is around 300 total deaths, most of these occurring in very young children, the elderly, and those with immune system deficiencies.

The Norovirus on Cruise Ships

It is on cruise ships that norovirus has had the largest impact, striking large groups of people on various ships in different places and times. In 2002, for example, more than 2,600 individuals became ill on 25 different cruise ships. While the percentage related to the total number of cruise passengers each year is low, it is still a startling number and a good reason for you to know what to expect.

The CDC has repeatedly tested and studied these outbreaks to ascertain their causes and has generally come to the conclusion that they are solely due to person-to-person contact and not a result of contaminated water supplies. It is generally the result of such a massive ship with so many passengers in constant contact with each other. You would not want to spend your cruise locked away in a cabin to avoid disease, and so you socialize, visit the various decks, and meet new people. In doing so, you risk becoming ill if there is an outbreak.

What You Can Do to Avoid Norovirus

Similar to the flu or the common cold, there are not too many things you can directly do while on a cruise ship to avoid becoming ill. If one out of 3,000 passengers enters the cruise ship with the virus before the symptoms have shown, it can spread rapidly to any number of other passengers. Additionally, you can come into contact with the disease and not know you are ill for a day or two, because of the time it takes to become ill.

The best way to avoid getting the norovirus on your first cruise is to be cautious. Wash your hands often — before eating, after using the bathroom, before and after exercising, and before or after using the pool. You will likely meet many people and shake a lot of hands. Avoid being rude because of a fear you might get sick, but try not to touch your mouth or face after shaking someone's hand. Wash your hands when you have a chance and be aware of everything you touch. Similar to how a parent worries about where their children's hands have been, you should be aware at all times what you have touched and how it might affect you.

While dining, avoid raw seafood and uncooked food items that carry a higher risk of illness. They may not have a direct correlation with illness on-board cruise ships, but if you eat raw oysters or clams, you are increasing the risk of illness and an outbreak on-board. Most of the time, common sanitary practices and general sense can keep you safe and healthy.

What to Do in the Case of a Norovirus Outbreak

When an outbreak occurs — meaning more than two people have become ill with the same symptoms — you should be more wary than before. Remember, though, that it is possible for the illness to remain isolated to those two individuals, and that you will be able to continue enjoying your cruise without too much worry.

However, if the illness continues to spread, you may need to take extra precautions against becoming ill. Staying in your cabin, avoiding physical contact with other passengers, and not using public restrooms on-board are all necessary steps you should take to keep from becoming ill when there has been an outbreak.

CASE STUDY JILL BUI

Jill Bui is a nurse at Harborview Medical Center in Seattle, Washington and has worked in the emergency room for much of the two years she has spent working there. When asked about the effects of the norovirus and whether it is commonly seen on cruise passengers, she had this to say:

"Norwalk or norovirus is not the most common source of admittance to the emergency room, but it does happen — possibly a small handful of times each month. The one thing I have noticed in these cases though is that usually those with the virus are either young children or the elderly. Rarely does the dehydration that accompanies the disease get anywhere bad enough for a normal, healthy adult to be admitted.

As for symptoms, the norovirus is no different than a standard case of the stomach flu or food poisoning, though its symptoms can be or severe in the short term, especially if dehydration sets in. Often, the fever associated is less than a traditional stomach virus and though gastroenteritis is a real concern, especially for someone who is ill enough to be in the emergency room, it is almost never life-threatening. Administration of intravenous fluids to hydrate the body, as well as some common stomach calming medications, are usually sufficient to help a patient recover from the illness.

Because of the number of outbreaks in recent years, cruise lines have plans in place for these instances. The medical facilities will usually try to pinpoint the disease if they can and treat anyone who starts to feel ill. They may also close certain activities and group events and, in extreme cases ,cancel the cruise and return to port — if enough individuals become sick. In these cases, you should be able to receive a refund for part or all of the cruise that was cancelled.

CDC Vessel Sanitation

The Center for Disease Control (CDC) does a lot of things to make sure that these kinds of outbreaks are as rare as possible though. Starting in the 1970s, the CDC instituted their Vessel Sanitation Program (VSP) to make sure this was the case. On average in the 1980s, 12 to 15 outbreaks occurred each year on cruise ships. In 1999 only 3 occurred and with many more ships sailing each year.

More than 150 cruise ships are inspected twice a year by the VSP to make sure they are sanitary. The ships are scored based on an established field manual with a score between one and 100. If a ship scores below 86 it fails and must be inspected again in four to six weeks with a passing grade.

Inspections include checks of the food, water, pools, spa environment, hygiene of the crew and staff, and the overall cleanliness of the vessel. These scores are then published on the VSP Web site where you can view them before booking your cruise. If you are worried about your upcoming cruise, you can view this report card and see when your ship was last inspected and how well it performed, and if any outbreaks have ever occurred on your ship. Many ships have never experienced an outbreak among their passengers and will likely remain that way.

It may be easy to worry about the possibility of becoming ill and having your vacation ruined, but with the right mentality and hygiene, you can put your worries aside and simply focus on enjoying your cruise as much as possible.

Chapter 10

The First Day On-Board

When you step aboard your first cruise, life as you know it will change. You are no longer responsible for the daily tasks that make up your life like cleaning, cooking, or shopping. You can do whatever you want and the cruise ship is designed to take care of the rest, especially on-board some of the more luxury cruises on which you quite literally do nothing but relax and enjoy yourself.

The list of amenities at your disposal is seemingly endless and will likely never get old, especially as you attend catered activities, enjoy full service dining, and a staff that is always at your side with something to do, directions, or a friendly smile.

Day one on-board a cruise, though, will be an overwhelming experience, spent trying to figure out where you are going, what you are doing, and who everyone is. It does not need to be so complicated, though. Simply focus on the basics during your first day and you can start slowly growing acclimated to the cruise environment.

The First Day On-board

Once you have finished the arduous process of passing through countless security checks, going through the long list of pre-embarkation tasks, and getting on-board, you will finally be within range of your cabin and walking into it for the first time.

After finding your cabin and starting to get settled in, your cabin steward will stop by and introduce himself. This person will be your liaison should you need anything for your room or have any questions. They will make sure that your room remains clean and tidy throughout your trip.

Before Anything Else

When you first get on-board, you will want to take care of a few basic tasks before you start touring the ship and having fun. First, find your dining card. This will usually be attached to your shipboard charge card or placed in your room somewhere. The card will tell you where you will be dining on the ship.

You may want to tour this area of the ship because you will be spending a lot of time here. If your cruise has a more relaxed dining atmosphere, start finding the various eateries and restaurants so that you do not wander aimlessly when you really are hungry. It also helps to check the information on your dining card early because making changes after the first day of a cruise can be very hard.

During your first meals on the ship, you may wish to spend a short amount of time reading through the first newsletter or bulletin provided by the ship staff. This will give you a general idea of the activities available on the ship the first day. You may be overwhelmed at this point by everything you have envisioned and a quick read through the newsletter may be able to focus your first-day activities a little bit.

Exploration

After you eat and read through the newsletter, it is time to start exploring your temporary home. You will be on the ship for days to come, so why not get familiar with it right away? A good first step is to tear out a copy of the deck plans from the brochure or borrow a map from the purser's desk. You can find smaller printed deck plans on-board as well, usually in your room.

Using your map, work your way through the cruise ship and soak in all of the facilities and public rooms that are available to you. Familiarize yourself with everything you see and you will be able to spend much less time wandering aimlessly on days two and three and more time getting to your next activity or meal.

At some point in your first 24 hours, the horn will sound and you will be forced to engage in the mandatory lifeboat drill. These drills are held at the beginning of each cruise and if you stay on-board for more than seven days, one will likely occur again at the beginning of your second week. They are quick and offer a good chance for passengers to feel safer knowing that the ship's staff is organized and has plenty of resources available in case of an emergency.

Setting Sail

After you have completed the drill and returned to your room, you may find that your luggage has yet to arrive. This is not uncommon as the stewards have thousands of pieces of luggage to sort through in a short period of time. You can expect that it will be in your room no later than that evening. Hopefully you have stored away a nice set of casual clothing in your carry-on. If not, do not worry too much. Many other passengers will still be sporting their travel clothes while they are waiting for their luggage to arrive.

Now it is time to watch the ship set sail. You can go above deck if you like and join the other passengers as they watch the shore trail away or you can stay in your room or on your balcony (if you have one) with your significant other.

Dinner Time

The first formal meal of your cruise may be chaotic. However, if you have sought out the right dining room, prepared for the meal properly, and know where you will be sitting, you are already a few steps ahead of some other new cruisers. Depending on your dining preferences and the time at which you are seated, the experience might be slightly different. No matter how it is planned, take advantage of the open atmosphere and meet some new friends. There could be any number of new people that you spend the next week getting to know.

Entertainment or Relaxation?

At the end of your first night, you have any number of options on how you will spend your evening. You can select from opening night shows or more laid-back, relaxed lounges. You may decide to visit the casino, or just spend your night walking with your loved one and enjoying the ambience. The options are limitless and you will have many more nights to spend exploring them, so do not feel rushed. The first day is about relaxing, getting to know your environment, and familiarizing yourself with all of the opportunities you will have in subsequent days. If you do that, you won't need to worry about day one at all.

The Food

What could be more basic than the food? While you might not eat anything on-board your cruise for a few hours, you will want to know exactly what to expect. There are so many stories and myths about cruise food and what you should and should not expect — some of them are true and others are increasingly not true. Regardless of what is or is not true, your options are wide open as you prepare for a week of catered meals and dozens of choices while on your cruise.

The Importance of Food

Many cruise lines have touted and advertised the variety of their menus and the importance of what they have to offer since they first went into service. Food is a big selling point for any vacation and on a cruise, where it is often fully included in the price, you want to know that you are getting the best food available.

Luckily, choice is not an issue. On-board a cruise ship, you will have so many options to choose from, your head may start to spin just thinking about it. You might wake up and try a selection of tropical fruit, French delicacies, and white wine for breakfast, followed by Italian soups, endive salad, and salmon for lunch, with a hearty rack of lamb, mushroom quesadilla, and chocolate mousse for dinner. The list goes on and on, with this just being a small sample size of what you might enjoy on a single day.

Choosing Your Meal Times

Different cruise lines have different rules for how they handle their meal times and how they serve their passengers. There are, however, generally some things you can count on needing to know.

Open Seating

Many cruises have started changing to an open seating option, made possible by the growth of cruise ships which are large enough for multiple restaurants and extra crew members. Open seating usually has its limitations, though, and does not necessarily offer food at any time during the day.

Single Seating

For someone eating alone, single seating is available, but usually allows no leniency on when. If you are eating alone and sign up for a single seating time, you may be placed in a specific location at a specific time, regardless of your needs. Generally, for those traveling or eating alone, this is less of a concern as they are not synchronizing their schedule with anyone.

Two Seating

Two seating offers two options, early and late seating. If you select one of these seating options, though, you will be stuck with it, so make sure you know which one will be best for throughout the cruise. The cruise ship's staff often needs to determine these seating plans as early as possible and stick with them.

Four Seating

If you are traveling with a larger group of people or have met friends on-board that you would like to sit with, you can select four seating and choose from nearly any time you like. This is the most flexible meal seating option available because it usually assumes you are already coordinating multiple schedules.

Captain's Table

At some point on the cruise, you may receive an invitation to sit at the captain's table for dinner. The food is generally the same but you receive much nicer service and usually a few extra amenities, such as photographs and the conversation of the ship's captain. Being selected to sit at the captain's table is a process varies from ship to ship, though.

Occasionally a hostess or cruise staff member may select someone they enjoyed talking to out of the crowd, or you may be rewarded in subsequent cruises to sit with the captain if you have traveled with them often. Marriage parties are often invited to dine with the captain, as are any individuals who do something special while on-board.

Preparation and Variation

The food on-board a cruise ship has changed a lot in the years since the famous all-day buffets of the 1980s. While the same hearty and rich food can be had, cruise lines today try to offer a more varied experience by hiring celebrity chefs or offering an assortment of expensive, inexpensive, and healthy options.

Additionally, themes might accompany cruises with the food. Costa Cruise Lines, for example, features Mediterranean- and Italian-themed cuisine, and different ships in the Carnival Cruise Lines carry different themes throughout their year-long voyage schedules.

The hiring of celebrity chefs has been an increasingly popular option for cruise lines as well. While they may not always be on-board a cruise, these celebrities will create a menu for a specific cruise that caters to various different dining preferences. Many cruises try to use a three-week or so menu cycle in which no dish is repeated in the same voyage. The cycle is then renewed with a new set of menus each year so that repeat visitors do not eat the same dishes.

Healthy Alternatives

With most people becoming increasingly health conscious, cruise menus have started to incorporate healthier dining options. While the majority of the menu may contain traditional or exotic food that caters to a wide audience, there are almost always specialty options available from the kitchen. Low-fat, low-salt, kosher, diabetic-friendly, low carb, or vegetarian meals are all available on most major cruise lines, offering the chance to eat well for those that do not want to return home with a couple extra pounds around their waist.

Spa Cuisine has become a popular option on many cruise lines because so many passengers want to have a good time without feeling guilty for eating the rich foods that cruises almost forced upon their passengers in years past.

The Midnight Buffet

The Midnight Buffet still exists and is a very popular option for first-time cruisers because it is something you do not find anywhere else. It is a unique experience that many people associate only with cruising. However, the image that many people have of a cruise because of that Midnight Buffet style of dining has become less accurate with time.

Today, while most cruise lines still offer buffets and 24-hour dining options, most veteran cruisers and healthy eaters take advantage of the lighter, more sensible dining options available. Along with a lighter menu, cruise ships are starting to incorporate more diverse menu, such as Thai or Indian food, options that have become increasingly popular on land.

Service Styles

The style of service on-board a cruise ship can vary greatly as well, depending on the quality of the restaurant, the style of dining, and the goals you may have for that meal.

Quick Alternative Dining

With so many more options now available on cruise ships for activities, at times some people would rather eat quickly and get back to their itineraries. Newer cruise ships are starting to integrate options such as pizza parlors or quick service food that does not necessarily skimp in quality but takes much less time than sitting for a meal in one of the larger restaurants.

Plate Service

A growing trend in cruise dining service is to offer plate service to each table. This allows the chefs to create a plate as they want it to appear and serve it to each of the diners. More complete, easier to cook meals are provided this way, similar to how a traditional restaurant on land might serve dinner. This also ensures that everyone at a table receives their meals at the same time.

Silver Service

The old style of cruise ship dining service was silver service. This involved the diner choosing from a vaster menu to select exactly what might appear on their plate. It gave the diners more options, but resulted in lower quality in each dish and a gap between service times for different diners. More cruise ships are moving away from this style of service to enhance quality. However, diners can often make special requests if they like.

The Black Tie Dinner

While the image of the tuxedo clad dinner may not be as prevalent on today's cruise lines, it is still widely available for those that want a romantic, fancier dinner option. However, many cruise lines are starting to institute dining options that require individuals to pay extra money for smaller, more personal meals with fancier accoutrements. More than 60 ships currently have this kind of service.

A Sample Dinner Menu

To give you an idea of the menu variety offered on a cruise ship over the course of seven days, here is a sample dinner menu taken from a Carnival Cruise Lines voyage. The menu shows what might typically be available over the course of a seven day trip.

Day 1

Appetizers
Lime Juice Drizzled Tropical Fruit
Barley and Beef Soup
Mixed Greens
Crema Di Funghi Selvatica
Smoked Salmon
Gazpacho Andalouse
Romaine Hearts with Cherry Tomatoes

Entrees
Vegetarian Dish — Madras Vegetable Curry
Sweet and Sour Shrimp
Ziti with Italian Sausage, Bell Peppers, and Mushrooms
Broiled Fillet of Fish
Rack of New Zealand Lamb
Grilled New York Sirloin Steak

Desserts
Orange Cake
Guava Napoleon
Black Forest Gateau
Ice Cream — Multiple Flavors
Sherbet — Multiple Flavors

Day Two

Appetizers
Tropical Berries
Roasted Pumpkin Soup
Strawberry Bisque
Mixed Greens

Mississippi Delta Prawns

Caesar Salad

Entrees

Trennette Putanesca

Fillet of Fresh Pacific Salmon

Broiled Lobster Tail

Whole Roasted Quail

Roasted Prime Rib Au Jus

Vegetarian Dish — Grilled Brochettes of Vegetables

Desserts

Banana Gateau

Swedish Almond Chocolate Cake

Passion Fruit Indulgence

Cherries Jubilee

Ice Cream — Multiple Flavors

Sherbet — Multiple Flavors

Day Three

Appetizers

Melon and Prosciutto

Palm and Artichoke Hearts

Lobster Bisque

Escargots Bourguignonne

Black Bean Soup

Chilled Cucumber Soup

Mixed Greens

Iceberg Lettuce Hearts

Entrees

Penne Mariscos

Fillet of Chilean Sea Bass

Paillard of Young Turkey

Jerked Pork Loin

Roast Leg of New England Lamb

New York Sirloin Steak, Marchand de Vin

Vegetarian Dish — Baked Herb Polenta

Desserts

Marbled Kahlua Cheesecake

Key Lime Pie

Chocolate Souffle

Ice Cream — Multiple Flavors

Sherbet — Multiple Flavors

Day Four

Appetizers

Grilled Vegetables

Breast of Long Island Duckling

Duet of Gratinated Mussels

Cream of Tomatoes — Touch of Gin

Won Ton Soup

Cream of Lyches

Mixed Greens

Artichoke Hearts, Ripened Tomatoes, Fennel Roots

Entrees

Farfalle with Smoked Turkey

Seared Fillet of Sole

Black Tiger Shrimp

Cornish Game Hen with Cherry Salsa

Grilled Chop of Veal

Tenderloin of Beef Wellington

Vegetarian Dish — Black Bean Enchiladas

Desserts

Coconut Cake

Old-Fashioned Apple Pie

Tiramisu

Ice Cream — Multiple Flavors

Sherbet — Multiple Flavors

Day Five

Appetizers

Vine-Ripened Tomatoes and Buffalo Mozzarella

Alaskan Snow Crabmeat

Southwestern Egg Roll

French Onion Soup

Corn Chowder

Mixed Greens

Curly Endive and Sliced Cucumbers

Entrees

Penne Tossed in a Tomato-Cream Sauce

Fillet of Fresh Fish with Roasted Garlic

Supreme of Chicken

Veal Parmigiana

Fillet Mignon with Cabernet Sauce and Gorgonzola

Vegetarian Dish — Lasagna with Spinach, Mushrooms

Desserts

Lemon Cake

Strawberry Cheesecake

Chocolate Mousse
Hazelnut Creme Brulee
Ice Cream — Multiple Flavors
Sherbet — Multiple Flavors

Day Six

Appetizers

Portabella Mushroom and Mesclun Lettuce
Atlantic Salmon
Game Consomme
Cream of Broccoli and Cheddar
Zucchini Soup
Mixed Greens
Caesar Salad

Entrees

Penne Siciliana
Halibut Steak with Herb Vinaigrette
Grilled Jumbo Shrimp
Long Island Duckling
Vegetarian Dish — Assorted Vegetable Princess

Desserts

Tropical Fruit Platter
Baked Alaska
Amaretto Cake
Dutch Apple Pie
Ice Cream — Multiple Flavors
Sherbet — Multiple Flavors

Day Seven

Appetizers

Supreme of Fresh Fruit

Louisiana Tiger Prawns

Chicken Fillets

Navy Bean Soup

Gumbo Creole

Mango Cream

Mixed Greens

Ripened Tomatoes and Cucumber Slices

Entrees

Fettuccine with Mushroom Cream

Fillet of Pacific Salmon

Oven-Roasted Turkey

Seared Pork

Roasted Prime Rib Au Jus

Vegetarian Dish — Zucchini and Eggplant Parmigiana

Desserts

Poached Williams Pear

Grand Marnier Souffle

Chocolate Fudge Cake

Cappuccino Pie

Ice Cream — Multiple Flavors

Sherbet — Multiple Flavors

Room Service and Staff

You can expect that while you are on your cruise, there is a substantial supply of quality service and interesting staff to keep your experience as well oiled as possible. Most often, you will rarely see the steward staff. Aside from your first introduction to your cabin steward and any subsequent interactions you may have with them regarding questions you may have, they will appear as ghosts who clean and disappear from your room while you are out.

They exist, though, and should you have any needs while on-board, they will be there in a second to offer assistance.

Room service is often available for snacks and drinks, things that the service staff has readily available. These items will be charged to your cruise charge card or to the credit card attached to your room number.

Liquor and spirits are often much less expensive on-board a cruise ship because of the lack of taxes on any purchases made at sea. It is a great chance to take advantage of your ocean-bound vacation. Just remember to have money on hand to tip any room service stewards that help you. They may return again later and it is in good taste to tip anyone you deal with on-board a cruise ship.

Your Shipboard Experience

When you set foot on-board your first cruise ship, your vacation has officially started. The overwhelming sensation of relief that will flood you after you pass through that final security checkpoint and actually enter the ship will be incredible. It may have taken months to get to this point, and with everything in place and all of the little details taken care of, there should be nothing to stand in the way of your relaxation and good time.

Chapter 11

Keeping Busy On-Board & Off-Board

After settling in, becoming more familiar with the resources on the ship and touring the vast and engaging facilities at your disposal, what will you do next? The beauty of a modern day cruise is that your options are nearly endless. From gambling at night to spending the day in a spa getting one of 12 different kinds of massages, there are many different ways to spend your vacation on-board a cruise.

Sports and Exercise

Many people have strict exercise regimens they would never want to abandon — least of all because they are on vacation. For that reason, almost all cruise ships have multiple forms of exercise equipment. Along with swimming pools, basketball courts, and tennis courts, ships often have full-sized gymnasiums, running tracks, or even golf courses to keep you occupied with the relaxing activities you enjoy at home. What facilities you can expect will often depend on which ship you select to cruise on. The larger and newer the ship, the more activities it often has available.

Sports On-Board

These sports on-board will keep you active throughout the cruise, and give you a great chance to meet new people who have similar interests.

Basketball Court

Basketball courts have been included on many of the largest ships on the sea, with half-sized basketball courts available for those ships without the space for a full-sized court. Basketball courts will often book up early, especially in the morning and evening hours, and if there are children on-board, good luck getting a spot on the court. For those interested in using the courts, the sports deck or desk will have equipment that you can check out using your cruise card.

Running Track

Almost every major ship on the sea has a running track and it will often take you above deck for a breathtaking view of the ocean. Often, you will be asked or reminded to wear the proper running shoes for the track. You should always pack the right clothing and equipment if you plan on taking advantage of the exercise equipment and facilities on-board.

Golf Simulator

For those ships that are too small for a course or that are stopping in ports with multiple golf courses, golf simulators offer a great option for the golf-loving cruiser. While the golf simulator often costs a little extra, it is usually staffed with a golf pro who can offer you advice if you are having trouble with your backswing.

Golf Courses

For the lucky few, there are cruise ships with golf courses on-board. Usually on the larger of the cruise ships, golf courses are small and only allow for short iron-play. Also, if you want to play golf on-board, you may want to sign up for a spot as early as possible. Golf becomes very popular as the cruise gets into the second and third day.

Tennis

Tennis on-board the ship can come in many different forms. It may be a simple, practice court in the gymnasium or it could come in the form of a full-sized court above deck. The options vary depending on the ship you choose. Equipment is usually available from the sports deck and courts are open to all ages, so check early for available times.

Volleyball

What better sport to play at sea than volleyball? On smaller ships, the tennis court or basketball court may convert to a volleyball court for certain hours of the day, while bigger ships may have a dedicated net and possibly even sanded areas for you to play.

Gymnasium

Any major cruise ship you select will have a gymnasium aboard, and that means you can take full advantage of the many different exercise options they have — from free weights to aerobics classes or machinery.

Aerobics

The aerobics programs available on-board a cruise ship are held often and by a trained instructor. Sign up for a class time when you first get aboard the ship to make sure you get in, otherwise you may be stuck doing your exercises alone.

Gym Equipment

The gym equipment provided aboard a cruise ship varies from ship to ship, but most ships today carry a large selection of equipment — enough for a good percentage of the ship's passengers to enjoy the facilities at any given time. Specific rules for use of the equipment will be posted and an instructor or fitness expert will be on hand to assist you if you have any problems or questions.

Fitness Programs

Fitness programs on-board a cruise ship vary depending on the staff currently under employment. Usually, experts in their fields will set up specific classes on-board certain ships. However, common programs offered include: Yoga, Total Fitness, Wellbeing, and General Health. The depth and detail of the programs will vary. See the bulletin and schedule posted in your room when you arrive on-board for which programs will be offered right away.

Water Sports Platform

For ships that have the space, a water sports platform can be lowered to offer a variety of additional recreation activities in the ocean.

Scuba Diving

Scuba diving options on-board a cruise ship vary, and often require a short to week-long course in diving. On some ships you can become scuba-certified by the Professional Association of Diving Instructors during the course of your cruise, taking home a certificate from your vacation. There are often scuba professionals on-board and you will be able to take "resort dives" after the first three days or so of instruction.

Snorkeling

Offering on-board courses in snorkeling techniques, many ships will teach you how to handle your equipment, provide a course in identifying fish and marine life, and then guide you to the best snorkeling spots on the islands you visit for shore excursions. These programs are usually purchased in advance through the cruise line.

Water-Skiing

Using the tenders (small ferrying boats) that the cruise ship has on hand, you can water-ski from the lowered water sports platform. There are usually no dress policies and the platforms are catered so that you can spend an entire afternoon there, enjoying the ocean.

Banana Boat Rides

Similar to water-skiing, banana boats allow you to relax in a smaller craft while being towed by a tender. The options vary from ship to ship, with banana boats more prevalent on the smaller cruise lines.

Wind Surfing

You can windsurf from the water sports platform if the weather is right. With paid instructors and professionals on hand, even those with minimal water sport experience can jump in and take advantage of these offerings.

Lido Deck

The lido deck, or pool deck, is one of the most frequented recreation areas on-board the ship. Every ship has one — some of them may even have multiple pools on more than one deck. You should expect that the pool will be the most crowded during midday hours. However, with a decent sized ship, there is often plenty of room for everyone to relax and enjoy the sun on the lido deck. If you want to exercise, however, you may want to return at night when the pool is slightly emptier — especially if there are children aboard.

Rest and Relaxation — the Spa

Alongside the cruise ship's fitness center is the spa — what has quickly become one of the most popular parts of any cruise ship. Relaxation is the sole purpose of your vacation, so it makes the most sense that a trip to the spa would be at the top of many cruise passengers' lists.

When you first step aboard the cruise ship, you should visit the spa and fitness center if you have the time. This allows you to get ahead of the rush that will overcome it in the next seven days. Most spas have a first night special as well. If you have time, you can take advantage of this and get to know the spa staff in the process. By visiting the spa first, you get initial pick of times and appointments, and possibly even a little extra notice on what special offers the spa will offer later in the week.

Included in Your Fare

Not everything on-board a cruise is free of charge. There are some luxury cruises that provide a truly all-inclusive fare, but most mid-range cruising options have a collection of caveats to your fare that will cost more as the week goes on.

The spa is one of those caveats. You do get free access to the steam and sauna rooms and the fitness center. Anyone on-board can use these any time they wish. Additionally, the staff will help you with any questions or issues you may have and are available most hours of the day. With free equipment and space, though, there is often a waiting list, so always arrive early and plan accordingly.

For a Nominal Fee

Almost every cruise ship uses the same service and product line to run their spas — Steiner Leisure and Elemis. This makes pricing easy as it will often be the same on any ship. The prices themselves are similar, if not slightly less than land resort spas, though the list of services is usually slightly smaller than a land resort.

Thermal Suite

A thermal suite is a collection of special steam rooms including amenities such as aromatherapy, mild steam bathing, fog/rain showers, and zero gravity loungers. They will cost an additional fee to use, but often that fee covers the extent of the cruise. Once the one-time fee is paid, you can access the thermal suite whenever you like as long as it is open and not occupied. If you sign up on the first day, you get the best deal because you can use the suite for the entire time you are on-board.

Sanctuary

For a half a day, you can pay a nominal fee (usually $10) and enjoy a sound secluded room with an ocean view. Some ships provide catering with waiters that bring you spa cuisine items and smoothies. In addition, you can purchase a massage while in these rooms to take advantage of the relaxation space.

Salon

You can find full salon services on most cruise ships, including shampoo, blow dry, cuts, coloring, manicures, and pedicures for similar prices to any land spa prices. There are barber services as well for men.

Teeth Whitening

Relatively new to most cruise ships, teeth whitening will cost slightly less than $200 on most cruise ships and last for about 40 minutes. The procedure is FDA approved and has moderate to decent results, and at a fairly inexpensive price compared to most dental office visits, it is an interesting addition to the spa treatment.

Acupuncture

Recently introduced by Steiner Leisure after the success of Acupuncture @ Sea on the Celebrity Cruises line, acupuncture is now a part of most spa menus on-board. Usually costing around $149/hour, it is slightly more expensive than land-based acupuncture.

Alpha Capsule

This body enclosure machine covers you up to your neck, while you wear an aromatic mask over your face and eyes. The machine will then produce heat, vibrations, various soothing sounds, and minimal colored lights to produce a relaxing effect on your mind. It costs about $45/hour.

Tipping

After a spa treatment is completed, it is customary, and almost expected, for you to tip the professional. They work on salary and do not receive percentages of each treatment they provide. With long hours, and mid-grade pay, tips are an important supplement to their income. For that reason, you should always tip the customary 10 to 20 percent.

When tipping, though, you have multiple options. While you can sign a tip on the charge slip, you may want to check with the spa and see how they handle tips before doing so. The tip may not reach the professional in some instances or may go through a series of hands and be skimmed down. It is good to carry cash for these instances so you know exactly where the tip is going when you offer cash.

Booking Your Spa Treatments

It can be a rush and a pain to get into the spa and book your appointments before they fill up on the first and second day of a cruise. If you have something in mind that you want, you need to do this right away. However, many cruise lines are making it possible to book your spa treatments much earlier now, using an online booking system. These systems allow you to view the various treatments that are offered on-board, along with the times you can select. You can then book before you board the ship — making sure you have the space you want.

Product Pitches

A big complaint made by many cruisers is the immediate and consistent product pitches that spa staff will give during and after treatments. It is common practice and will be the same on any ship you travel on, largely because Steiner Leisure operates all of these spas. Slightly before the end of your treatment, you will receive a product pitch from your massage therapist or spa professionals. This is normal and everyone experiences it, but if you do not want to hear the product pitches, politely let them know before the treatment begins to avoid losing any of their time or your time because of an unwanted sales pitch.

Massage

One of the most popular and frequented selections in a cruise ship spa is massage. With multiple massage professionals on staff, varying in style and experience, you can rest assured you will find whatever type of massage you are looking for. These are some of the most common massage options available on-board. Not every option is always available though — it will depend on who is working on the staff at any given time.

- ❀ Wellbeing Massage

- ❀ Shiatsu Massage

- ❀ Hot Stones Massage

- ❀ Ayurvedic Massage

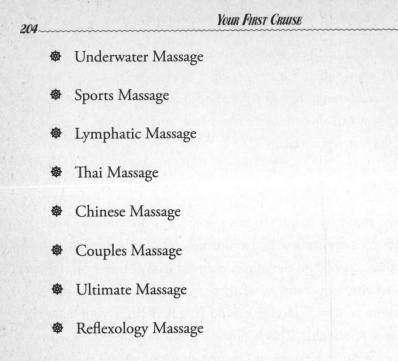

- Underwater Massage

- Sports Massage

- Lymphatic Massage

- Thai Massage

- Chinese Massage

- Couples Massage

- Ultimate Massage

- Reflexology Massage

Massage Tips

Remember to book your massages as early as possible. Time slots can fill up completely by the third day of a cruise, leaving you without a chance to experience what so many people enjoy about — a relaxing massage.

To best enjoy your massage, make sure you communicate with your massage therapist. It may seem hard to communicate with the masseuse because of your position and the embarrassment of asking them to adjust or move. However, he wants you to tell him how you are feeling and if he can make any changes. Make suggestions — comment if something hurts or is effective and help him make your massage better.

As a final note, remember to drink plenty of water after a massage. A massage opens your pores and releases toxins from your body. If you do not flush these toxins, they will settle back into your muscles and cause you to be sore the next day. By drinking plenty of water, you will retain that relaxed, good feeling the next day and not have a negative impression of a perfectly good masseuse.

Organized Entertainment

The organized entertainment on-board a cruise ship has been famous since the early days of the modern industry when stars of film and stage would take month-long tours on cruise ships and offer nightly shows to vacationers. The same style of entertainment is still available, but with much more variety involved.

Because a cruise ship is so large and so varied, there are multiple forms of entertainment scheduled throughout the day for all age groups, interests, and styles. In many places there will be music playing on a steady basis. The lido deck will usually have a steel drum band (for those in the Caribbean) or will have, at a minimum, a DJ to keep the mood festive.

Daytime entertainment is by far the most creative. You will find everything from art auctions and wine tastings to lessons on napkin folding, scuba diving, or snorkeling.

Nighttime entertainment may consist of as many as a dozen different venues — and those are just the active venues. There are still plenty of laid-back options available for those not interested in spending the night dancing or drinking.

Nightlife and Partying

The nightlife aboard a cruise ship will vary depending on the type and style of cruise you select. If you are on-board a Disney Cruise Line ship, you will not find a casino and the adult options that are offered are slightly more limited due to the addition of extra family activities. Other cruise lines, though, have varying degrees of late night attractions available for adults to choose from. Some of the common late night entertainment options are included here to give you an idea of what you can do on your cruise.

Discos

The open lounge space in which you can grab a cocktail and discuss your activities during the day will often convert to thumping disco space at night. With professional DJs, a wide array of dance music, and a varying selection of eras on different themed nights, discos offer a little bit of something for everyone. If you like to dance, this is the place to be at night.

Live Music and Shows

Each cruise line has a different style when it comes to live music and shows. Some still produce the gaudy, large shows made famous in the 1980s. Others focus on smaller, talent filled shows, and some hire celebrity talent to entertain throughout the cruise. It generally does not matter which cruise line you select — they all provide plenty of entertaining shows and a wide variety of different styles. From piano players, to singing or scripted, large shows — a single cruise will have more than enough shows and options to keep you busy.

Casinos

Almost every cruise ship has a casino on-board. As one of the few places that Americans can legally gamble, cruise ships provide a wide array of different gaming options in an elegant, almost always open environment. It may not be Las Vegas, but a cruise ship casino is where you will most likely meet the most new friends and have a good time. Check the bulletin when you get on-board to see the operational hours and best times to visit the casino.

Lounges

For those that do not want to dance or take in a show, there are plenty of lounges to relax in and have a drink and some good conversation. But be aware that drinks on-board a cruise ship are often charged in addition to your fare. When you order a drink you will likely be asked for your cruise card or credit card.

On-board Activities

There are dozens of activities on-board any given cruise ship for you to choose from. You will receive a bulletin with a list that includes the scheduled times and locations of the activities. The daily newsletter will keep you updated on any changes and of any one-time event. Here is a sample of a major cruise line's activities list from their sample newsletter.

Activities for Children

* Reading Hour (All Ages) 1:30 pm - 2:30 pm - Club Room

* Soda and Ice Cream Social (6 - 11 yrs) 5:30 pm - Dance Club

* Babysitting (2 - 11 yrs) 10:30 pm - 3:30 am - Playroom

Activities for Teens

* Ping Pong 10:30 am (15 & up) - Veranda

* Teen Game Shows (15 - 17) 3:30 pm - 4:30 pm - Lounge

* Basketball (15 - 17) 4:30 pm - 5:30 pm - Veranda

* Disco (12 - 18) 9:30 pm - 10:30 pm - Disco

* Outdoor Disco (15-17) 11:30 pm - 12:30 pm - Disco

Breakfast

* 7:30 am Continental Breakfast - Bar and Grill

* 8:30 am -10:30 am Open Seating - Dining Room

- 8:30 am - 10:30 am Lido Breakfast - Lido Deck

- 8:30 am - 12:30 pm Breakfast - Bar and Grill

Lunch

- 12:30 pm - 2:30 pm - Dining Room

- 12:30 pm - 2:30 pm - Bar and Grill

- 12:30 pm - 2:30 pm - Bar and Grill

- 12:30 pm - 6:30 pm - Bar and Grill

Main Seating Dinner

- 5:45 pm Dining Room - Pacific Deck, Aft

- 6:45 pm Dining Room - Pacific Deck, Fwd

Late Seating Dinner

- 8:30 pm Dining Room - Pacific Deck, Aft

- 8:30 pm Dining Room - Pacific Deck, Fwd

Seaview Bistro

- 6:30 pm - 9:30 pm - Bar and Grill

Pizzeria

- Open until 4:30 am - Bar and Grill

Casino Gaming Lessons

❀ 11:30 am - Casino

Art Auction

❀ 1:30 pm Art Preview - Lounge

❀ 2:30 pm Art Auction - Lounge

❀ 7:30 pm Art Gallery Open until 8:30pm - Promenade

Comedy Show

❀ R-Rated Comedic Fun 12:30 am - Lounge

Bingo

❀ 10:30 am - Lounge

Music and Dancing

❀ Piano Music
8:30 pm - 8:30 pm - Piano Bar

❀ Cocktail Piano Music
4:45 pm - 6:45pm, 7:30pm - 9:30 pm - Bar
6:30 pm - 8:30 pm - Piano Bar

❀ Party Sing-a-Long Piano Music
9:30 pm - 1:30 am - Piano Bar

❀ Karaoke
8:30 pm -11:45 pm - Lounge

❀ Dance & Party Music
9:30 pm - 1:30 am - Bar

❀ Live Music
9:45 pm - 1:45 am - Lounge
10:30 pm - 10:45pm Couples & Lovers - Lounge

❀ Teens' Disco
9:45 pm - 10:45 pm - Dance Club

❀ Dance Music (18 & up)
11:30 pm - Late - Dance Club

Big Screen Movie

❀ 10:00 am - Lounge

Crazy Olympic Pool Party

❀ 1:30 pm - Pool

Horse Racing Fun

❀ 1:30 pm - Lido Deck

Newlywed, Not So Newlywed Game

❀ 2:30 pm - Lounge

Who Wants to be a Millionaire?

❀ 3:30 pm - Lounge

Casino

❀ Tables open from 10:30 am until late

Blackjack Tournament

❋ 2:30 pm - 4:30 pm & 7:30 pm - 10:30 pm

Finale: 10:45 pm

Photo Gallery

❋ 10:30 am - 10:30 pm - Atlantic Deck Aft

Port Shopping

❋ 7:00 pm - 8:30pm - Promenade

Shopping

Shopping on-board a cruise ship can be an exciting experience. This is in large part because everything is duty-free. The majority of shopping is handled by a small handful of firms that provide goods, so you will likely see the same items on many cruise ships. However, if you are looking for souvenirs to take home or a good bottle of wine for your cabin, there are plenty of options at your disposal here.

Shops are usually open from 9 am to 10 pm or so, though the times may change depending on the cruise ship. The options provided in the shops are very similar to what you have seen in the airport shops or other duty-free shops, but with a little more ocean-bound flavor. You can find items you may need for your trip, such as sunblock, flip flops, or t-shirts and also souvenir items, such as postcards, keychains, and coffee mugs.

Jewelry, perfumes, and other fine goods that you can save a significant amount of money on by purchasing duty-free from the cruise ship shops are also available.

Art auctions are a popular addition to many cruise ships. The art auctions give you a chance to purchase a piece of art at a classic-styled auction, adding a bit of flavor to the sensation of affluent pampering. However, if you attend multiple cruises, you may start to notice that the art offered in these auctions is very similar and likely mass produced. While the quality is suspect, the experience is always entertaining.

Chapter 12

Ports of Call: What to Expect

When you pull into a port of call, the tone and mood of your vacation may change immediately, because of the change from the party, town-like atmosphere of the cruise ship to the more exotic, foreign exchange with a local culture. Do not worry because this is a good thing. Before and after stepping off the boat in one of the many ports-of -all you will visit, there are plenty of resources to help you better access and enjoy what these faraway locales have to offer.

Preconceived Notions

Many people carry around with them a set of preconceived notions about a culture or a specific country. These can be completely wrong. You may be pleasantly surprised by what you find when you visit a new port of call and should be willing to accept the differences that surround you. It is a part of the experience of traveling abroad.

The Language Barrier

Language is the first problem many people assume they will encounter. While it can be an issue in some cases, keep in mind that a port of call in the Caribbean or other foreign country with consistent cruise traffic from America or other English-speaking countries is going to be prepared to deal with English-speaking customers. How else would they make money?

If you know you will be visiting a country in which another language is predominant, it does not hurt to learn a few of the more basic greetings and niceties of that language, but you do not need to purchase a bulky phrase book and carry it in your back pocket while on land.

Not only will you likely have a tour guide and a set area onshore in which you will spend your time, you will likely be able to speak English to local store owners and not make a fool of yourself. Be prepared, but do not overcompensate.

Safety Preparedness

While it is true that you are not quite as safe onshore as you are on-board the ship, you do not need to walk around constantly on guard. Ports of call are often well secured and organized port cities in which extra police are present, if only because of the importance of the cruise industry's tourism dollars to the local economy. If every tourist that stepped foot in St. Thomas was mugged, cruise ships would stop going there because of lack of passenger interest.

Always be prepared, but mostly just try not to stand out. If you do not walk with the gaudiest clothing you can find and a camera hanging around your neck, you will be much less likely to attract the additional attention of the criminal element. Be polite, be courteous, and be safe, but do not be overly protective and standoffish. You are on vacation. Enjoy it as much as possible.

Common Questions

These common questions may arise when you pull into a new port of call. The purser's desk will usually have additional information available regarding further questions you may have.

Do you need to get off the cruise ship for every port of call?

At no point during the cruise are you required to get off the ship. If you have previously visited a port before and do not want to disembark, it may be a good chance to enjoy certain activities on-board that are usually too crowded. You can find discounts in the Spa and for training courses during port days, as well as a slightly less crowded environment.

How do I get to the pier from the ship?

While some ships can dock directly to the pier and allow you to disembark from a portal on the ship, others may require that you shuttle to the port on a tender. Shuttling is free of charge, however, and is usually done as quickly as possible.

Does my shipboard account work while in port?

The card on which you charge your expenses on the ship does not work while in port. You will need to carry a major credit card or traveler's checks for additional purchases. You can usually find an ATM to withdraw cash, but be wary of openly carrying cash with you while you are on land.

What kind of planned activities are available on land?

While you hopefully booked shore excursions well in advance, you can usually find excursions through the ship's shore excursion desk as well. These last minute bookings may be just a simple shopping tour in the port city or a bicycle ride on the island. You are also free to spend your time exploring the port of call on your own if you like.

What is available to do in a port-of -all on my own?

If you decide to explore a port of call on your own, you should bring a guide book with you. Lonely Planet makes great guide books that show you not only the popular tourist attractions in a location, but the smaller, off-the-beaten-path locations you can explore. Do a little research and you will not run out of things to do while in port.

Are meals included while in port?

Your meals are only paid for when you are on-board the ship. If you decide to spend the day in the port of call, you are responsible for all expenses incurred there.

What to Expect in Various Ports

Every port of call has something different to offer. Depending on where you are stopping and how long you will be there, you can likely find many things to do for every member of your family. Here you will find some of the most popular excursions, shoreside activities, dining, and shopping options for each of the most popular ports of call.

Third Party Options

Most of the most interesting and extensive excursions offered in Alaska are available through third party companies that you would book well in advance of your trip. There are many companies to choose from, and the best way to approach them is through a travel agent who can provide you with a list that has a good solid safety record and plenty of recommendations from experts in the field. In addition, make sure there is a money-back guarantee clause with your excursions because the cost of a shore excursion in Alaska can quickly be negated by bad weather, especially when you get closer to low seasons.

Cruise Line Options

If you book your excursions through the cruise line, there is still a good selection of options available. Currently, large cruise lines like Royal Caribbean offer as many as 100 or more excursions from the ship throughout their summer long cruising schedule in Alaska, ranging in cost from $25 to $500. In addition, you can select from a wide variety of different pre- and post-cruise tours. Many of these excursions are no longer offered after September because of the severe shift in weather. Some excursions, such as dog sledding, can be removed from your choices as early as August depending on high elevation weather shifts.

Port Tours

When you pull into port in cities like Juneau, you will notice a wide selection of tour guides set up outside the cruise ship pier. Similarly, in cities like Skagway you can find more than a dozen different companies offering tours in town as soon as you step off the boat. This allows those who did not book early to find a good selection of touring and excursion options after they get off the ship.

For anyone looking for a specific adventure, it is necessary to book as early as possible and plan accordingly. With the number of cruises and tourists growing every year and the number of facilities and tour guides starting to lag behind, many excursions book up as much as six months in advance. If you want to take a float plane or helicopter tour of the glaciers or mountains, you should book as early as possible.

Alaska

In recent years, the shear volume of activities available in Alaska for shore excursions and port of call days has increased exponentially. Partially, this is due to the growing interest by the cruise lines and passengers to visit the north and enjoy the great outdoors. While Alaskan cruises were once relegated to companies like Cruise West, larger companies with more access to ample resources have started sailing to the northern most parts of North America and have brought larger collections of passengers, experts, and interests with them.

Today, you can enjoy a large selection of shore excursions in Alaska, including kayaking, bicycling, rafting, fishing, dog sledding, wilderness tours, hiking, and traditional culture and history related tours. Every year, more activities and tours are added.

Skagway

One of the most interesting and historically rich locations you will enter when on a cruise in Alaska is Skagway. The city was founded during the Klondike gold rush and currently sits on the National Register of Historic Places. You will be shuttled into the town when you arrive, taking you to Broadway, the central street of the town and location of many of the Gold Rush's original buildings.

The Klondike Gold Rush National Historical Park Visitor Center is a good place to stop as well for anyone looking to learn more about Alaskan history and the Gold Rush. If you decide to tour the city on your own, make sure to pick up a walking-tour map from the Visitor Center between Second and Third Avenue. It will give you a list of the surrounding buildings, when they were built, and what for.

You can find classic, 19th century Gold Rush entertainment here as well, with shows like the Days of '98 at Eagles Hall. Various shops, including some historically renovated shopping spaces, are available to buy souvenirs from. You can also visit the Jewell Gardens, a massive garden and tourist destination in Skagway that shows off the plentiful vegetation and good soil in the city.

Outside of the city there are plenty of additional options for sightseeing, especially if you book a car rental well in advance. Whitehorse, located in the Yukon, is a good two-hour drive away and offers plenty of different sightseeing and hiking opportunities. Additional activities here include horseback riding, photo safaris, salmon fishing, and float tours.

The list of possible activities you can enjoy in Skagway and the surrounding areas stretches on, including helicopter tours, the famous Yukon Route Railway and White Pass. Research the area thoroughly before arriving to uncover one of the most naturally and historically rich segments of United States, still very much like its original, 19th century self.

Juneau

In Juneau, the state capital of Alaska, you will find a wide selection of activities and a slightly larger selection of options with which to enjoy those activities. After leaving the cruise ship, you will be in the midst of downtown Juneau. You can find the visitor's bureau office next to the pier where you disembark along with maps, tour times, and local hot spots.

Along the waterfront are a number of memorials and historical sights that you can see as you make your way out of downtown. State and city museums, the world famous Red Dog Saloon, and an ample selection of shops are all present for you to choose from.

One of the first things you will see as you disembark from the cruise ship is the Mt. Roberts Tramway. This 1,800 foot tramway ascends the slope beside the pier and allows you to see for miles in any direction on a clear day. Tram tickets cost $21.95 and are good for the entire day, providing you with plenty of sightseeing, restaurant, and shopping opportunities at the top of Mt. Roberts.

Outside the city, you can visit the Mendenhall glacier, only 20 minutes from the city, making it the easiest glacier to visit from a city in Alaska. You can take a shuttle for $5 and reach the glacier in just a few minutes where a visitor center, a lake, and plenty of hiking trails are located. Be wary of the trails, though, and walking off alone. Park rangers provide guided hikes and with bears in the area, you should take advantage of these options.

Hiking in other regions is another great thing to do in Juneau, though again because of bears, you should hire a guide for your hikes to remain safe when you leave the city. If you do decide to take a hike, you can choose from plenty of locations, such as Mt. Roberts or the surrounding hills. Juneau has many more options available that you can take advantage of with the right planning and tour companies. Contact a travel agent early and learn more about what you can enjoy while in Juneau.

Ketchikan

For those interested in sport fishing and cultural heritage, Ketchikan is a great place to stop while on a cruise. Fishermen can select from any of five different species of salmon, with a fishing spot right in the town's marina. Snorkeling has become a recent attraction as well, allowing you to enjoy the sealife directly without fishing.

The ship docks in downtown Ketchikan alongside the visitor information center where you can find pay phones, maps, ATMs, and guides to help you get around town. In addition, you can rent a car or a bicycle and arrange your local sightseeing and fishing excursions directly through the local marina with ease.

Like Skagway, Ketchikan is a great place to take a walking tour with one of the many tour maps and guides provided at the visitor center. The Southeast

Alaska Discovery Center is a great place to start learning more about the culture and history of the region, while Creek Street provides a historic, stilt supported walkway above the Ketchikan Creek, filled with salmon. You will also find Dolly's House, a museum devoted to the lawless ways of the town in the 19th and early 20th centuries. You can also take a cable car up to Cape Fox Lodge where a restaurant is located. The view allows you to see the entire town and the trip is only $2.

The lumberjack show is run three times every day, regardless of the weather and allows you to see a bit of the Alaskan sporting and classic competition the area is known for.

For native culture, the Totem Bight Historic Park and Saxman Native Village are entertaining and educational places to visit. Saxman Village is only two miles outside the town and has one of the world's largest displays of totem poles. Artists carve, dancers perform native dances of the Tlingit, Tsimishian, and Haida people, and you can purchase souvenirs and local arts and crafts.

Another popular destination out of Ketchikan is the Misty Fjords National Monument. You can book a flight with a company like Taquan Air for $199 to the 2.3 million acre national monument and view some of the most breathtaking scenery in the vast and wildlife filled state. The same touring company also offers bear-viewing flights to the Tongass National Forest. The excursion involves a 45-minute flight and one hour of bear watching for $299. There are also slightly longer tours that go farther into the wild for an additional fare.

New England and Canada

Cruises taken to the northeastern corner of the United States and Canada frequent many ports with a wide variety of different excursions available. The ports are in English-speaking locations, with plenty of options for activities that do not need to be booked through the cruise line — saving you vast amounts of time and potentially money. Provided below are some of the most common locations to visit in the area and the various options you will have when you reach these locations.

Newport, Rhode Island

In Newport, you can almost entirely rely upon your own two feet to get around the area and enjoy the outdoor activities. Walks through the historic sites in town and day-long hikes into the surrounding landscape allow you to see the foliage and outdoors of the Northeast.

In addition, you can take walking tours to the Newport mansions in the hills, though you will need to book early, before the cruise, to make sure you actually make it into the mansions. There are plenty more things you can do and enjoy in Newport, beyond the basic options provided by the centuries-old mansions in the hills.

After you disembark from the cruise, you can visit the tourist center on America's Cup Drive, only seconds from the cruise terminal. The shops and restaurants in the area, on Thames Street, include 18th and 19th century buildings and New England-style locations that you can spend time touring or purchasing souvenirs from.

You can visit Trinity Church, modeled after the Old North Church in Boston in 1726 or visit the oldest synagogue in North America, the Truro Synagogue, built in 1763.

Martha's Vineyard

The world famous Martha's Vineyard, located on an island just off the northeastern coast has been home to summer cottages and vacationers for decades. One of the best options for touring the island is a day pass to get you away from the tourist-heavy parts of the island. Visit the Victorian Oak Bluffs, the beaches along the island's small coastlines and Edgartown for a more diverse experience while docked here. No matter where you visit, you can walk to the closest attractions, making it an easy to explore destination. Bike paths and historic districts all serve to make the island more entertaining for those with a day to spend there.

Boston

If your cruise ship stops in Boston, you should have a good idea of what you want to do well before arriving because the options are seemingly endless. You can spend an entire day exploring the city and not see more than a small fraction of the cultural and historic offerings it provides. The best way to explore the classic, colonial center of American history is to purchase a one-day pass for the MBTA, the Boston transit system. From the cruise terminal, you can usually find taxi service, bus routes, and paths that will take you to the center of the city and to the midst of the MBTA system, with subways, trains, street cars, busses, and trolleys to get you across town.

A very popular outing in Boston is the Freedom Trail, a 2.5 mile walk that begins in Boston Common and takes walkers along a redbrick path through Quincy Market, Faneuil Hall, North End, the Old North Church, Cropp's Hill Burial Ground, The USS Constitution, and the Bunker Hill Monument, nearly 235 years old. The tour can easily take half a day depending on how many stops you take and how long you walk. Have a good map and an idea of which places you most want to visit to best budget your time.

Another good walk is along the waterfront, taking from Rowes Wharf to the North End. You will walk past the ferry landings, whale-watching boats, and plenty of other classic, interesting attractions along the waterfront.

From the MBTA, you can visit any of the famous and popular Boston neighborhoods, both Cambridge and Harvard Universities, the Museum of Fine Art, or the Isabella Stewart Gardner Museum. If you decide to get a day pass, the cost is quite reasonable, while individual fares are also equally well priced.

If you are interested in leaving Boston for a short while, you can take a train to Salem, only 30 minutes outside the city where the Peabody Museum and residential district are great historical reminders of the importance of the small town in the Witch Trials. Farther north are the fishing communities of Gloucester and Rockport.

Saint John

Farther north, in New Brunswick, you will find Saint John, an walkable city with classic architecture, beautiful landscapes, and historical significance to keep you occupied for a day. Visit the Victorian town square or Old City Market for souvenirs and plenty of pictures, or visit the Reversing Falls, where the Saint John's River actually reverses its flow at high tide, making for incredibly unique rapids that are perfect for jet boating.

A 90-minute drive outside the St. John's is St. Andrews, a popular destination for tourists in the area. The originally Acadian settlement later became a center of residential and resort atmosphere thanks to the railway built through the city and the famed 19th century Algonquin Hotel.

Fall foliage brings out millions of tourists to St. John's with more than 100 years' worth of different varieties of trees losing their foliage and, with plenty of reds, yellows, oranges, and a hint of remaining green — the perfect backdrop for a relaxing stroll through the city.

Halifax

After disembarking from the cruise ship in Halifax, you will be within a quick walk of the city center along the boardwalk. You can visit the maritime museum, 19th century Public Gardens, and plenty of tourist information located in nearby tourist information centers.

The Canadian immigration museum located on Pier 21 has plenty of artifacts, photographs, and videos from 1928 to 1971 when the Pier was used for processing and admitting immigrants into Canada from overseas, as well as returning soldiers and their wives. There is another immigration depot located across the street where the immigrants who had recently arrived in Canada would depart for the Western Provinces.

From the waterfront, you can climb the hill past the Old Town Clock to the Citadel where the Army Museum is located. Every day at noon, a canon is fired, as has been done since the middle of the 1800s. You can visit the Public Gardens from here, first built in 1836 and continue to enjoy the Spring Garden Road, and Old Burial Ground near St. David's Church.

Hawaii Ports

Hawaiian cruises have become much more popular in recent years. With year-round nice weather, plenty of activities to keep you busy, and a half-dozen major port cities to choose from, there is little wonder that the Aloha State has developed such a big cruise industry following. Your options are varied, with smaller cruises offered while you are in Hawaii or large cruise lines sailing from California or Seattle with the purpose of providing a week-long or more trip to the islands.

Activities in Hawaii will vary depending largely on what you are most interested in. Hawaiian history is a major draw for many visitors, with Polynesian culture and the well-documented history of the Hawaiian monarchy on islands such as Oahu. The Kilauea volcano on the Big Island is another major attraction, having been continually erupting since 1983. Cruising along beside the ocean at night while the lava pours into the sea allows cruisers to watch with the perfect lighting.

Whale-watching is a popular opportunity for cruisers, with humpback whales spending their winters in Hawaiian water, often as many as 3,000 of them each year.

Oahu — Honolulu

Oahu is the most populous and active of the Hawaiian islands, known as the gathering place for a good reason. The state capital is located here along with Waikiki Beach, Diamond Head Monument, and Pearl Harbor. You can spend your day combing the beach, or simply eating from one of the dozens of local and international eateries. Nightlife on Oahu is also among the most active in the islands, with a Polynesian show held in almost every hotel in Waikiki and plenty of clubs open as late as 4 am.

Kauai — Nawiliwili

On Kauai, you will find more natural attractions — things such as the Waimea Canyon or the Wailua River and its popular Fern Grotto where many Hawaiian weddings are held each year. With plenty of valleys, gardens, beaches, and groves in which you can spend your day ashore, Kauai offers one of the most relaxing outdoor-oriented stops on your Hawaiian cruise.

Maui — Kahului/Lahaina

Maui is formed by two dormant volcanoes, one of them sitting at 10,000 feet in elevation. It features a wide variety and selection of valleys and beaches as well as the Haleakala National Park. Golf courses, as on every Hawaiian island, are plentiful, with some of the most amazing vistas on any courses in the world. If you are interested in whale-watching, Lahaina is the best port to find a whale-watching boat to purchase passage on. You will also find one of the first missionaries and plantations formed in Hawaii, along with plenty of other historically important locations to visit.

Hawaii — Hilo/Kailua

The Big Island, also known as Hawaii, is home to the Hawaii Volcanoes National Park. On this island you will find plenty of volcanic formations, fern tree forests, lava tubes, and sightseeing locations to watch the world's largest active volcano, Mauna Loa, at 13,600 feet. From Hilo, you can reach the most attractions quickest.

The Bahamas

Not quite a part of the Caribbean, the Bahamas are a popular location just off the Florida coast in the Atlantic Ocean. Millions of people visit every year for honeymoons, vacations, or as part of a cruise. As a result, there are countless things you can do while in port at Nassau. Located on New Providence Island, Nassau is home to plenty of historic and sightseeing options, as well as entertainment opportunities, such as world-class casinos, shopping, and restaurants. Water sports, diving, and hiking are also very easy to seek out and enjoy while in port.

Nassau

As the heart of the 700-island chain of the Bahamas, Nassau is rich in history. Pirates, Spanish invaders and explorers, British colonists, and rumrunners in the 1920s all claimed Nassau at some point in the port's long history. Today, with more than 210,000 permanent residents, Nassau is home to more than 60 percent of the entire country's population.

Nassau is a great place to visit, with plenty of opportunities to relax and have fun, but be aware of the various different locals who will try to sell you souvenirs, offer you services, and entice you into tours or restaurants. While many of these opportunities may be interesting, do not feel obligated if you are not interested. Simply shake your head no and politely move away.

For those interested in gaming, there are two large casinos in Nassau, the Atlantis Resort and Casino and the Crystal Palace Casino. The casinos are open 24 hours a day, though tables are only open from 10 am to 4 am. While your cruise ship will likely contain a decent casino, you can find a much larger selection of gaming choices on the island casinos.

Shore excursion options to Nassau are about as wide and varied as any Caribbean island you might visit. However, you can also go it alone and spend as much time as you like exploring the port, without having booked ahead of time. A surrey ride around the town is a great option, which allows you to view the town comfortably and quickly. Queen Victoria's statue and 19th century British government buildings are interesting and unique sightseeing destinations that many tourists enjoy visiting.

Busses can be flagged down from most street corners for a one dollar fare, while rental cars, motorcycles, and bicycles are freely available for daily use. Taxis are equally accessible, while water taxis can take you back and forth from Paradise Island, where one of the cities two major casinos is located.

If you are looking for a wide variety of dining options, Nassau is the perfect destination. With a worldwide selection of eatery options, you can choose from ethnic options of almost any culture, or if you are looking for something quick and familiar — an American fast-food restaurant.

Local delicacies and specialties are equally as common and should not be overlooked. Guava duff pastry and well-prepared Conch are unique dining options that you can find nowhere else in the world, at least not made properly. It is almost impossible to leave without trying some other seafood delicacies — such as Bahamian lobster or fried Johnnycake.

The shopping in Nassau is equally diverse and interesting for the first-time visitor. Bay Street has a world-famous collection of shops offering many different options. Colombian Emeralds has a wide selection of jewelry and stones from around the world while Little Switzerland is a popular location to find perfumes and watches. Local liquor is a great purchase, with specialties to take home, such as Nassau Royale, and clothing options range from traditional batik cotton clothes to Straw Market.

There are many shoreside sporting options for those interested in getting a little exercise or relaxation while off the ship. The 18-hole golf course at

Cable Beach is among the world's best, providing plenty of scenic views and breathtaking holes.

Additionally, water sports are very popular for those stepping ashore for the day. Scuba diving, snorkeling, fishing, parasailing, windsurfing, shark diving, and swimming on Cable and South Ocean beaches are among the most popular activities for anyone visiting the island. The water is clear, dozens of companies offer lessons and provisions along the beaches, and you can find nearly anything you might want by simply asking for assistance. Booking ahead for some water sports such as windsurfing or parasailing is necessary in most instances, but if you are merely looking for a diving instructor, there are almost always more than enough.

The Caribbean

St. Martin

The island of St. Martin is known for its dual cultural influences, with one side being French and the other being Dutch. It has long since become a favorite destination for many Caribbean cruises and features a wide array of options for stepping out and becoming more active or just enjoying the fine dining, shopping, and relaxation.

As for the division between French and Dutch sides of the island, the border was supposedly first created in 1648 when a French and Dutch man each walked as far as they could, the French man 21 miles and the Dutch man 16. The borders were created to match their distances. Today, the island may be split down the center, but both sides live together peacefully, with no border crossing routines or customs of any kind.

When you arrive in St. Martin, you will dock in Philipsburg, the Dutch capital. Here alone you can find 12 different casinos and plenty of shopping opportunities. On the other side of the island, you will find the French-influenced collection of restaurants, beaches, and the clothing optional Orient Beach. For those looking to shop, duty-free items such as French perfume and leathers are easily purchased in the French district of the island.

If you are interested in an organized shore excursion, the ships offer many different options for you to select from, with water sports, hiking, sightseeing, and other opportunities plentiful. However, if you like, you can rent a motorcycle and see the island on your own terms, visiting as many locations as possible.

St. Thomas

Located in the U.S. Virgin Islands, St. Thomas is a prime destination for those looking to find quality shopping in the Caribbean. The islands of St. Thomas, St. Croix, and St. John were originally discovered by Christopher Columbus in 1493 and named the Virgin Islands then, but have been home to various tribes of native populations since 1500 B.C. Both the culture and the history represented by the island make for popular destinations while in port.

The Virgin Islands have been controlled by many different nations, and have a long history of pirate activity, with Blackbeard, Edward Teach, and other famous plunderers having scoured the waters around the islands.

From 1671 until the 1910s, St. Thomas was a primarily Dutch port, home to a free port by the Dutch Trading Companies. They sold the port to the United States during World War I for $25 million.

There are plenty of shore excursions to St. Thomas and the other Virgin islands, and with as many as 12 different cruise ships in port at the Crown Bay Marina any given day, it is no wonder that shopping provides so many choices. Contact your cruise line directly for more information about the different excursions available in St. Thomas or to learn where you can go to visit the historical and cultural remnants of the 500-year-old port island.

Aruba

The island of Aruba is an incredibly popular annual destination for college students, cruisers, and honeymooners alike. It is here you will find clear blue waters, palm trees as far as the eye can see, and a year-round temperature in the mid-80s, all beyond the reach of most hurricanes and in the center of the cruise industry's largest service area.

The island is actually a member of the Kingdom of the Netherlands and operates under its own democratic government, sitting only 15 miles off the coast of Venezuela. Additionally, the island is English-speaking and uses the U.S. dollar as currency, provides clean drinking water, and drives on the right side of the road. The tourism industry has had a profound effect on how the island's economy both operates and works in tandem with the tourists constantly visiting.

Your cruise ship will dock in Oranjestad, the capital of the island and only a few short minutes away from both the town and Palm Beach, the biggest and most popular beach on the island.

Shopping in Oranjestad is plentiful, with Smith Boulevard loaded with shops featuring items from around the world. However, be aware of the small tariffs that are required on most imported goods here.

A short distance outside the capital is Arikok National Park, which includes plenty of trails, huge rocks, and free-roaming goats and other wildlife walking along above your heads. You can find ancient native drawings on rock walls in Cunucu Arikok and a massive rock ledge home to thousands of bats. Adobe homes from the 1800s are still intact where people lived until only a short while ago.

The Natural Bridge, a 100-foot long, 25-foot high rock formation above the water along the coastline is one of Aruba's most recognizable and popular destinations. On the other side of the island, you can find many more beaches, with more secluded, relaxing locales. This side of the island is less developed and home to rockier, rougher terrain but a more natural appearance.

The island's highly respected and pricey golf course can cost as much as $120 for a single round of golf, but offers multiple discounts for those who visit or play more than once.

The Aruba tourism board caters to more than a half a million cruise ship visitors each year and has boasted that there is no location on the island that is not safe for you to visit. For that reason, visitors are encouraged to freely roam the island and explore without fear of wildlife or dangerous terrain. Additionally, poverty is not as large an issue on Aruba, reducing crime rates and dirtier parts of town. Aruba has come to be known as one of the most cruise ship friendly islands in the Caribbean for a good reason.

Mexican Riviera

The Mexican Riviera, a popular cruise destination throughout the year has plenty of opportunities for cruisers looking to do everything from whale-watching to landscape-viewing. Many of the excursions provided at this destination are wildlife and touring related.

If you are interested in viewing humpback, gray, or blue whales near Cabo San Lucas, you have a window between January and March in which to go on a smaller ship expedition and view the whales for a short period of time, up close and personal. Dolphins are nearly as often viewable from these locations as well.

Sightseeing also includes trips to see things like Los Arcos, the rock formations near Cabo San Lucas and the sea lion colonies located in the region. You can rent an ATV for as little as $100 and take a Baja Adventure tour for half the day, touring the countryside with a trained guide. You can also enjoy a similar tour on a mountain bike, known as an Eco-Ride.

If you choose to disembark in Cabo San Lucas and select your own excursions, there are plenty of options available, though not nearly as many resources at hand. For these locations, cruise lines usually offer the best excursions and should be booked as early as possible to ensure you have something to do when you reach the location.

Other ports in the Mexican Riviera, such as Puerto Vallarta and Mazatlan, offer additional options such as city tours and folklore shows that allow you to enjoy and learn more about the local culture and history. A fun excursion that differs from the traditional snorkeling, kayaking, and hiking options of most cruise excursions is the touring of local factories that create everything from saddles and sandals to tequila and beer.

Local rainforests, such as the Puerto Vallarta location, where Arnold Schwarzenegger's "Predator" films were shot, provide a perfect backdrop for afternoon tours and wildlife sightseeing. For a complete list of the many options now available in the Riviera port cities, you should contact your travel agent and start booking early. That list can quickly shrink as your fellow cruisers start booking their own excursions.

There are certain things to remember when cruising to Mexico, as the provisions are not always as modernized as they are in some of the Caribbean port cities.

Always bring your own bottled water ashore. Because of the possibility of water-born pathogens you have not built up immunity to, you can become ill by drinking the water in town. If you do purchase water in town, make sure it is in a sealed bottle. Also, bring clothing to protect you from the sun such as a hat, loose clothing, good walking shoes, and sunscreen. Even if it is slightly cloudy outside, you will want this material to keep yourself safe from the still powerful sun rays. Also, bring small bills with you to pay for items and tip your guides or servers. Most locations in the Riviera will accept U.S. money, but will not accept anything larger than a $20 bill.

Shopping in Another Country

Shopping in another country can be exciting and different from what you are used to. Not only do you have a chance to interact with local cultures and learn more about a far way society, you can bring home souvenirs and intricate artistic pieces that would be nearly impossible to find otherwise.

Souvenirs and Customs

When you visit a foreign country, you will want to bring home a selection of souvenirs to remember your trip by. Without those items, how else can you show your friends and family the kinds of shopping opportunities you were able to take advantage of on your trip? However, keep in mind that there are many rules and regulations in place as to what you can buy and how much you can bring back into the United States.

Do not purchase anything that appears to be an antique unless you can acquire an official, printed receipt or a certificate of authenticity with the date of its creation. Items older than 100 years brought back into the country are often considered cultural or historical artifacts and may be confiscated if you cannot prove you purchased it legally.

Additionally, buying any one item in bulk may cause customs to stop and question you. Because the rules regarding duty-free exemptions include a clause about personal use or gifting to a friend or family member, a purchase of 600 strands of beads may cause customs to raise an eyebrow. This kind of purchase often appears to be for resale purpose, and would require additional taxes and duties paid on your part. Buy souvenirs conservatively and be aware of the response customs might have, both in the country you are visiting and in the United States.

Here are a few things to remember when traveling and buying goods overseas.

Duty-Free Shopping

On your cruise, you will encounter many instances of duty-free purchases you can make. Because items are taxed differently in different countries, there is often a duty placed on items brought into a country. However, there is a duty-free exemption that allows you to carry goods home with you without paying any additional taxes. This exemption is usually $400, though there is a limit to how much of that total can include alcohol and tobacco — two of the most common duty-free items purchased overseas.

You must meet the following requirements to receive the duty-free exemption:

* All items purchased are for personal or home use.

* You have been outside the country for longer than two days (48 hours).

* All items claimed in the exemption are with you. You cannot mail home goods and claim exemptions on them. However, you can mail home goods you brought with you that were purchased in America, such as dirty clothes. Label your packages "American Goods Returned" to claim duty-free status on returned items.

* The exemption has not been used in the last 30 days. The $400 exemption is only valid after 30 days has passed between uses.

* All items you purchased while outside the United States are claimed when you re-enter the country.

It can be confusing to know what items must be claimed when you re-enter the country — so it is often best to claim everything. If the customs officials presume you are trying to trick them, they may decide to confiscate all of your items.

The Duty-Free Shop

The cruise ship will have many duty-free shops on-board, and most of the goods you buy in port will be labeled "duty-free." However, this does not automatically mean they are free of taxes or duty. These items are only free of taxes in the country in which you are buying them. You pay the labeled price for a shirt you purchase in St. Marten, for example. However, your $400 exemption is applied to all items brought back with you to the United States. If you purchase $500 worth of duty-free goods in a port of call, you will be assessed duty for $100 of them.

Many of the items in a duty-free shop can be very good deals. You may find, as many travelers do, that cosmetics, liquor, tobacco, and perfume are much cheaper without duty applied, saving you large sums of money on luxury goods. However, not every item sold in a duty-free shop is a good deal. Before making any large purchases in a local shop in port, look around and make sure it is a fair price. It defeats the purpose of buying an item duty-free if you pay too much for it.

The Personal Exemption

The $400 personal exemption you receive is almost always the maximum value you can claim when returning to the United States. However, there are occasions when you can claim a higher exemption, such as in the case of a Caribbean island or U.S. territory. For the following countries, your duty-free exemption is a bit higher at $600:

- Antigua
- Bermuda
- El Salvador
- Nicaragua
- Aruba
- Granada
- Panama
- Bahamas

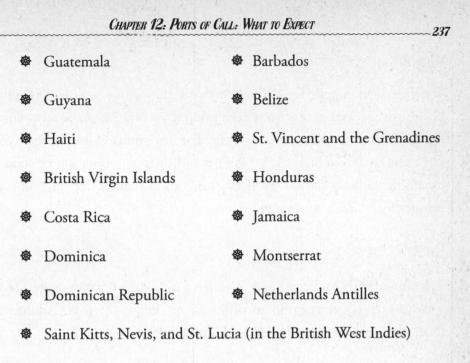

- Guatemala
- Guyana
- Haiti
- British Virgin Islands
- Costa Rica
- Dominica
- Dominican Republic
- Barbados
- Belize
- St. Vincent and the Grenadines
- Honduras
- Jamaica
- Montserrat
- Netherlands Antilles
- Saint Kitts, Nevis, and St. Lucia (in the British West Indies)
- Trinidad and Tobago (in the West Indies.

Exceptions and Special Cases

There are some items that carry exceptions to the duty-free rules put in place by U.S. customs. These include the following.

Fine Art

Any artwork or antique that is more than 100-years-old is considered fine art and is not subject to duty, regardless of your exemption. However, folk art and crafts purchased while in port will be subject to duty.

Tobacco

The purchase of tobacco can be much less expensive in another country, but is limited to 200 cigarettes and 100 cigars. Anything after this limit and you are subject to duty payments, regardless of how close you are to your total exemption. Additionally, you cannot bring back cigarettes or cigars from another country if they were manufactured in the United States.

Alcohol

The general rule applied to alcohol purchases allows only one liter of alcohol be brought back as part of your exemption if you are 21-years-old and if it is intended for personal use or as a gift. For the countries listed above, you can bring back two liters. Anything beyond these amounts will be subject to additional taxes and duties. If you bring in too much alcohol, you may be questioned as to your intent.

Restrictions

You cannot bring back any items considered to be drug paraphernalia, illegal substances, nonprescription medication, or dangerous toys. Additional restrictions apply to a variety of agricultural goods:

Meat — The exact rules regarding the import of meat vary, but generally, you are not allowed to bring back any fresh, canned, or dried meat from an international trip. Check with the USDA before leaving if you plan on doing so.

Other Food Products — Most food products are subject to additional inspection and some food products are disallowed altogether. Baked goods and cheeses are generally allowed, and many processed foods are considered safe.

Wildlife and Fish Products — Due to a wide variety of regulations, there are many laws in place regarding the import of wildlife and fish products. Before purchasing or returning to the United States with any such items, you should check with the U.S. Fish and Wildlife service to make sure an item is not made from an endangered species and that wildlife or fish you may be trying to important will not be quarantined. There is a long list of items that are prohibited, restricted, or subject to additional taxes.

Fruits and Vegetables — The rules change widely depending on where you acquired the fruit and what it was. If you have ever been to Hawaii, you know that the state screens all incoming and outgoing agricultural goods.

The same is true for the United States itself, as it tries to keep infestations of outside bugs from destroying crops or killing strains of necessary insects already here. Contact the USDA for more information about what is allowed and not allowed.

Cultural Property

Items found to be culturally important to another country or society are often restricted from being imported, both by that country's laws and by the United States. This may include any of the following items:

- ❀ Pre-Columbian murals or sculptures from Central and South America

- ❀ Native American items from Canada

- ❀ Pre-Columbian archeological, architectural, or mural items from any Central or South American Country

- ❀ Period paintings or ritual items from Peru

The list goes on to include many of the culturally significant items you may find in a foreign country. In most cases, this issue will not apply to Caribbean islands. If you do find a particularly good deal on what looks to be an old, cultural artifact, be aware that you may be questioned about its purchase and should be able to show ownership. Even then, you may be forced to relinquish the item.

What Is the Duty Rate After the Exemption?

For those that go over their exemption, there is a duty charged of 10 percent for the next $1,000 of merchandise brought into the country. After the $1,000, specific duties will be charged based on the items being taxed. You must pay the duty as you re-enter the country and with cash, check, or money order.

Trusting the Tour Guides

The men and women working aboard most cruise ships are fair and trustworthy individuals, but be aware of the circumstances in which your tour guides might be working with local shops. Often, the tour guides will receive a commission on any sales made by a local shop to members of a cruise ship whom they referred. These may be unspoken agreements at times and can lead to advice from your tour guide that might not be entirely truthful or accurate.

If a price seems particularly high or misrepresented in a shop, look around at a few other shops in the area. Visit a shop or two that the tour guide did not mention and look for similar items being sold. If they are of a similar price, your original recommendation was probably fair. However, if you notice significant differences in price between shops, you may want to look elsewhere for souvenirs.

You can often ask your tour guide pointedly if they receive commissions for referrals to shops in port. It may feel as though you are being rude, but there is nothing actually wrong with them receiving such commissions, so they should tell you readily. It is when they act as though they have something to hide that you might end up paying too much money for an item. Be a savvy shopper and you can bypass the possibility of being taken advantage of in a port city.

Interacting with Native Cultures

There is no one right way to interact with a foreign culture, but there are plenty of ways in which you should not act, to avoid being insensitive or embarrassing your fellow cruise passengers.

Remember first that any port of call you visit is a major tourist destination. Unless you are on-board a smaller, more intimate cruise ship, the ports of call you visit see millions of cruise ship passengers and other tourists every year and are used to handling those who do not speak their languages and do not understand their culture.

In many cases, shop owners, restaurant owners, and guides will speak English to a certain degree and will be able to communicate with you efficiently. It does not hurt, however, for you to bring a guidebook and phrase book to help make communication slightly easier between you and the natives. Most commonly, Spanish, French, or English are already spoken in these countries and cheap, easy-to-use guidebooks can be found to help you communicate.

In addition to being prepared for any differences in language, be prepared to see and participate in varying cultural styles. Dishes may be different from what you expect in a local restaurant — either served differently or including foods you have not heard of or tried before. Be daring and willing to accept what you are offered. Asking what is in a dish is not rude. Spitting it out after you find out is.

Always be polite and patient in another country as well. You are essentially a guest in someone else's home. If someone visited your home and started offending your family, talking loudly, and being pushy, you would not be happy either. Treat the local citizens with proper respect and you can expect the same in return.

Finally, try not to be too much of a tourist. This is a hard point of advice because there is a fine line involved that you may not realize you are crossing. There are many things you will want to do and try because you are on vacation in a different country and are experiencing a different culture. You will want to take pictures, buy souvenirs, and try new foods. However, try not to walk around with a camera around your neck and a fanny pack around your waist. It may be convenient, but it announces to anyone within 300 feet that you are a tourist and there are always some individuals who seek to take advantage of that fact. Stay with your tour group when you can and if you decide to explore alone or with your family, be on your guard and be as inconspicuous as possible.

Chapter 13

The Return Home

Unfortunately, it is time to return home. After seven or more wonderful days on-board a cruise ship for the first time in your life, you need to return to your home, job, and possibly family. Disembarking from a cruise ship can be a hectic, confusing ordeal. You need to be prepared in advance for a full day and for whatever might happen; make sure you have everything in place, and have all of your post cruise travel plans in place. Just like the time leading up to your cruise, the time between leaving the ship and returning home will benefit greatly from careful planning.

Pulling Into Port

When your ship prepares to pull into port, everything can start to seem very hectic. After a full week of relaxation and having all of your needs catered to, you now must resume the roll of the organizer and make sure things are in place for disembarking. While you do not want to start the packing and preparation process too early — it is a vacation after all — start organizing your things the night before you return to the port.

This means that anything you have unpacked, unfolded, or placed on the nightstand should be repacked on your final night at sea. This allows you to focus on a pleasant departure from the ship the next morning.

If you have children, make sure their things are all packed and prepared to return home. Their things can find ways into nooks and crannies all over the ship, so confer with your packing lists to make sure you do not forget anything on-board. It will ultimately save you a lot of time and energy that can now be spent relaxing on your final night on-board.

The morning you disembark, organize all your luggage into a single location. The ship's staff will move it off the ship for you, but you will want to make sure everything is present before leaving. Trying to get a lost bag or item back from a cruise line is a complex process that you hopefully never need to undergo.

With your things organized and your family ready to leave, start saying goodbye to anyone you made friends with on-board. You may want to exchange email addresses and phone numbers with anyone you have not done so with yet. These people may take cruises often, or may even live close enough to you for future visits. Share information now and you can start preparing for the next time you take a cruise.

Disembarking

Shortly before you disembark from your cruise, the cabin attendant will leave you a disembarkation questionnaire. This questionnaire will ask you what your plans are after you leave the ship. Your answer to this question will decide what color tags are placed on your luggage before you get off the cruise ship. The color of your tags will determine the time at which you leave the ship and the group number in which you pass through customs and security.

The tags are organized by urgency. Those with flights and tours that require they be off the ship as quickly as possible will be given priority while those who are driving or taking public transportation will probably be given a longer wait on the way off the ship.

U.S. Customs

Now that you have disembarked, the cold hard reality of getting home will start to kick in. The first stop in that trip is U.S. Customs. Whenever individuals return to the country from overseas, they must pass through Customs and declare any items they did not leave the country with. This is a tricky situation, especially if you brought anything with you that may not have been seemingly domestic.

The best thing you can do before leaving the ship is to create a list of the items you purchased on-board the ship and in any ports of call. These items will all count toward your duty-free exemption and should be clearly catalogued now so the customs agents do not assume you are trying to cheat them when you leave the ship. If they suspect you are not being completely honest, you may be forced to step out of line and go through all of your possessions.

U.S. Customs at a Glance

To give a rough idea of what U.S. Customs handles on a daily basis, here are some figures taken from the U.S. Customs Web site at **http://www.customs.gov:**

- Customs processes more than 1.3 million passengers daily.

- Customs processes more than 340,000 vehicles daily.

- Customs processes more than 45,000 trucks and containers daily.

- Customs processes more than 2,500 aircraft and 550 vessels daily.

- Customs seizes more than 3,900 pounds of narcotics daily.

- Customs seizes more than $1.2 million in currency daily.

- Customs seizes more than $500,000 in commercial merchandise daily.

The list goes on to include many other actions taken by U.S. Customs on a daily basis and with that kind of constant load, you can see why they are easily overwhelmed and need you to cooperate.

What You Must Know Before Returning to the United States

Many actions you might take can set off red flags for customs officials and result in extra delays that you do not want to incur on your way home. Be aware of the various laws that affect what you bring back into the country and what they can mean.

Medication

When you bring medication out of the country, take several precautions. Keep the medication in its original container and do not bring excessive amounts. While you should bring a backup of any medication that is necessary for daily operations, make sure they are clearly labeled, in their original containers, and stored safely. It is illegal to bring prescription drugs back from other countries.

Electronics

If you bring any electronics overseas, you should make sure to register your ownership before you leave home. You can either register the item with the manufacturer using your proof of purchase or with a Form 4457 through U.S. Customs. This form keeps you from needing to pay duty on any electronics you may already own that were manufactured in another country when you re-enter the United States.

Alcohol and Tobacco

There is a limit on how much alcohol and tobacco you can bring with you back to the United States. In most cases, this limit is one liter of alcohol, 200 cigarettes, and 20 cigars. However, in the case of many Caribbean countries, as well as Canada and Mexico, you can double those numbers accordingly. Check with the Customs department to receive accurate, up-to-date numbers on what you are allowed to bring back into the country with you.

Items That Must Be Declared

The list of items you must declare upon re-entering the United States includes all of the following:

- All items bought, including from airports, airplanes, or on the ship.

- All items inherited or received as gifts.

- All items brought home as a gift for a friend or family member.

- Anything brought home for use in your business.

- Any alterations or repairs on items you brought with you — this includes tailoring or electronics repair.

- All items bought in the Caribbean and being shipped to your home.

In addition, you must claim any foreign currency you return with in excess of $10,000 (after conversion). The best way to handle these declarations is to keep your receipts for anything you purchased overseas and to pack all of the returned items in a carry-on if possible.

While on the ship, you will be given a U.S. Customs form and asked to fill it out. Upon disembarking, you can hand this form to the customs agents and show them your items if they request.

What Happens if You Break the Law by Accident?

The Customs department is not going to incarcerate you or take away your things if you merely forgot to enter an item on the claim forms. For the most part, travelers are honest people and mistakes happen. However, it is still safest to claim anything you bring back into the country that you did not already have when you left.

If you accidently forget you stored a small item in your purse, you may be forced to hand it over, but as long as it does not violate the import list, you can keep it after it is declared. But if you appear to be lying on your customs forms or have sneaked back illegal substances, Customs will not be so accommodating.

If, for some reason, you are pulled out of line for questioning or a search, expect the customs officials to be as kind as possible. If they are not, contact the U.S. Customs office and let them know the circumstances. The process should be quick and easy, without you needing to be concerned about your possessions or how you are treated.

Getting Home

The process of getting home from your vacation, if you have planned properly, should be as quick and painless as getting to the cruise terminal on the way out. You should have all of your tickets and paperwork on hand, ready to pull them out when you arrive at the airport, rental car outlet, or terminal.

Before leaving the ship, you should contact anyone who may be picking you up or is currently watching children, pets, or your home. Remind them you are returning home and make sure the plans you made two or three weeks earlier are still in effect.

Do not expect to be able to step off the boat, waltz through customs, and relax comfortably on a plane trip home. There are a number of tasks you will need to complete and be aware of on the way home if you do not want to be lost, behind schedule, or just plain frustrated. Plan your return trip while you plan your initial trip to the cruise ship and you should be able to synchronize everything and save time.

More Recovery

Getting home after your first cruise will be a bittersweet experience. You may have been away from your house for as long as two or three weeks. Your children, pets, or garden are likely begging for attention and the mail is piled up at the post office. On top of all that, walking into your home might be only a reminder of the fact that you will need to return to work in a very short time.

Before you allow any of the pressures and realities of your vacation's end to sink in, take a deep breath and relax, making sure to give yourself plenty of time to unwind following your vacation. When you book your vacation, hopefully you gave yourself at least two or three days after returning from the cruise to unwind before returning to work.

Cruisers tend to squeeze their itineraries too close together and end up returning to work a day or two after they get home. This is a bad idea for a few different reasons.

First, you will need time to get your house and your life back in order. Putting everything on hold for two or more weeks can result in a lot of errands and chores that will need doing. You probably have very little food in your refrigerator, a few recently arrived bills, and some shopping to do. It is best to give yourself the time to take care of these tasks without returning to work as well and juggling everything. What good is a vacation if you become stressed-out and overworked the day after you get home?

Second, your vacation probably resulted in a lot of new possessions, dirty clothes, piles of items that need to be put away carefully, and a few hundred other tasks that might take longer than you anticipate. The day or evening you return will most likely be devoted to lying down and taking a good long rest, so give yourself time to put away your possessions and souvenirs.

Third, and something that many people overlook because it is an unpleasant thought, is that you may still become ill. Because illnesses such as the norovirus have as much as a 48-hour incubation period, you could still carry the virus without showing any symptoms before you get home and return to work. By waiting an extra two or three days to return to work and the general pace of life, you give yourself enough time to know if you returned safe and healthy. It keeps the virus from spreading unnecessarily and keeps you from throwing yourself headlong back into a busy lifestyle.

By giving yourself plenty of time to rest and recover, you can be sure that your life will not look nearly as daunting or unpleasant as it might if you simply jumped directly back into work and errands the same as before you left. Do not waste a wonderful vacation by overwhelming yourself with stress after only two days back home.

The Bill

While you may have paid the bill for your plane tickets, luggage, and cruise fare well before you set sail, there will be a bill waiting at your home some time shortly after you disembark. This bill, including all of the items you charged to your cruise card while on-board, should already be factored into your expenses.

Because the bill might arrive as much as two or three weeks after you return home, it is best to keep a careful record of the items and goods you use or charge while on-board. Every time you buy a bottle of wine or visit the spa, make a note somewhere of the charge so you can keep track of what you will owe. This allows you to not only keep from overspending while on-board, but gives you a detailed record of the items you purchased so you can compare your numbers with the bill in case of a discrepancy.

You can additionally request a receipt for any items purchased with your cruise card on-board. Keep these receipts organized together. Your final bill will usually be due within 30 days of the invoice being sent, giving you slightly less than one month to pay your bill.

If you have a particularly large bill or an unexpected financial hardship, simply contact the cruise line and try to work out a payment plan with them. Usually you can split your bill up into a number of smaller, monthly payments. Make sure to do this right away, however. If you fail to pay your bill within the 30 days, you may be subject to additional charges, late notices, or collections fees. The bill is the same as any credit card bill and must be treated accordingly.

Getting a Refund

In some rare instances, you may have had a poor experience on-board or felt that you did not receive what you paid for. In such a case, getting a refund for your cruise fare is not unheard of. However, it is rare.

If you have a problem, contact the purser's desk on-board as quickly as possible to inform them of your displeasure, and usually you will be able to work out a solution. This also documents your complaint and makes it easier to bring up your circumstances later if you try to receive a refund from the cruise line.

There are also some cruise lines that will allow you to disembark early if you are displeased with your cruise experience. You must inform the purser's desk before the first port of call at which point you are allowed to disembark and are refunded the portion of your cruise fare you did not use. The cruise line will then fly you back to the United States for free.

If you have a problem with your cruise and feel you should be entitled to some or all of your money back, contact the cruise line as early as possible, preferably while still on-board. Most cruise lines have terms that disallow refunds in all but the most extreme circumstances — such as an outbreak of illness, severe weather, or ship malfunction. However, if your situation warrants special consideration, the cruise lines will often work with you to provide some form of compensation or fair recompense.

Conclusion

The first time you take a cruise, it will be an engaging, unforgettable experience. Millions of individuals embark each year on cruises to escape the daily grind of their lives — to get away from everything and be pampered for a week or more in the Caribbean or another exotic locale. By now, you should have all of the necessary tools at hand to start the cruise planning process, contact a travel agent, choose which cruise line and ship, and start packing for that first ocean-bound vacation.

It will be a stressful process at first as you try to organize all of the bits and pieces of your life into a set of luggage, an organized itinerary, and eventually a boat that caters to the needs and desires of everyone you are traveling with.

Like any other vacation, or part of life for that matter, anything can go wrong at any time. You must be willing to accept that, even on your first cruise, when you might hope and wish for everything to go right. But because things go wrong, there are safeguards that can be put in place or taken advantage of on-board a cruise ship. Things such as travel insurance, a working knowledge of the ship's staff and medical officers, and a detailed list of necessary items for long distance travel can make every aspect of your trip that much easier.

With the right tools at hand, there is no telling how much easier your first cruise will be compared to what it might have been if you tried to vacation without the proper preparation.

You are one of the few careful planners that has taken the time and exerted the energy necessary to make sure you will not have any issues on-board your first cruise and for that alone you should feel comforted. After all, while many couples or families on-board that cruise ship may be worrying over a lost prescription bottle or missing luggage, you will be laid-back, relaxing in the sauna because you thought of everything.

Do not let your vacation be wasted. Take precautions, plan carefully, and be ready to have the most fun possible on-board your first-ever cruise.

Section 2

What You Need to Know
About the Cruise Lines

Section 2 provides details about 11 different cruise lines. These cruise lines sat down and answered questions about their services, what they offer, and where they sail. This section outlines the differences between the various cruise lines so that you can make a better informed decision on which one you would like to set sail. Please keep in mind that there are other cruise lines that you can choose from.

Cruise Line Case Studies

Butterfield & Robinson

Contact: Erika Nigalis, Sales Manager
70 Bond St. Suite 300
Toronto, ON Canada, M5B 1X3
Phone: 1-800-678-1147
E-mail: erika.searles@butterfield.com
Web site: **www.butterfield.com**

© *Butterfield & Robinson. Reprinted with Permission*

Q. **What is the history of your cruise line?**

A. *Butterfield & Robinson (B&R) started the "By Sea" program in 2000; however we have been running biking and walking trips since 1966. We have found that the best way to bring our travelers to hard-to-reach places is to go by water. Our group sizes are small and intimate — about 30 people per departure — and give our travelers an unparalleled experience.*

Q. **What should readers know about your cruise line?**

A. Some of the best biking and walking on earth is inaccessible by land. So we take the finest small ships you can imagine, turn them into boutique hotels, and cruise to those out-of-the-way places that larger vessels cannot access.

Q. **How many ships are in your fleet?**

A. We use the Isabela II in the Galapagos Islands and the Callisto in the Mediterranean, Black Sea, and the Adriatic. We use the Queen Karia II to sail along the Turquoise Coast. We sometimes charter other boats (small ships and yachts) for our private Bespoke trips.

Q. **What features are unique to your ships?**

A. Our trips feature active travel by small ships and yachts. Our ships are small and boutique — we charter them exclusively, and they are ours for the duration of the B&R trip. We pride ourselves on making each trip as unique as the people on-board. We have frequent, spontaneous swim stops whenever our travelers want a dip, and snorkeling gear is always available. We also have kayaks on the Isabela II and the Callisto, perfect for when we see a blue grotto that we just have to experience.

Other features:

❀ Our trips are all inclusive (food, alcohol, events, and activities)

❀ Bicycles on-board, customized for B&R and fitted to each traveler by expert bike mechanics

❀ Plethora of choices for travelers each day, and all activities are optional

❀ Mix of meals on-shore and on-board

❀ Three to four B&R guides plus a shipboard crew

Q. **What kinds of staterooms and/or suites do you offer?**

A. *This depends on the boat, but we offer Queen, Double, and Twin categories on all of our ships. Each stateroom has a private bathroom. The cabins are small but well-appointed.*

Q. **What kind of on-board entertainment do you offer?**

A. *Our B&R guides are knowledgeable and entertaining. They often live in the region, and have a unique perspective on the region we are visiting. Depending on the trip, we occasionally invite a special guest on-board to lead discussions and bring out some of the best of the politics and cultural climate of the region.*

Q. **What unique activities do you offer to guests?**

A. *Butterfield & Robinson has taken a different approach to cruising then most regular cruise lines. We are active. We offer either hiking or biking everyday on the different islands we are visiting. We immerse our travelers in the culture and create unique events for our travelers. We interact with the locals, who in many cases are our friends. We offer our travelers access to places and things they cannot do or find on their own.*

Q. **What dining options are offered on-board?**

A. *We like to experience meals onshore to enjoy the local delicacies and flavors. So every day we have either lunch or dinner in a restaurant, trattoria, or taverna, depending on what part of the world we are in on that day.*

Q. **What special services (for example, laundry or medical) are available on-board?**

A. *There is a doctor on-board the Isabela II. We offer a laundry service, access* to Internet, and other amenities as well. On all our trips we offer an all-inclusive bar, and meals.

Q. **To what areas do you travel? Any unique locations?**

A. *Butterfield & Robinson travels "By Sea" to the Classic Greek Islands, Crete and the Peloponnese, the Black Sea, the Turquoise Coast, Sicily and the Aeolian Islands, the Tunisian Coast, the Galapagos Islands (include "With the Kids" departures for families), the Dalmatian Coast, and Athens to Dubrovnik.*

Q. **What are the most popular shore and land excursions in which guests participate?**

A. *The hiking and biking are the most popular activities with our travelers — they allow them to experience a place much more intimately than a bus or car. Also well loved are winery tours and tastings, cooking demonstrations, language lessons, dancing, and more. Each trip strives to highlight the best of the region through the people.*

Q. **Do you have luggage restrictions?**

A. *We do not have luggage restrictions for our "By Sea" trips. We do recommend collapsible luggage that can be stored underneath the cabin beds. Some storage is available, though not abundant.*

Q. **What items are passengers prohibited from bringing on-board?**

A. *We do not restrict what can be brought on-board.*

Q. **What is the average cost per day?**

A. *B&R "By Sea" trips range in price from $900 to $1,500 per person per day, depending upon the cabin.*

Q. Do you offer and special promotions?

A. *No.*

Q. How would you describe your typical guest?

A. *There is no such thing as a typical B&R traveler, but they do tend to share some characteristics: an adventurous streak, a love of active travel, and a desire for authenticity and immersion in local cultures.*

Q. What is the one item guests always seem to forget?

A. *We can usually supply whatever is forgotten for our travelers.*

Q. What is the question you are most frequently asked by guests?

A. *A frequent question is "Is everything included?" And in a word: yes. In ninety words? Signature B&R guides who are adept at wearing many hats; local experts of all kinds; swimming whenever you want; sea kayaking; awesome biking and walking routes; custom made hybrid bicycles; on-shore excursions every day; private tours; a traveler to staff ratio of two to three; authentic local meals; incredible on-board meals; lessons and demonstrations of all kinds; local artisanal wines; wine tastings; well-appointed cabins; all victuals and libations; all the endorphins you can handle; new insight; interesting, fun, and like-minded travel companions; a feeling of total freedom; and in short, an unforgettable, hassle free journey full of discovery.*

Q. What is your cruise line known for?

A. *Active travel by small ship while slowing down to see the world.*

Cruise West

Phone: 888-851-8133

Web site: **www.cruisewest.com**

© *Cruise West. Reprinted with Permission*

Q. **What is the history of your cruise line?**

A. *The West family celebrates more than 60 years in the adventure travel business. Chuck West was affectionately referred to as "Mr. Alaska" for his pioneering efforts in developing Alaska into a dynamic, sought-out destination for travelers seeking an exploration experience.*

Today, Richard (Dick) West serves as the chairman and managing director. As the company's visionary, Dick West satiates his passion for travel by personally exploring each locale to develop truly unique and memorable itineraries.

Q. **What should readers know about your cruise line?**

A. *Cruise West's Alaska itineraries call at 24 Alaskan and Russian ports —
more than all other cruise lines in Alaska.*

Q. **How many ships are in your fleet?**

A. *Cruise West's small cruise ships — nine in all — hold between 78 and
138 guests. Our ships include:*

- ❀ *Spirit of Oceanus — Flagship, 120 guests*

- ❀ *Spirit of '98, 96 guests*

- ❀ *Spirit of Endeavor, 102 guests*

- ❀ *Spirit of Discovery, 84 guests*

- ❀ *Spirit of Alaska, 78 guests*

- ❀ *Spirit of Columbia, 78 guests*

- ❀ *Pacific Explorer, 100 guests*

- ❀ *Spirit of Yorktown, 138 guests*

- ❀ *Spirit of Nantucket, 102 guests*

Q. **What features are unique to your ships?**

A. *Small ship cruising allows for up-close and personal cruising not offered
by the traditional larger cruise lines.*

Q. **What kinds of staterooms and/or suites do you offer?**

A. Queen-size beds are available in select cabin categories on the Spirit of Endeavour, the Spirit of '98, the Spirit of Discovery, the Spirit of Columbia, and the Spirit of Yorktown. King-size beds are available in all categories on the Spirit of Oceanus and in the Owner's Suite aboard the Spirit of '98.

Q. **What kind of on-board entertainment do you offer?**

A. To further enrich the travelers' experiences, we offer on-board narratives, lectures, and presentations by local experts and interpreters from a wide variety of backgrounds.

Q. **What unique activities do you offer to guests?**

A. We offer everything from kayaking off a remote island in the Sea of Cortez, Mexico, or hiking in a rainforest in Alaska, to strolling through the ancient villages of Qui Nhon, Vietnam. Each unique itinerary is designed to an engage all the senses.

Q. **What dining options are offered on-board?**

A. Meal times on-board vary depending on the day's scheduled activities. Generally, we provide an early riser continental breakfast starting every morning at 6 a.m. A full breakfast is served in the dining room starting around 7:30 to 8 a.m., lunch is around noon, and dinner is served around 7 to 7:30 p.m. Appetizers are also served at Social Hour each evening before dinner.

We are able to accommodate most special dietary needs. Prior to your cruise, visit **www.cruisewest.com,** and select Booked Guests, where you'll find the Special Meals form. Completing this form will ensure that the chef has enough notice to prepare for your needs. The chef or hotel manager on-board will check in with you upon your arrival to the ship to confirm your request.

Q. **What special services (for example, laundry or medical) are available on-board?**

A. *We have fee-per-item laundry service available on the Spirit of Oceanus. There is no laundry service on our other ships, but laundry services can be found in many of the towns we visit.*

Each Cruise West vessel has a trained first responder on-board at all times. The Spirit of Oceanus has a doctor on-board for all itineraries.

Q. **To what areas do you travel? Any unique locations?**

A. *We sail to North and Central America, the South Pacific, and Asia. We offer 21 itineraries that visit 18 countries and have 237 departures. We have cruises from three to 24 nights that explore wilderness regions extending from the southern tip of the Alaska Panhandle to the Arctic Circle in the Bering Strait, including Southwest and Southeast Alaska, Prince William Sound, and the Bering Sea, with an emphasis placed on wildlife, fjords, glaciers, natural and pioneer history, and native cultures. Numerous land tour options are available including Anchorage, Denali National Park, and Fairbanks. Guests also have the opportunity to lodge at select wilderness properties in Denali and remote areas known for wildlife viewing just a floatplane ride away from Anchorage.*

Q. **Do you have luggage restrictions?**

A. *We recommend you limit your luggage to one standard piece and one carry-on per person. This is due to limited space on some motor coaches and storage space limitations on-board. Please also check with your specific air carrier as most airlines have specific luggage limitations and additional fees.*

Q. **How would you describe your typical guest?**

A. With Cruise West, guests are not just visitors, but participants.

Q. **What is the question you are most frequently asked by guests?**

A. Guests often ask us how active the tours are. Our answer is that each itinerary varies with regard to activity level. Travelers should look at their specific itinerary details. A variety of activity levels are also available when choosing optional shore excursions.

Crystal Cruises

Phone: 888-722-0021

Web site: **www.crystalcruises.com**

© *Crystal Cruises. Reprinted with Permission*

Q. **What is the history of your cruise line?**

A. *Crystal Cruises was created in 1988 and currently operates two luxury ships: the Crystal Symphony and the Crystal Serenity. The Crystal Harmony (launched in 1990), was retired in 2005. Crystal is wholly owned by Nippon Yusen Kaisha (NYK), the largest shipping company in the world.*

Q. **What should readers know about your cruise line?**

A. *Crystal Cruises is committed to developing plans for preventing pollution, complying with worldwide environmental regulations, and continually improving our environmental management system to reduce the environmental impact of our operations.*

Q. **How many ships are in your fleet?**

A. *Two: the 940-guest Crystal Symphony (launched in 1995) and the 1,080-guest Crystal Serenity (launched in 2003).*

Q. **What features are unique to your ships?**

A. *We have a full 360° open air teak Promenade Deck with the exclusive WOW® — "Walk on Water" — fitness program. We also have a wine cellar with more than 200 vintages including Crystal's exclusive "C" label.*

Q. **What kinds of staterooms and/or suites do you offer?**

A. *We offer a variety of different rooms, including:*

❂ *Two Crystal Penthouses with verandahs*

❂ *19 Penthouses with verandahs*

❂ *214 Deluxe Staterooms with verandahs*

❂ *176 Deluxe Staterooms*

❂ *Five Staterooms for guests with disabilities*

❂ *10 connecting Staterooms and 89 Staterooms with third berth for families*

❂ *470 Staterooms*

Q. **What kind of on-board entertainment do you offer?**

A. *We offer a nightclub for nightly dancing and karaoke, recent release films in the Dolby-equipped Hollywood theatre, a full orchestra, a ballroom and dance lounges, cabaret acts, and bridge instructors.*

Q. **What unique activities do you offer to guests?**

A. *We have an "Avenue of the Stars" shopping arcade with three boutiques offering upscale clothing, jewelry, and specialty items. Guests can also take advantage of our casino, galaxy lounge, Hollywood theatre, Computer University@sea, Fantasia children's center and Waves teen center, and our library, which features over 3,000 books, DVDs, and audio books.*

Q. **What dining options are offered on-board?**

A. *Crystal Cruises offers 24-hour room service. Our Crystal Dining room provides distinctive international cuisine and a world renowned wine list. There is also our Prego restaurant for classic Italian cuisine; sophisticated Jade Garden for contemporary Asian dining; The Vintage Room, Classic boardroom and wine cellar for winemakers dinners; the outdoor Trident Bar & Grill serving hot dogs, hamburgers, pizza, sandwiches, wraps, and fruit; and a complimentary ice cream and frozen yogurt bar.*

Q. **What special services (for example, laundry or medical) are available on-board?**

A. *Our services include:*

- ✸ *24-hour front desk service*

- ✸ *24-hour e-mail and Internet service*

- ✸ *24-hour medical center*

- ✸ *Complete laundry, dry cleaning, and valet services*

❀   Beauty services for men and women

❀   Telefax and secretarial services available upon request

❀   Satellite phone service

❀   Wi-Fi service

❀   European-trained Concierge

❀   Complimentary safety deposit boxes

❀   Interdenominational religious services

Q. To what areas do you travel? Any unique locations?

A. Crystal Cruises travel all over the world, stopping in different ports such as Chile, Norway, Vietnam, Mozambique, Mexico, and Russia.

Holland America Line

Contact: Erik Elvejord
300 Elliott Ave W.
Seattle, WA 98119
Phone: 206-298-3057
Web site: **www.hollandamerica.com**

© *Holland America Line. Reprinted with Permission*

Q. **What is the history of your cruise line?**

A. *Holland America was founded in 1873 as the Netherlands-America Steamship Company (NASM), a shipping and passenger line. Because it was headquartered in Rotterdam and provided service to the Americas, it became known as Holland America Line (HAL).*

Within 25 years, HAL owned a fleet of six cargo and passenger ships, and operated between Holland and the Dutch East Indies via the newly constructed Suez Canal. The line was a principal carrier of immigrants from Europe to the United States until well after the turn of the century, carrying 850,000 to new lives in the New World.

Though transportation and shipping were the primary sources of revenue, in 1895 the company offered its first vacation cruise. Its second leisure cruise, from New York to the Holy Land, was in 1910. In 1971, HAL suspended its transatlantic passenger trade and, in 1973, the company sold its cargo shipping division.

In 1989, HAL became a wholly owned subsidiary of Carnival Corp., the largest cruise company in the world. Today, it operates 13 ships to seven continents with nearly 700,000 cruise passengers a year.

Q. **What should readers know about your cruise line?**

A. *In the 2006 Portrait of Affluent Travelers survey by Yesawich, Pepperdine, Brown, and Russell, Holland America Line topped the list of cruise lines sought after by affluent leisure travelers.*

Holland America Line's elegant staterooms are 25 percent larger than the industry standard and offer ample closet and drawer space. Through Holland America Line's Signature of Excellence™ initiatives, all staterooms are outfitted with Premium Plush Euro-Top mattresses, featuring 250-thread-count cotton linens, large extra-fluffy Egyptian cotton towels, and plush terry bathrobes. New amenities also include Elemis Aromapure "Time to Spa" specialty soaps, shampoo, conditioner, and lotion used in the award winning Greenhouse Spa. Guests also enjoy massage showerheads, lighted magnifying make-up mirrors, stylish hair dryers, a complimentary fresh fruit basket, and an elegant stainless-steel ice bucket and serving tray for in-cabin beverages.

Also, suites are outfitted with comfortable duvets on the beds, fully-stocked mini-bars, DVD players and access to a well-stocked DVD library, and personalized stationery.

Q. **How many ships are in your fleet?**

A. *Holland America Line's fleet of 13 ships offers nearly 500 cruises to more than 320 ports. Two- to 108-day itineraries visit all seven continents, including Antarctica, South America, Australia/New Zealand and Asia voyages; a Grand World Voyage; and popular sailings to ports in the Caribbean, Alaska, Mexico, Canada/New England, Europe, and Panama Canal.*

Q. **What features are unique to your ships?**

A. *To provide guests with new and unique enrichment experiences that inspire and delight, Holland America Line will introduce a number of enhancements, including:*

❁ *A groundbreaking interactive Culinary Arts Center featuring: chef presentations, cooking demonstrations, and wine and specialty shops.*

❁ *The new Explorations Café, powered by The New York Times, offers guests an opportunity to sip coffee, browse one of the most extensive libraries at sea, and enjoy diverse music at one of several listening stations or surf the Internet.*

❁ *An expanded Exploration Speakers Series.*

❁ *Expanded Club HAL and teen programs. Children ages three to seven enjoy creative arts, watch big-screen television, and having a play area. Older children, ages eight to 12, have an area featuring arcade games, air hockey, foosball, Karaoke, Internet access, and Sony PlayStations. Teens, ages 13 to 18, can enjoy The Loft, a teens-only lounge, which is connected to a secluded teens-only sun deck called The Oasis.*

Q. **What kinds of staterooms and/or suites do you offer?**

A. *Amenities in all staterooms include:*

❀ *Complimentary 24-hour room service*

❀ *Complimentary ice service twice a day or as requested*

❀ *A complimentary souvenir canvas tote bag for shopping*

❀ *Guest Services Directory describes all the services available on-board and the room service menu*

❀ *Turndown service each evening ensures that guests returning to their staterooms are greeted by soft lighting and "Sweet Dreams" chocolates*

❀ *Staterooms include privacy cards and a breakfast card for in-room breakfasts*

❀ *Daily program listing the next day's activities placed on the bed each evening*

❀ *An eight-page satellite edition of the New York Times, delivered by 8 a.m.*

❀ *Stationery, envelopes, postcards, and pen provided and replenished as needed*

❀ *Complimentary shoeshine service available*

❀ *Self-service laundry/ironing facilities (not available on Zuiderdam, Oosterdam, Westerdam, or Noordam)*

❀ *Men's and women's hangers (with skirt clips) in each of the three closets along with laundry, dry cleaning bags, and price lists (padded silk hangers in Deluxe Verandah Suites and Penthouse Verandah Suites)*

❋ *Flat-screen televisions featuring CNN, and subject to satellite availability: TNT or TCM, Boomerang, Cartoon Network, and CNN, and also shore excursions information, safety information, ship programming, and feature movies*

❋ *Non-allergenic pillows (feather pillows available upon request)*

❋ *Complimentary use of beach towels and shore excursion towels available upon request*

❋ *A premium line of Elemis Aromapure amenities are provided in each stateroom including Pure Shine Shampoo, Pro-Vitamin Conditioner, Citrus Slice Soap, Sharp Shower and Bath Gel, Pure Zest Cleaning Soap, and Vitamin Rich Body Lotion*

❋ *All staterooms have private bathrooms and individually controlled air conditioning, telephone with a computerized wakeup service, and a multi-channel music system*

❋ *All staterooms have sofas, hair dryers, and voicemail on the telephone*

❋ *Most staterooms have convertible twin-to-queen beds; Deluxe Verandah Suites have convertible twin-to-king beds; and Penthouse Suites have king-size beds*

❋ *Accessible staterooms to accommodate guests with special needs*

❋ *Numerous staterooms on-board the Ryndam, Maasdam, Veendam, Rotterdam, Volendam, Zaandam, Amsterdam, Zuiderdam, Oosterdam, Westerdam, and Noordam have connecting doors*

Q. What kind of on-board entertainment do you offer?

A. *The best in live entertainment is offered each night including an award-winning production spectacular designed by Broadway's finest, vocalists, musicians, comedians, and illusionists direct from Las Vegas and Atlantic City — the variety is endless. Film buffs can enjoy a wide variety of recently released movies on our big screen in the Queen's Lounge or Wajang Theater, depending on the ship. There are a variety of musical styles featured in our bars and lounges, from a string ensemble to a rock band. Cruises 30 days and longer have male social hosts for dinner hosting and dancing.*

Q. **What unique activities do you offer to guests?**

A. *Greenhouse Spa*

Our Greenhouse Spa offers a complete menu of massage and body treatments, facials, detoxification therapy, and a full-service salon. The Greenhouse fitness center features state-of-the-art weight and cardio machines. Fitness classes such as Pilates, yoga, and spinning are available at a nominal charge.

Culinary Arts Center Presented by Food & Wine Magazine

Holland America Line, in partnership with Food & Wine magazine, presents an exciting culinary program featuring demonstrations and seminars conducted by top chefs, wine experts, and leading cookbook authors on select sailings in a state-of-the-art demonstration kitchen.

Explorations Café powered by The New York Times

The Explorations Café, powered by The New York Times, offers a comfortable, living room-style environment where guests can sip a cup of coffee, browse through a selection of more than 2,000 books, spend time enjoying a wide selection of music, and surf the Internet. Wireless "hot spots" are available throughout the ship for guests traveling with personal laptop computers. A limited supply of laptops and wireless network cards are also available for rent.

Explorations Speaker Series

Cruises 10 days or longer have a guest speaker on-board who provides lectures about the culture or geography of the ship's itinerary along with a bridge director who leads games and provides instruction.

Gaming

The casino offers a friendly, non-intimidating place to just have fun. Guests can test lady luck on many of the favorite games including Blackjack, Poker, Craps, Roulette, and Slots. Complimentary gaming lessons are held at the beginning of the cruise. Bingo games are also scheduled throughout the cruise.

Shopping

Duty and tax-free shopping and Signature Shops are just steps away from guest staterooms. There is a great selection and fantastic prices on everything from fine jewelry and watches to leading brand fragrances and cosmetics. Also available are gifts, popular name brand liquor, tobacco products, and stylish Holland America Line wear.

Each cruise also features relaxed and entertaining auctions of art by masters such as Rembrandt, Picasso, Dalí, Chagall, and Erté, and also sports memorabilia and animation art, all priced below gallery prices.

Sports

There are two swimming pools, walking and jogging decks, and a basketball and volleyball court.

Q. **What dining options are offered on-board?**

A. *Holland America Line offers The Pinnacle Grill, a popular Northwest-themed, reservations-only restaurant, featuring distinctive Bulgari china and elegant Riedel stemware; one-on-one service in the main dining room; four dinner seating times in the main dining room; introduction of all-white table linens and new main course plates in the main dining room; made-to-order dinner entrees and table-side waiter service in Lido's popular casual dining alternative; and As You Wish dining provides open seating from 5:15 to 9 p.m.*

Q. **What special services (for example, laundry or medical) are available on-board?**

A. *Self-service laundry/ironing facilities are available (except on Zuiderdam, Oosterdam, Westerdam, or Noordam). We also provide men's and women's hangers (with skirt clips) in each of the three closets along with laundry, dry cleaning bags, and price lists. Padded silk hangers are available in Deluxe Verandah Suites and Penthouse Verandah Suites.*

Q. **To what areas do you travel? Any unique locations?**

A. *We visit all seven continents, including Antarctica, South America, Australia/New Zealand and Asia voyages; a Grand World Voyage; and popular sailings to ports in the Caribbean, Alaska, Mexico, Canada/ New England, Europe, and Panama Canal.*

Norwegian Cruise Line

Contact: Anne Marie Matthews, Director PR
7665 Corporate Ctr. Drive
Miami, FL 33126
Phone: 305-436-3699
E-mail: amathews@ncl.com
Web site: **www.ncl.com**

© *Norwegian Cruise Line. Reprinted with Permission*

Q. **What is the history of your cruise line?**

A. *NCL was first established in 1966 when one of Norway's oldest and most respected shipping companies, Oslo-based Klosters Rederi A/S, acquired the M/S Sunward and repositioned the ship from Europe to the then obscure Port of Miami. With the formation of a company called Norwegian Caribbean Lines, the cruise industry was changed forever.*

The late-1980s brought new ships, new itineraries, and a new corporate name, as Norwegian Caribbean Lines became Norwegian Cruise Line in 1987 to reflect an expanded route structure.

NCL further expanded the fleet in November 1997, with the purchase of the 1,050-guest M/S Royal Majesty (built in 1992) from Kvaerner ASA. The re-named Norwegian Majesty provides seven-day cruises from Boston to Bermuda and from Charleston, South Carolina to the Bahamas and Mexico.

In addition, NCL contracted with the Lloyd Werft shipyard in Bremerhaven, Germany, to stretch three of its vessels in 1998 and 1999. Sister ships M/S Dreamward and M/S Windward were lengthened by inserting a prefabricated midsection into each vessel.

The 50,760-ton, 1,748-guest ships were re-introduced to the marketplace in 1998, each with 40 percent increased capacity. In 1999, NCL lengthened Norwegian Majesty, increasing the ship's capacity from 1,056 to 1,462 guests, and its tonnage from 32,400 to 40,876 GRT.

Between 2005 and 2009, over 8,000 berths will leave the NCL fleet, as part of the company's new building program that is under way to replace those transferred berths and to continue to grow the fleet as well.

Q. **What should readers know about your cruise line?**

A. *NCL today has the youngest fleet in the industry (based on major North American cruise lines), providing guests the opportunity to enjoy the flexibility of Freestyle Cruising on the newest, most contemporary ships at sea, and has recently added its latest new ship, the 2,400 passenger Norwegian Gem.*

In May 2000, NCL announced Freestyle Cruising, which challenges the conventional model of cruising, and is designed to meet the changing needs of today's cruise passengers. Hallmarks of the innovative on-board program include up to 10 restaurants, open seating and extended hours in the main restaurants, "resort-casual" attire each night, simplified tipping procedures, and a more leisurely disembarkation procedure.

The company recently announced it will take its signature Freestyle Cruising to the next level with the introduction of Freestyle 2.0, a major enhancement to its on-board product fleet-wide, that will further improve the guest experience, including an increased investment in food of $50 million over the next two years, and an upgrading of stateroom bedding and amenities across the fleet. The company also announced a new travel agent program, Partnership 2.0, which includes major changes to the way NCL does business and is designed to strengthen its relationships with travel partners.

Q. **How many ships are in your fleet?**

A. *There are 13 ships in service and 2 under construction.*

- ❀ *Norwegian Dawn*
- ❀ *Norwegian Dream*
- ❀ *Norwegian Gem*
- ❀ *Norwegian Jade*
- ❀ *Norwegian Jewel*
- ❀ *Norwegian Majesty*
- ❀ *Norwegian Pearl*
- ❀ *Norwegian Spirit*
- ❀ *Norwegian Star*

✽ *Norwegian Sun*

✽ *Pride of America*

✽ *NCL America Fleet*

✽ *Pride of Aloha*

✽ *Unnamed (2010)*

✽ *Unnamed (2010)*

Q. **What features are unique to your ships?**

A. *Recognized as an innovator in on-board and onshore programming, NCL pioneered a number of industry "firsts" that include:*

✽ **Freestyle Cruising:** *NCL created this innovative cruising experience that challenges the conventional cruise model. It is designed to meet the changing needs of today's cruise passengers offering NCL passengers a more relaxed, resort-style cruise with complete flexibility and non-intrusive service of the highest standard.*

✽ **Shore Options:** *NCL's "Dive-In" snorkeling program was the first of its kind in the industry. NCL was the first cruise line to provide an uninhabited "out island" experience at Great Stirrup Cay in the Bahamas.*

✽ **Entertainment:** *NCL was the first in the industry to offer big-name entertainers and full Broadway productions within fully equipped theaters.*

✽ **NCL's Children's Program "Kid's Crew":** *Created for junior cruisers ages 2 to 17, the Kid's Crew programs offers organized activities, games, parties, and menus.*

❋ ***Comprehensive Pricing:*** *NCL was the first cruise line to offer a nationwide air/sea program combining cruise, hotel, and transfers from more than 150 U.S. and Canadian cities.*

❋ ***Internet Cafés, Wi Fi Access, and Cell Phone Service:*** *An Internet Café — the first ever at sea — was introduced on Norwegian Sky in 2000. Internet Cafés are now available fleet wide. NCL recently became the first line to offer remote wireless Internet access (Wi Fi) at sea and cell phone service. NCL was also the first cruise line to launch a Web site –* **http://www.ncl.com** *– in 1997.*

❋ ***First Bowling Alley at Sea:*** *In 2006, NCL introduced the first bowling alley at sea with the introduction of Norwegian Pearl. Another bowling alley was introduced on Norwegian Gem.*

❋ ***Ship-Within-A-Ship Concept:*** *NCL's Jewel-class ships—Norwegian Jewel, Pride of Hawaii (soon to be Norwegian Jade), Norwegian Pearl, and Norwegian Gem — offer the very popular Villa complex at the top of the ship. Here guests can enjoy an exclusive private haven while still experiencing all the amenities and Freestyle flexibility, of a big ship.*

Q. **What kinds of staterooms and/or suites do you offer?**

A. *We offer:*

❋ *Garden Villas*

❋ *Courtyard Villas*

❋ *Suites: Deluxe Owner's Suites; Owner's Suites; Romance Suites; Mini-Suites*

❋ *Penthouses: Deluxe Penthouses; Penthouses*

❀ *Balcony Staterooms*

❀ *Oceanview Staterooms*

❀ *Inside Staterooms*

Q. **What kind of on-board entertainment do you offer?**

A. *NCL offers a variety of Broadway style shows that vary by ship. Additionally, enrichment classes are offered during each ship's itinerary along with an on-board casino (except for NCL America ships).*

Since 2005, NCL has partnered with famed improvisational group, Second City. Customized specially for NCL guests, the troupe performs "The Best of Second City," a laugh-out-loud revue filled with memorable improvised skits and songs. During each of Norwegian Gem's sailings, the troupe also performs two script-free improv shows in the Spinnaker Lounge.

The Second City ensemble also hosts up to six workshops on-board each sailing. Based on guest demand, these classes cover areas from musical improv to lecture workshops. Troupe members also teach customized acting and improv classes to Kid's Crew and Teen's Crew participants.

Second City performances are currently available on six NCL ships.

Q. **What unique activities do you offer to guests?**

A. *From a four-lane, 10-pin bowling alley to a rock climbing wall to Broadway-style shows and Freestyle Private Tours, NCL offers guests a variety of activities to its guests.*

NCL Freestyle Private Touring are private tours exclusively created for our guests. These carefully chosen tours offer a truly different experience allowing guests to customize time ashore and discover the things they want to do and see at your own pace. The different modes of transportation are by plane, skiff, Hummer, and other vehicles. With these options, guests create their own itinerary and visit destinations in more depth. And since tours include only those with whom guests choose to travel, their experience is intimate. The advantages of choosing NCL Freestyle Private Touring are value, flexibility, privacy, comfort, and personalized guide service. In Alaska, Freestyle private tours are available in Juneau and Ketchikan.

Q. **What dining options are offered on-board?**

A. NCL's Freestyle Cruising provides the following for its guests:

- *NCL ships have up to 10 restaurants.*

- *Guests can eat in a different restaurant every night of the week if they choose.*

- *Open seating and extended hours in the main restaurants allow guests to dine when they want, where they want, and with whom they want.*

- *Guests can dine in their choice of main restaurants any time between the hours of 5:30 p.m. to midnight with seating until 10 p.m.*

- *Guests have the option to choose their dinner companions and request tables of any size from two to 10 each evening rather than being assigned to a specific table for the length of the cruise.*

- *Meals cooked to order instead of prepared banquet style.*

- *Guests can linger over dinner or dessert without feeling rushed.*

- *NCL's newest ships feature a Restaurant Reservation and Table Management system. Flat-screen TVs placed in key, high-traffic areas around the ship show each restaurant's current availability status.*

Indicator bars reflect when each restaurant is "full," "short wait," "filling up," or "empty." Screens also show an estimated wait time in each restaurant and the different table sizes available. If a restaurant is full and guests would like to wait for an opening, the hostess will quote a wait time and issue a pager that works all over the ship. This allows passengers to sit down in a bar, enjoy a pre-dinner cocktail, and listen to one of the ship's many entertainers until their table is ready.

Dining highlights of NCL's new Freestyle 2.0 initiative include:

❀ An increased investment in food of $50 million before we deliver our first F3, equating to a 20 percent increased investment in food per passenger per day, plus major fleet-wide capital investments.

❀ Lobster Galore — Lobster served in the main restaurant on multiple days and in one restaurant every night of the cruise.

❀ A signature specialty dish in every restaurant (for example, 48 oz. Porterhouse in the steak house and a chocolate fondue tower in the action station restaurant).

❀ An enhanced nighttime dining/ambience in the action station restaurant with table cloths, muted lighting, and enhanced service.

❀ One or two alternative restaurants open for lunch on sea days.

❀ A new and expanded room service menu.

❀ A "bubbly welcome" — a welcome glass of bubbly for everyone.

❀ A Taste of Freestyle on embarkation day — samplings from all of the specialty restaurants.

❀ A major hardware investment to bring all buffets to Norwegian Gem/ Norwegian Pearl "action station restaurant."

❀ *An investment in the back of the house to refine the reservations process and system.*

Q. **What special services (for example, laundry or medical) are available on-board?**

A. *We provide:*

❀ *Library*

❀ *Fitness rooms*

❀ *Internet Café art auctions*

❀ *Casino (not available on NCL America ships)*

❀ *Card room*

❀ *Bowling alley (available on Norwegian Pearl and Norwegian Gem)*

❀ *Sports courts*

❀ *Cinema*

❀ *Players Club*

❀ *Beauty salon and spa services*

❀ *Gift shops that feature duty-free shopping, fine jewelry, perfumes, clothing, cosmetics, and sundry items*

❀ *Laundry and dry-cleaning services*

❀ *Photographs taken throughout the cruise*

❀ *A physician and nurse*

Q. To what areas do you travel? Any unique locations?

A. *Seasonal: Alaska, Bahamas and Florida, Bermuda, Canada and New England, Europe, Mexican Riviera, Pacific Coastal, Panama Canal and South America, Transatlantic*

Year–round: Caribbean, Hawaii

Q. What are the most popular shore and land excursions in which guests participate?

A. *Shore excursion popularity varies by destination. On warm-weather itineraries, activities such as snorkeling and SCUBA are popular. In Alaska, flight-seeing excursions are very popular. And in Europe, shore excursions to major attractions (for example, The Colosseum in Rome, The Anne Frank House in Amsterdam, The Acropolis in Athens, and St. Andrews in Scotland) are popular.*

Q. Do you have luggage restrictions?

A. Each person is allowed up to four pieces of personal luggage on-board, with each piece weighing a maximum of 50 pounds.

Q. What items are passengers prohibited from bringing on-board?

A. ❀ *Firearms, explosives, or weapons of any kind*

   ❀ *Animals, except for service animals*

Q. What is the average cost per day?

A. *Prices range according to itinerary and stateroom category.*

Q. Do you offer any special promotions?

A. Yes. At certain times during the year (such as Wave Season), NCL offers special consumer and travel partner promotions.

Q. How would you describe your typical guest?

A. NCL is a mainstream cruise line appealing to a broad audience of all ages. NCL's research shows that the types of people who are attracted to Freestyle Cruising see themselves as individualists who prefer vacations without organized activities or set schedules. NCL guests want to enjoy their cruise on their terms without the structure and regimentation that is still the central feature of traditional cruises.

Q. What is the one item guests always seem to forget?

A. They tend to forget their passports.

Q. What is the question you are most frequently asked by guests?

A. Is there a formal night? Resort casual dress is the norm throughout the fleet. One completely optional "formal night" (two on cruises longer than seven-nights) are offered in various areas of the ship for those who enjoy dressing up for dinner.

Q. What is your cruise line known for?

A. NCL is most widely known as the inventor of Freestyle Cruising, but is recognized as an innovator in on-board and on-shore programming.

Princess Cruises

24305 Town Center Drive
Santa Clarita, CA 91355
Phone: 1-800-PRINCESS
Web site: **www.princess.com**

© *Princess Cruises. Reprinted with Permission*

Q. **What is the history of your cruise line?**

A. *From its modest beginnings in 1965 with a single ship cruising to Mexico, Princess has grown to become one of the premiere cruise lines in the world. Today, its fleet carries more than a million passengers each year to more worldwide destinations than any other major line.*

Considered one of the most recognized cruise lines in the world, Princess Cruises was catapulted to stardom in 1977 when Pacific Princess was cast in a starring role on a new television show called "The Love Boat." The weekly series, which introduced millions of viewers to the still-new concept of a sea-going vacations, was an instant hit and both the company name and its "seawitch" logo has remained synonymous with cruising ever since the show aired.

Q. What should readers know about your cruise line?

A. *In addition to incorporating a wide range of choices, vessels in the Princess fleet are specifically designed to provide the ultimate in affordable luxury, with an emphasis on "big ship choice with small ship feel." No matter the size of the ship, public spaces are designed to feel intimate and are decorated in a contemporary style, allowing passengers to enjoy themselves in an informal, relaxed on-board atmosphere that mirrors today's lifestyles.*

Q. How many ships are in your fleet?

A. *Princess' modern fleet has grown considerably in recent years to include Caribbean Princess (2004), Coral Princess (2003), Crown Princess (2006), Dawn Princess (1997), Diamond Princess (2004), Emerald Princess (2007), Golden Princess (2001), Grand Princess (1998), Island Princess (2003), Pacific Princess (1999), Regal Princess (1991), Royal Princess (2007), Sapphire Princess (2004), Sea Princess (1998), Star Princess (2002), Sun Princess (1995), and Tahitian Princess (1999). An additional ship, Ruby Princess, will join Princess' fleet in 2008, making it one of the most modern fleets on the high seas.*

Q. What features are unique to your ships?

A. *Today, the line's emphasis on choice is apparent across the fleet, with each vessel offering its own unique version of a host of multiple dining options and locations; flexible and varied entertainment selections; renowned customer service; and a full complement of on-board activities including a variety of ScholarShip@Sea enrichment classes featuring computer training, ceramics, culinary arts, finance, and photography.*

Q. What kinds of staterooms and/or suites do you offer?

A. *The company has long been the leader in building ships specifically designed to accommodate an extensive number of the most sought-after shipboard luxury — the private balcony. In the mid-1980s, Princess pioneered the concept of the affordable veranda, once an exclusive feature incorporated in only the most expensive suites. Today, Princess' fleet offers one of the highest percentages of balcony cabins in the industry, across all cabin categories.*

Q. What kind of on-board entertainment do you offer?

A. *Some vessels sport a Times Square-style "Movies Under the Stars" LED screen showing poolside movies and concerts. Often imitated but never duplicated, the Princess concept of cruise customization has been adopted as the touchstone of new ship design for the entire cruise industry.*

Q. What unique activities do you offer to guests?

A. *As befits the cruise line that starred in "The Love Boat," Princess continues to emphasize romance with a variety of special on-board features designed to help couples celebrate their love. Princess was the first, and currently the only, major North American cruise line on which passengers can be wed at sea by the ship's captain. In addition, the line regularly hosts vow renewal ceremonies, anniversaries, and even marriage proposals with the unique "Engagement Under the Stars" program for passengers who want to "pop the question" on the ship's 300-square-foot LED Movies Under the Stars screen. Special room service packages help passengers enjoy time alone together with all the ingredients for a romantic evening.*

Q. What dining options are offered on-board?

A. *Each vessel offers its own unique version of a host of multiple dining options and locations.*

Q. **To what areas do you travel? Any unique locations?**

A. *Princess' philosophy of choice is also reflected in its sailing schedule. Offering voyages to more worldwide cruise destinations than any other major line, Princess has nearly 100 itineraries ranging from seven to 102 days. The line sails to all seven continents and calls at approximately 280 ports around the world. Princess passengers can enhance their cruise experience through the Adventures Ashore® program featuring more than 2,000 in-port excursions worldwide, and the company's expanding cruise tour offerings enable passengers to combine their cruise with a full land tour. Destinations include the Caribbean, Alaska, Panama Canal, Europe, Mexican Riviera, South America, Australia/New Zealand, South Pacific, Hawaii, Tahiti/French Polynesia, Asia, India, Africa, Canada/ New England, Antarctica, and world cruises.*

Q. **What are the most popular shore and land excursions in which guests participate?**

A. *Having led the way in Gulf of Alaska cruising, Princess maintains a strong presence in Alaska. Through its Seattle-based Princess Tours division, the company operates a wide variety of spectacular land and sea experiences in the majestic "Land of the Midnight Sun." The largest cruise and tour operator in the state, Princess operates as many as eight cruise ships, five riverside wilderness lodges, luxury Princess Rail domed rail cars, and a fleet of deluxe motor coaches; these tours allow cruise passengers to connect seamlessly to a landside tour and experience several distinctly unique facets of the Alaska wilderness in a single trip.*

Q. **What is your cruise line known for?**

A. *The physical design and décor of the ships, coupled with Princess' hallmark service excellence, creates an on-board atmosphere of relaxed luxury in which passengers can enjoy their perfect vacation experience.*

Regent Seven Seas Cruises

Contact: Brian Major, Account Supervisor
1000 Corporate Drive, Suite 500
Fort Lauderdale, FL 33334
Phone: 646-442-6762
E-mail: bmajor@mmgmardiks.com
Web site: **www.rssc.com**

© *Regent Seven Seas Crusies. Reprinted with Permission*

Q. **What is the history of your cruise line?**

A. *In 1992, Carlson Companies of Minneapolis, the huge privately-held hospitality enterprise entered the cruise business. Under the Radisson banner, the 350-guest Radisson Diamond was launched in London in May of that year.*

In 1994, it became evident that the line could not prosper with just one vessel. At the same time, another one-ship operator, Seven Seas Cruise Line, was in similar circumstances. Their vessel, the intimate 200-guest

Song of Flower, had built a loyal following offering soft adventure cruises in more exotic venues such as Asia, but the business model, which had bet heavily on a strong revenue base from Japan and other Far East markets, did not materialize. The two lines agreed on a merger and in January 1995, Radisson Seven Seas Cruises was born.

The line quickly became known as a luxury operator offering a mixture of exotic and traditional cruise deployment, with the Radisson Diamond covering the more traditional Caribbean and European destinations, while the Song of Flower offered the more exotic (and longer) cruises to Asia and Africa.

In 1995, an agreement was signed with a French ship owner to market and sell a new ship which was to be based in Tahiti. This new build, the 320-guest Paul Gauguin, was launched at the end of 1997 and sailed immediately to Tahiti, where it has been ever since, establishing itself in a destination that had seen other ships fail, and creating somewhat of a legend for itself in the process.

In 1997, the first of the new all-suite vessels, the 490-guest Seven Seas Navigator, was ordered, and was duly delivered in September of 1999.

The delivery of the Seven Seas Navigator allowed RSSC to market the all-suite concept, with the vast majority of the suites boasting private balconies, walk-in closets, and marble bathrooms with full tub and separate glass-enclosed shower stall. These spacious accommodations were an instant hit, and encouraged the company to become more ambitious with its next new build — the world's first all-suite, all-balcony ship, the Seven Seas Mariner.

The 700-guest Seven Seas Mariner was introduced in March 2001 to instant acclaim. The 700-guest Seven Seas Voyager was launched in March 2003 during the "perfect storm" — United States and Allied forces were entering Baghdad, the U.S. economy was in recession, and a recent _outbreak of SARS had put a damper on international travel. The line was forced to re-deploy the Radisson Diamond to offer year-round cruising in the Caribbean, and occupancies and rate took a hit all around. Having six ships in the fleet, the line introduced a season of cruises to Bermuda in the summer, with Canada/New England in the fall. It was the first time a luxury cruise line had offered a full season of sailings to this island destination._

With the new generation of ships established, RSSC shed its two original vessels, the Song of Flower and Radisson Diamond, in 2003 and 2005, respectively, leaving the line with the three newer "Seven Seas" ships, plus the Paul Gauguin, and an annual charter of the acclaimed adventure ship Explorer II in Antarctica.

In March 2006, Carlson Companies decided to align their luxury hotel brand, Regent International Hotels, with the cruise line, thus creating a re-branded Regent Seven Seas Cruises. Becoming more focused on the customer and personalized luxury, the company is offering The Regent Experience both ashore and on the ships. The two brands — cruises and hotels — are now managed under one Regent umbrella, once again, a first in the industry.

Q. What should readers know about your cruise line?

We have won several awards, including:

* ❊ _"Best Large-Ship Cruise Line," Condé Nast Traveler Readers' Choice Awards (2006)_

* ❊ _"Best Luxury Cruise Line," Travel Weekly (2006, 2005, 2004)_

* ❊ _Condé Nast Traveler "Gold List" (2007)_

* ❊ _"World's Leading Luxury Cruise Line," World Travel Awards (2006)_

❀ *"2006 Above & Beyond Award," Ensemble Travel Group (2006)*

❀ *"Cruise Line Receiving Best Customer Feedback," 2007 TravelAge West WAVE Awards (2007)*

❀ *Among Top Five, "World's Best Value — Cruise Lines," Travel + Leisure (2007)*

❀ *"Best Luxury Line," Porthole's "Readers' Choice Awards" (2006)*

❀ *"Best South Pacific Itinerary," Porthole's "Readers' Choice Awards" (2006)*

❀ *"Best Cruise Line Spa," Condé Nast Traveler's "Best in the World" Readers' Choice Awards (2006)*

❀ *"Best Luxury Cruise Line," Caribbean World Magazine (2006)*

❀ *"Five Ribbons: Econoguide's Best Luxury Cruise Lines," Econoguide Cruises (2006)*

❀ *"Best Cabin Configuration and Amenities for a Standard Outside Cabin," Travel Age West WAVE Awards (2006)*

❀ *"Best Large Ship Cruise Line," Cruise Report (2005)*

❀ *"International Star Diamond Award," The American Academy of Hospitality Sciences (2005)*

❀ *"Cruise Innovation Award," Cruise Critic (2005)*

❀ *"Best Large-Ship Cruise Line," Departures "Readers' Favorites Survey: Travel" (2004)*

❀ *"Best Value, Ultra-Deluxe Six+-Star Category," Ocean & Cruise News (1992 - 2004)*

Q. How many ships are in your fleet?

A. *There are four. They include the 700-guest Seven Seas Voyager, the 700-guest Seven Seas Mariner, the 490-guest Seven Seas Navigator, and the 330-guest Paul Gauguin.*

Q. What kinds of staterooms and/or suites do you offer?

A. *The Seven Seas Voyager and Seven Seas Mariner are all-suite, all-balcony ships. The Seven Seas Navigator offers all-suite accommodations (90 percent with balconies).*

Q. What kind of on-board entertainment do you offer?

A. *Our new program features a nine-piece orchestra, an emphasis on live musical performances, and five new productions with "The Regent Singers and Dancers."*

Q. What unique activities do you offer to guests?

A. *The ships have casinos, libraries, and Internet lounges.*

Q. What dining options are offered on-board?

A. *There are four open-seating main restaurants plus the Pool Grill. Select wines and spirits are served with dinner, or you may select an alternative reserve vintage available for purchase from the wine cellar. The room service menu is available 24 hours a day.*

Q. What special services (for example, laundry or medical) are available on-board?

A. *Each ship has a licensed and registered doctor and nurse for professional and emergency services. Laundry and valet services, including pressing and dry cleaning, are available with charge.*

Q. To what areas do you travel? Any unique locations?

A. *Celebrated for delivering fine dining experiences, impeccable service, and outstanding value in the luxury niche, the line's four-ship, six-star fleet calls at over 300 ports worldwide, reaching all seven continents, including chartered explorations of Antarctica.*

Q. Do you offer and special promotions?

A. *Yes.*

Q. What is the question you are most frequently asked by guests?

A. *Guests often ask about the dress code on-board the ships. The attire ranges from Country Club casual to informal to formal.*

Q. What is your cruise line known for?

A. *Apart from the spacious all-balcony suite concept, the line is known for offering interesting, port-intensive itineraries on all seven continents, and delivering a product that is as good as any other, without some of the formality of its competitors. By partnering with brands such as Le Cordon Bleu culinary institute, the famed Carita of Paris spa, and other upscale marks, RSSC is firmly established in the luxury cruise market.*

Royal Caribbean Cruises. Ltd.

Harrison Lui, Manager, Brand
Communications
1050 Caribbean Way, 6th Floor
Miami, FL 33132
Phone: 305-982-2363
E-mail: hliu@rccl.com
Web site: **www.royalcaribbean.com**

© *Royal Caribbean Cruises. Reprinted with Permission*

Q. **What is the history of your cruise line?**

A. *Royal Caribbean was founded in 1969. In May 2007, we welcomed the newest addition to our fleet, Liberty of the Seas, sister ship to the popular Freedom of the Seas. Liberty and Freedom feature amenities such as the FlowRider surfing simulator, a 14-person family suite, and cantilevered whirlpools suspended 112 feet above the sea. Liberty of the Seas will be followed by a sister ship, Independence of the Seas, in May 2008.*

Q. **What should readers know about your cruise line?**

A. *We deliver friendly and engaging Gold Anchor Service to our guests and travel partners every day. Not only that, but Royal Caribbean invests in community organizations and initiatives to enhance the quality of life in communities all over the world.*

Q. **How many ships are in your fleet?**

A. *There are 21 ships in our fleet.*

Q. **What kinds of staterooms and/or suites do you offer?**

A. *Our staterooms vary by ship, but every room offers a television, telephone, private bath, shower, vanity, and a hair dryer. We offer four main categories of staterooms: Suite/Deluxe, Balcony, Oceanview, and Interior.*

Q. **What kind of on-board entertainment do you offer?**

A. *We offer Broadway-style musical productions, hilarious comedians, live musicians, cooking and wine classes, and even professional ice-skating shows on some ships.*

Q. **What unique activities do you offer to guests?**

A. *Our ships offer activities such as:*

* *Rock-Climbing Walls*

* *Miniature Golf Courses and Golf Simulators*

* *Sports Courts*

* *Jogging Tracks*

* *In-Line Skating Tracks*

* Center Ice at Studio B

* Bungee Trampolines

* FlowRider

* Day Spa

* Royal Caribbean Online

* Cybercabin

* Wi Fi

Q. **What dining options are offered on-board?**

A. *The elegant main dining room offers five-course meals, while the Windjammer Café offers buffets and incredible views. We offer Italian cuisine at our Portofino restaurant. Chops Grille, Johnny Rockets, the Seaview Café, and Jade also offer traditional favorites and exciting new dishes. For snacks, visit the Café Promenade, Ben & Jerry's, or Latté Tudes. We also offer 24-hour room service.*

Q. **What special services (for example, laundry or medical) are available on-board?**

A. *Self-service laundry facilities are not provided, but we do offer full laundry and dry cleaning services.*

Q. **To what areas do you travel? Any unique locations?**

A. *We travel to Alaska, Asia, Australia/New Zealand, Bahamas, Bermuda, Canada/New England, Caribbean, Europe, Hawaii, Mexico, Panama Canal, and South America.*

Q. **Do you have luggage restrictions?**

A. *Each passenger is permitted to carry up to 200 pounds of luggage.*

Q. **What items are passengers prohibited from bringing on-board?**

A. *Passengers may not bring any controlled substances, live animals, weapons, firearms, explosives, or other similar property without written permission from the Carrier.*

Q. **Do you offer any special promotions?**

A. *Royal Caribbean offers special prices and discounts for groups such as senior citizens and military.*

Q. **How would you describe your typical guest?**

A. *Royal Caribbean appeals to couples and singles in their 30s to 50s as well as family vacationers. The median age is low-40s, slightly lower on three- and four-night cruises and slightly higher on longer cruises of 10 or more nights.*

Q. **What is the question you are most frequently asked by guests?**

A. *Guests often ask if they can check-in for their cruise in advance. The answer is yes. You can use our Online Check-In process to expedite your boarding.*

Q. **What is your cruise line known for?**

A. *With more than 170 destinations worldwide and an amazing array of exciting shore excursions, there are multiple options for the vacationer including cave-tubing in Belize, glacier-trekking in Alaska, and experiencing the wonders of China.*

Viking River Cruises

Contact: Lisa Juarez, VP, Marketing
Communications
5700 Canoga Ave. Suite 200
Woodland Hills, CA 91367
Phone: 818-227-1234 ext. 8402
E-mail: lisa.juarez@vickingrivercruises.com
Web site: **vikingrivercruises.com**

© *Viking River Cruises. Reprinted with Permission.*

Q. **What is the history of your cruise line?**

A. *Viking River Cruises, a global corporation with U.S. headquarters in Los Angeles, CA, was established in 1997 by a Scandinavian and Dutch consortium with the purchase of four Russian ships. The following year, more ships were purchased and the company continued to cater to European passengers. U.S. headquarters was established in Los Angeles in 2000, and Viking River Cruises expanded into the American market.*

Q. **What should readers know about your cruise line?**

A. *Recipient of multiple awards from Conde Nast Traveler and Travel + Leisure, Viking River Cruises offers travelers comfortable, affordable, and all-inclusive river cruise vacations along the great rivers of Europe, Russia, and China.*

Q. **How many ships are in your fleet?**

A. *Viking River Cruises operates a fleet of 21 ships and over 3,800 berths.*

Q. **What features are unique to your ships?**

A. *We offer roundtrip air to Europe, Russia, or China with included transfers for each departure. U.S. Market Cruises also offer fully escorted tours led by English-speaking guides. In China, full escorted, English-speaking land and tour programs are provided with on-site Western management. We also offer non-smoking throughout ship interiors.*

Q. **What kinds of staterooms and/or suites do you offer?**

A. *We offer deluxe river cruise vessels with on-board amenities including a restaurant, bar, lounge, library, sun deck, air-conditioned staterooms, telephones, and private bathrooms. There are comfortable and spacious river-view outside staterooms equivalent to ocean cruise ship accommodations. Additionally, there are all-balcony staterooms on the two new China vessels.*

Q. **What kind of on-board entertainment do you offer?**

A. *Old World Highlights® featuring lectures, demonstrations, and folkloric entertainment.*

Q. **What dining options are offered on-board?**

A. *All on-board gourmet meals are served in a single, open-seating dining room featuring gourmet cuisine and regional specialties adjusted for American tastes. In China, alternate meals of Western fare and Chinese multi-course menus are created by world-famous chef Martin Yan.*

Q. **To what areas do you travel? Any unique locations?**

A. *Cruises range from eight to 17 days along Europe's Rhine, Main, Danube, Seine, Saône, Rhône, and Elbe Rivers; Russia's Volga and Svir; Ukraine's Dnieper; and China's Yangtze.*

Q. **Do you offer any special promotions?**

A. *Yes. We offer early booking incentives and are currently offering specials on trips from Paris to Prague, our Grand European Tour, China's Cultural Delights, and Waterways of the Czars. These offers will expire May 30, 2008.*

Q. **What is your cruise line known for?**

A. *Viking River Cruises has 22 vessels built specifically for river travel. We operate the world's largest fleet of river vessels and have over 175 years of heritage in European river cruising. Viking was also the first to offer river trips in Russia.*

Windstar Cruises

Contact: Jenny Mowrer, Marketing
Coordinator
2101 4th Avenue, Suite 1150
Seattle, WA 98121
Phone: 206-292-9606
E-mail: infor@windstarcruises.com
Web site: **www.windstarcruise.com/Media.asp**

© *Windstar Cruises. Reprinted with Permission*

Q. **What is the history of your cruise line?**

A. *What started in 1984 as an idea to bring together the freedom of sailing with the luxury of a resort vacation has developed into the ultimate getaway. Windstar is a vacation experience that is truly "180 Degrees from Ordinary." Extreme efforts are made to ensure a luxurious yacht-like feel aboard all three Windstar vessels. Privacy and pampering service are the operative words.*

Q. **What should readers know about your cruise line?**

A. *Windstar's commitment to providing the most casually elegant, enriching, and luxurious cruise vacation has been rewarded with accolades from the most prestigious names in travel. In 2006, the line enjoyed recognition as a "Top Ten Small Ship Cruise Line" by Travel + Leisure, and all three ships were lauded among "The World's Best Small Ships" by Condé Nast Traveler's readers. Yet it is the line's devotion to its guests that continues to reap the best rewards — including the "World's Best Service" award in the 2006 Travel + Leisure Readers' Choice Poll. It is that same devotion that drives the Seattle-based Windstar team to create vacations that truly are 180 degrees from ordinary.*

Q. **How many ships are in your fleet?**

A. *Three: Wind Spirit (1988), Wind Star (1986), and Wind Surf (built in 1990 as Club Med I; Acquired in 1998).*

Q. **What kinds of staterooms and/or suites do you offer?**

A. *On the Wind Surf boat, the all ocean-view staterooms and suites provide comforts of home with additional amenities including sitting area, DVD/ CD player, safe, mini-bar/refrigerator, international direct-dial phones, bath toiletries, hair dryer, plush robes, and plenty of closet space. The library stocks an array of international newspapers, books and games, and a multi-media selection of more than 500 DVD titles and CDs available for complimentary use. We have 123 deluxe, ocean-view staterooms, with queen beds (converts to two twins), and a sitting area. Some offer a third berth. The 31 deluxe ocean-view suites are 376 square feet or 35 square meters. Two luxury Bridge Suites are 495 square feet each.*

On the Wind Surf/Wind Star we have a total of 74 staterooms: 73 deluxe ocean-view staterooms and one Deluxe owner's cabin with queen bed (converts to two twins), and dining/sitting area. Some staterooms offer a third berth and some side-by-side staterooms offer an adjoining private door.

Q. **What kind of on-board entertainment do you offer?**

A. *The Wind Spirit and Wind Star have a library, casino, fitness center, and fly bridge. The Wind Surf offers a library and a fitness center.*

Q. **What unique activities do you offer to guests?**

A. *On all of our boats we offer water-skiing, windsurfing, kayaking, sailing, ski-tubing, and snorkel gear. Scuba diving is available for a fee.*

Q. **What dining options are offered on-board?**

A. *On the Wind Surf boat we offer two restaurants. The Restaurant and Degrees accommodate all passengers at one sitting. Menus are created by renowned chef Joachim Splichal of the Patina Group in Los Angeles. Windstar offers an open seating program allowing guests to dine when and with whom they like. Degrees seats 124 in an alternative casual setting serving a steakhouse menu four nights a week. Other nights feature rotating menus from Northern Italy, France, and Indonesia. Sail Light and Vegetarian cuisine is developed by Jeanne Jones. The Veranda and Terrace serves breakfast and lunch, while continental breakfast and afternoon tea are served in the Compass Rose.*

Q. **What special services (for example, laundry or medical) are available on-board?**

A. *On the Wind Surf boat, we have reception, signature shop, sports program, 24-hour room service, WindSpa, infirmary with a full-time physician and nurse, laundry service, computers, Internet and e-mail, cell phone service, DVDs, CDs, iPod nanos, laptops, games, and books.*

The Wind Spirit/Wind Star reception, signature shop, sports program, 24-hour room service, salon, massage, infirmary with a full-time physician, laundry service, wireless Internet, computers, DVDs, compact discs, iPod nanos, laptops, games and books are available for checkout.

Q. **To what areas do you travel? Any unique locations?**

A. *We travel to several locations, including:*

❀ *Caribbean: Lesser Antilles, Virgin Islands, French West Indies, Barbados, Tobago*

❀ *Costa Rica*

❀ *Europe: Western/Eastern Mediterranean and Greek Islands*

❀ *Panama Canal*

❀ *Transatlantic*

Q. **How would you describe your typical guest?**

A. *The average age is 52 for past guests and 50 for new guests. Average annual household income is $175,000 and above. Windstar cruisers are active and adventurous, sophisticated travelers ranging from their 20s to 70s. Guests represent a broad spectrum, for example, business owners, executives, retirees, honeymooners, stockbrokers, lawyers, engineers, entrepreneurs, artists, authors, researchers, doctors, educators, and so on.*

The Yachts of Seabourn

Contact: Bruce Good, Director PR
6100 Blue Lagoon Drive, Ste 400
Miami, FL 33126
Phone: 305-463-3105
E-mail: bgood@seabourn.com
Web site: **www.seabourn.com**

© *Yachts of Seabourn. Reprinted with Permission.*

Q. **What is the history of your cruise line?**

A. *Seabourn Cruise Line was founded in 1987 by Norwegian industrialist Atle Brynestad. Its first ultra luxury cruise ship, the Seabourn Pride, made her maiden voyage in November 1988. Her sister ship, the Seabourn Spirit, sailed on her maiden voyage in November of 1989. A third sister ship, the Seabourn Legend, was acquired in January 1996. In 1991, Carnival Corporation (NYSE:CCL), the largest and most successful operator of cruise vacations in the world, purchased 25 percent of Seabourn, and in 1996 purchased an additional 25 percent. In 1998,*

Seabourn Cruise Line and Cunard Line merged to form Cunard Line Limited when a consortium including Carnival Corporation acquired Cunard Line from Kvaerner ASA. In 1999, Carnival Corporation exercised its option to purchase the merged company in total. In 2004, subsequent to the formation of Carnival Corporation and plc (NYSE & LSE: CCL and NYSE: CUK), Seabourn Cruise Line was reorganized as a stand-alone company with Miami, Florida headquarters.

Seabourn will be adding a new ship, the Seabourn Odyssey, in June 2009. Seabourn has already started booking tours for this new ship. They will also be launching new ships in 2010 and 2011.

Q. **What should readers know about your cruise line?**

A. Ultra luxury cruise pioneer Seabourn Cruise Line has earned unanimous accolades from cruising guidebooks, travel critics, and traveler polls since its founding in 1987. Its fleet of three identical, all-suite ships, Seabourn Pride, Spirit, and Legend are renowned for:

❁ Extraordinary levels of personalized service, with nearly one staff member per guest

❁ Sumptuous suites of 277 square feet or more, 40 percent with balconies

❁ Award-winning cuisine served in a single-seating restaurant

❁ Exceptional shoreside experiences in the world's most desirable destinations

Q. **How many ships are in your fleet?**

Seabourn currently has three ships in operation, with three more planned for the future. The following chart details each ship's years in service, tonnage, and how many guests and crew members it can accommodate.

SHIPS IN SERVICE				
Current Ships	Year in Service	Tonnage Ships	Guests (D/O)	Crew
Seabourn Pride	1988	10,000	208	165
Seabourn Spirit	1989	10,000	208	165
Seabourn Legend	1993	10,000	208	165
Seabourn Odyssey	2009	32,000	450	330
Newbuild Two	2010	32,000	450	330
Newbuild Three	2011	32,000	460	330

Q. **What kinds of staterooms and/or suites do you offer?**

A. *We have 104 Ocean-View Suites and 42 Balcony Suites. All suites include:*

❀ *Sitting area and bedroom*

❀ *Five-foot wide picture window or balcony*

❀ *Walk-in closet*

❀ *Flat-screen television with DVD player*

❀ *Bose Wave radio/CD stereo system*

❀ *Bar stocked to guests' request*

❀ *Spacious bathroom with tub, shower, and large vanity*

❀ *Hair dryer*

❀ *110/220 volt outlets*

❀ *Private electronic safe*

The categories of suites include: Owner's Suites, Double Suites, Classic Suites, Seabourn Balcony Suites, and Seabourn Suites. Square footage is between 277 and 575.

Q. **What kind of on-board entertainment do you offer?**

A. *Seabourn offers a variety of entertainment options nightly, from cabaret performances and classical recitals to music for dancing and local entertainment from ashore in selected ports of call. We also offer movies under the stars.*

Q. **What unique activities do you offer to guests?**

A. *We offer:*

* *Boutique*

* *Beauty salon*

* *Gymnasium equipped with variable resistance lines, treadmills, stairmasters, stationary cycles, rowers, and free weights*

* *Massage Moments on deck*

* *No tipping policy*

* *Indoor/outdoor Veranda Café*

* *Three outdoor whirlpools, outdoor swimming pool, and enclosed steel mesh pool, allowing guests to swim in the ocean*

* *Kayaking, sail boating, windsurfing, pedal boating, banana boat rides, snorkeling, and water skiing*

Q. What dining options are offered on-board?

A. *We offer fine dining in an open-seating restaurant. There is also a more casual alternative dining offered nightly and complimentary wines and spirits are offered throughout every voyage.*

Q. What special services (for example, laundry or medical) are available on-board?

A. *We offer:*

- *Complimentary French champagne upon arrival*

- *24-hour room service, in-suite dinner service from restaurant menu*

- *Personalized stationery*

- *Fruit basket replenished daily, in-suite bar stocked to guests' request*

- *Egyptian cotton bed linens*

- *Towels and robes*

- *Designer soaps and Molton Brown toiletries*

- *Pure Pampering aromatherapy bath menu*

- *Nightly turndown service with pillow sweet*

- *Daily newspaper*

- *Umbrella*

- *Direct-dial telephone*

❀ *Hair dryer*

❀ *Private safe*

❀ *World atlas*

❀ *Flat screen TV/DVD player, Bose Wave radio/CD stereo, and 3-channel music*

❀ *Self-service launderette; laundry and dry cleaning*

Q. **To what areas do you travel? Any unique locations?**

A. *Summer: Riviera, Greece, Turkey, Mediterranean, Dalmatian Coast, Italy, France, Scandinavia and Russia, British Isles, and Norwegian Fjords*

Fall: Mediterranean, Red Sea, Riviera, Spain, and Caribbean

Winter: Thailand and Vietnam, South America, Caribbean, Panama, Belize and Costa Rica, Hong Kong, Singapore, and Malaysia and India. In 2010, we will begin doing a world tour.

Christmas Holiday: Caribbean, and Thailand and Vietnam

Spring: China, Amazon, South America, South East Asia, Red Sea, India, Rivers of Western Europe, Mediterranean, Caribbean, and Transatlantic

Seabourn also provides a wide range of other travel experiences ashore — overland tours, journeys, and excursions. The crème de la crème of shore excursions are Seabourn's exclusive Signature Series, from a private visit to the Peggy Guggenheim Museum in Venice to a Czarist-era extravaganza in St. Petersburg's Yusupov Palace.

Q. How would you describe your typical guest?

A. *Seabourn guests are affluent, knowledgeable travelers who want the "best of the best." They may not necessarily be experienced cruisers. They avoid large ships and are frequent guests at exclusive hotels and resorts or top-end luxury tours.*

Additional Resources

CDC's Vessel Sanitation Program: **www.cdc.gov/nceh/vsp/default.htm**. The CDC Web site will provide you with everything you need to know to trust your cruise ship when you head out. Here you will find the sanitation scores for your cruise ship as they were recorded most recently. Each ship is scored at least every six months, so it is good to know how well your ship has performed in recent sanitation reviews by the cruise line.

Fodor's: **www.fodors.com/cruise.** Fodor's not only provides much of the same information you will find in this book, it offers updated travel information for ports, ships, and new cruise lines as they are developed. If you have a quick question that you cannot find an answer to elsewhere, visit Fodors and search through their well-organized listing of cruise resources.

Cruise Critic: **www.cruisecritic.com**. Cruise Critic provides detailed reviews of each cruise ship from individuals who have been on each ship. The reviews are not basic reviews either. You will find information that pertains to specific ships, their quirks, and how you will interact with them. If you might have trouble navigating the lido deck on a particular cruise ship, the reviews here will likely mention it. Before you book, check these reviews.

Cruise411: **www.cruise411.com**. Cruise 411 goes slightly above and beyond what many other cruising Web sites provide, offering dozens of different reviews, information for each of the biggest of 30 different embarkation ports, and ground transportation and facility information for the 400+ airports you might interact with. The depth of information provided at this site is very impressive and will fill in any of the gaps you might have as you book and prepare to leave on your first cruise.

Cruise Lines International Association: **www.cruising.org**. As one of the oldest and best organized cruising groups in the world, the CLIA provides a detailed cruise- and travel agent-finding tool, as well as a database of past press releases, news-related to the industry, and important safety information and resources. You can find nearly anything you need on this site to better prepare in booking your cruise and learning more about the current state of the cruise industry.

Cruise Mates: **www.cruisemates.com**. Cruise Mates provides a large selection of personal stories and articles from cruisers that have been to many of the largest and most popular destinations in the world and have spent a great deal of time learning more about the cruise industry than most average vacationers. You can find both humorous personal stories and detailed instructions and help for basic cruising tasks.

Bibliography

Accessible Journeys, **http://www.travelers-with-wheels.com**, October 12, 2007.

Atlantis Cruises, **http://www.atlantiscruisesandtours.com**, October 22, 2007.

Anonymous, "A Brief History of the Cruise Line Industry," **http://www.jobmonkey.com/cruise/html/a_brief_history.html**, October 9, 2007.

BudgetTravel.com, **http://www.budgettravel.com/bt-dyn/content/article/2005/06/04/AR2005060400664_pf.html**, October 13, 2007.

Bunting, Chris, "Weddings at Sea: Say 'I Do' to Cheaper Weddings," April 29, 2005.

Carnival Cruise Line, **http://www.carnival.com**, October 25, 2007.

Carr, Kelby, "Family Reunion Cruises: Planning a Destination Reunion on a Cruise Ship," April 24, 2007, **http://familytravel.suite101.com/article.cfm/family_reunion_cruise**, October 12, 2007.

Celebrity Cruise Line, **http://www.celebritycruises.com**, October 25, 2007.

Costa Cruise Line, **http://www.costacruise.com**, October 25, 2007.

Anonymous, "Crossing U.S. Borders," **http://www.dhs.gov/xtrvlsec/crossingborders/**, November 11, 2007.

Anonymous, "Cruise Industry Overview," **http://www.cruising.org/press/overview%202006/2.cfm**, October 15, 2007.

Anonymous, "Cruise Line Comparison," **http://www.asource.com/incentive/cruiselines.htm**, October 29, 2007.

Cruise Line International Association, **http://www.cruising.org/press/sourcebook2007/index.cfm**, October 15, 2007.

Anonymous, "Cruise Line Security," **http://www.iccl.org/pressroom/security.cfm**, November 12, 2007.

Cruise Mates, **http://www.cruisemates.com**, October 5, 2007.

Anonymous, "Cruise Ship Consumer Fact Sheet," **http://www.uscg.mil/hq/g-m/cruiseship.htm**, November 14, 2007.

Anonymous, "Cruise Travel: New Ships," **http://www.cruiseserver.net/travelpage/other/new_build.asp**, October 9, 2007.

Anonymous, "Cruise Weather Info," **http://www.cruise-links.com/cruise_weather_information.htm**, October 13, 2007.

Cruise West, **http://www.cruisewest.com**, October 25, 2007.

CSA Travel Protection, **http://www.csatravelprotection.com**, October 26, 2007.

Cunard Cruise Lines, **http://www.cunard.com**, October 9, 2007.

Dickinson, Bob and Andy Vladimir, *Selling the Sea: An Inside Look at the Cruise Industry*, John Wiley & Sons, Inc., New York, 1997.

Anonymous, "The Different Kinds of Cruise Vacations," **http://www.bookrentbuy.com/The-Different-Kinds-Of-Cruise-Vacations.shtml**, October 14, 2007.

Disney Cruise Line, **http://disneycruise.disney.go.com**, October 25, 2007.

Easy Cruise, **http://www.easycruise.com**, October 23, 2007.

Family Cruises, **http://www.familycruises.com**, October 15, 2007.

Freighter Trips, **http://www.freightertrips.com**, October 13, 2007.

Garrison, Linda, "Gay and Lesbian Cruises," **http://cruises.about.com/cs/gaycruises/a/gay_lesbian.htm**, October 13, 2007.

Garrison, Linda, "Ten Most Popular Cruise Lines for Families," **http://cruises.about.com/od/cruisingwithkids/tp/top10family.htm**, October 14, 2007.

Heil, Scott and Terrance W. Peck, eds., *The Encyclopedia of American Industries*, 2nd ed. Gale Research, Detroit, 1998.

Holland America Cruise Line, **http://www.hollandamerica.com**, October 25, 2007.

Anonymous, "How Much Does a Cruise Cost?" **http://www.cruisecheap.com/faqs.asp?pageID=176**, October 11, 2007.

InsureMyTrip.com, **http://www.insuremytrip.com**, October 26, 2007.

Anonymous, "Luggage logic: choosing and using bags with care help ensure you'll have something to wear when you get there — Brief Article," March-April 2002, **http://findarticles.com/p/articles/mi_m0FCP/ is_5_23/ai_83582781**, October 26, 2007.

Maisel, Sally J., "Sinking the cruise myths — Cruise News," Cruise Travel. July-August 2003, **http://findarticles.com/p/articles/mi_m0FCP/ is_1_25/ai_104609911**, FindArticles.com, October 12, 2007.

Majestic America Cruise Line, **http://www.majesticamericaline.com**, October 25, 2007.

M.H. Ross Travel Insurance Services, **http://www.mhross.com**, October 26, 2007.

Anonymous, "Norovirus Technical Fact Sheet," **http://www.cdc.gov/ Ncidod/dvrd/revb/gastro/norovirus-factsheet.htm**, November 16, 2007.

Norwegian Cruise Line, **http://www.ncl.com**, October 25, 2007.

Olivia Travel and Tours, **http://www.olivia.com**, October 22, 2007.

Princess Cruise Line, **http://www.princesscruises.com**, October 25, 2007.

Regent Seven Seas Cruise Line, **http://www.rssc.com**, October 25, 2007.

Rotman, Ann, "Cruising for Love," **http://www.cruisingforlove.com**, October 13, 2007.

Royal Caribbean Cruise Lines, **http://www.royalcaribbean.com**, October 25, 2007.

RSVP Vacations, **http://www.rsvpvacations.com**, October 22, 2007.

Anonymous, "The Safest Way to Travel: Passenger Safety on Cruise Ships." **http://www.iccl.org/pressroom/passafetyfactsheets.pdf**, November 14, 2007.

Sarna, Heidi and Matt Hannafin, *Cruise Vacations for Dummies: 2007*, Wiley Publishing Inc, Hoboken, NJ, 2007.

Sarna, Heidi and Matt Hannafin, *Frommer's Cruises & Ports of Call 2008: From U.S. & Canadian Home Ports to the Caribbean, Alaska, Hawaii & More*, Wiley Publishing Inc.,Hoboken, NJ, 2007.

Seabourn Cruise Line, **http://www.seabourn.com**, October 25, 2007.

Anonymous, "Seasickness," **http://www.seasickness.co.uk/**, October 11, 2007.

Showker, Kay and Sehlinger, Bob, *The Unofficial Guide to Cruises*, John Wiley and Sons, Inc., Hoboken, NJ, 2007.

Anonymous, "Special Interest Guide to Theme Cruises," **http://www.cruising.org/planyourcruise/guides/theme.cfm**, October 15, 2007.

Transportation Security Administration: Information for Travelers, **http://www.tsa.gov/travelers/index.shtm**, November 11, 2007.

Anonymous, "Travel Agency Directory," Travel Hub, **http://www.travelhub.com/travel_agencies/cruise_category/11_startAt/**, October 24, 2007.

Anonymous, "Travel Fraud," **http://www.fraud.org/tips/internet/travelfraud.htm**, October 23, 2007.

Travel Safe Insurance, **http://www.travelsafe.com**, October 26, 2007.

Anonymous, "Travel Scams." **http://www.cruisecritic.com/cruiseplanning/articles.cfm?ID=88**, October 22, 2007.

Uniworld River Cruises, **http://www.uniworld.com**, October 22, 2007.

U.S. Customs, **http://www.customs.gov**, November 17, 2007.

Ward, Douglas, *Berlitz 2008 Complete Guide to Cruising and Cruise Ships*, Berlitz Guides, London, 2007.

West, Jim, *The Essential Little Cruise Book, 3rd: Secrets from a Cruise Director for a Perfect Cruise Vacation*, Globe Pequot Press, Guilford, CT, 2003.

Anonymous, "What is SOLAS?" **http://www.acebi.com/Solas.htm**, November 15, 2007.

Windstar Cruise Line, **http://www.windstarcruises.com**, October 25, 2007.

Wilkinson, Brooke, "Family Reunion on a Cruise Ship?" August 2, 2007, **http://www.concierge.com/cntraveler/blogs/perrinpost/2007/08/family-reunion-.html**, October 12, 2007.

Yangtze River Cruises, **http://www.yangtzeriver.org**, October 24, 2007.

Author Biography

T. Brian lives and writes in Seattle, Washington. He previously wrote *The MySpace.com Handbook: The Complete Guide for Members and Parents* published in early 2008.

Index

THE SAVVY BUZINESS TRAVELER'S GUIDE TO CUSTOMS AND PRACTICES IN OTHER COUNTRIES: THE DOS AND DON'TS TO IMPRESS YOUR HOST AND MAKE THE SALE

Pack your bags and travel around the world. With this book you can proceed confidently through foreign travel and negotiations in over 40 countries on six contintents.

Did you know red roses should be avoided as gifts in Switzerland, or that women should cover their mouths when they laugh in South Korea? Not every country shares the same customs, religions, and ideas as America, so it is useful to have a guide on how to behave if and when you are doing business in a foreign country. Now, *The Savvy Business Traveler's Guide to Customs and Practices in Other Countries* can be your hand-held guide to accompany you as you travel to countries near and far.

This book takes you through each country individually and explains its economic conditions, proper greetings, native foods, religions, etiquette, bargaining and deal making, and customs. By reading and understanding the behaviors expected when you are in each country, you will be better prepared to make the sale and leave a great impression of your company. This book makes it easy for you to navigate yourself around the world and flip the page to whichever country you may be visiting.

ISBN-13: 978-1-60138-013-5
288 Pages • $24.95

How to Plan Your Own Wedding and Save Thousands:
Without Going Crazy

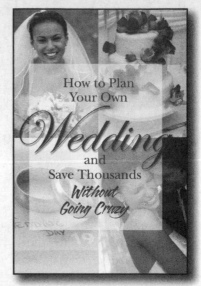

Congratulations! You are getting married and want a beautiful, memorable event, yet you need to stick to a tight budget. Do not despair! There are hundreds of proven ways to have your dream wedding without breaking your budget.

The average cost of a wedding in the United States in 2007 was approximately $30,000, a 73 percent increase since 1992. What is astonishing is how quickly all the other smaller expenses, like stationary, invitations, announcements, and hair and makeup, add up. Just imagine what you could do if you could save $30,000 as you start out your new life together.

Whether your budget is $1,000 or $50,000, *How to Plan Your Own Wedding and Save Thousands* will teach you hundreds of ways to cut down on your wedding expenses without serving a roomful of guests hamburgers and hot dogs at your reception. Reading this book will help reduce your stress and relieve your wallet so you can walk down the aisle in peace.

ISBN-13: 978-1-60138-007-4
288 Pages • $24.95

DID YOU BORROW THIS COPY?

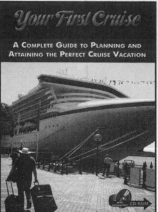

Have you been borrowing a copy of *Your First Cruise: A Complete Guide to Planning and Attaining the Perfect Cruise Vacation* from a friend, colleague, or library?
Wouldn't you like your own copy for quick and easy reference? To order, photocopy the form below and send to:
Atlantic Publishing Company
1405 SW 6th Ave • Ocala, FL 34471-0640